WHAT IS HAPPENING TO NEWS

OTHER BOOKS BY JACK FULLER

NONFICTION

News Values

FICTION

Abbeville
The Best of Jackson Payne
Legends' End
Our Fathers' Shadows
Mass
Fragments
Convergence

What Is Happening to

NEWS

The Information Explosion and the Crisis in Journalism

JACK FULLER

THE UNIVERSITY OF CHICAGO PRESS : CHICAGO AND LONDON

Jack Fuller is the author of numerous books, including
The Best of Jackson Payne, Fragments, Convergence, and *News Values,*
all available from the University of Chicago Press.
A Pulitzer Prize–winning journalist, he served as editorial page editor,
editor, and publisher of the *Chicago Tribune.*
He retired as the president of Tribune Publishing
Company at the end of 2004.

The University of Chicago Press, Chicago 60637
The University of Chicago Press, Ltd., London
© 2010 by The University of Chicago
All rights reserved. Published 2010
Printed in the United States of America

19 18 17 16 15 14 13 12 11 10   1 2 3 4 5

ISBN-13: 978-0-226-26898-9 (cloth)
ISBN-10: 0-226-26898-5 (cloth)

Library of Congress Cataloging-in-Publication Data

Fuller, Jack.
What is happening to news : the information explosion
and the crisis in journalism / Jack Fuller.
p. cm.
Includes bibliographical references and index.
ISBN-13: 978-0-226-26898-9 (cloth: alk. paper)
ISBN-10: 0-226-26898-5 (cloth: alk. paper)
1. Journalism—United States.   2. Journalistic ethics.   3. Information society.
4. News audiences.   5. Affective neuroscience.   I. Title.
PN4867.2.F85 2010
070.4—dc22
2009039090

FOR DEBBY

Messages are sent with flares and set about with barbs.

ROBERT WIEBE

CONTENTS

Never before have human beings had so much information so ready to hand. The resources of the Web spread endlessly before us, promising instantly to answer any question our minds have the wit to ask. Our computers link us with people from Antarctica to the tropics; mobile devices put us only a few keystrokes away from most of the human beings on the planet. The technology also permits others to access us—anytime, anywhere. Messages come at us ceaselessly—at the speed of light. We can read the latest word posted by anyone in the world on an election halfway around the world at least as easily as we can learn the tally in a referendum in our hometown. Images of violence that only a couple of decades ago would have taken days to reach our eyes, now explode before us in real time, before the event has had the opportunity to ripen into what we used to call news.

Messages are so ubiquitous that we cannot avoid them. They speak to us from every corner of the airport, from the screen in the elevator, from the scrolling words at the bottom of the multiple TV screens looking down on us as we sweat in exercise facilities. Many of them aim at us personally, either because someone we know sent them or because we have signaled to a computer what we're interested in. These messages are particularly compelling. It is as if they call out our name.

Often we engage several streams of information at once: Talking on the cell phone while driving behind a bus striped with advertisements—one ear cocked for the traffic report on talk radio. Or window-shopping on the Web while sitting in on a conference call with the phone on mute, every now and then reading a document from the leaning tower of papers on the desk.

Paradoxically, all of this makes the fundamental question for American journalism today how to reach people. The old ways don't work so well anymore. And we don't know how to discipline the use of the new ones. That is because we don't understand the deep sources of the change in the behavior of the news audience. This is where we have to begin.

One problem is that some of the sources of change seem so obvious that they tempt one to look no further. They had been gathering steadily and hardly unnoticed in the late twentieth century—the arrival of cable television offering viewers an order of magnitude more choices than they had before, then the rapid growth of digital interactive media, the relentless spread of wireless technology that made the introduction of a new telephone a major news event. Meantime, various voices were issuing dire warnings. As early as 1985 Neil Postman saw television's entertainment values replacing print's invitation to rational discourse.[1] Today 1985 seems to belong to journalism's Golden Age.

Somewhere along the way, the profession, which had felt courageous in its coverage of the Vietnam War and virtuous in its pursuit of the misdeeds of the Nixon administration, began to sense the ground shifting under it. Circulation was drifting downward (though much more slowly than network or local TV news ratings). Economic slumps, spikes in newsprint prices, and the relentless financial market demands for growth drove technological changes in the way newspapers were produced, eliminating production jobs by putting the work into the news departments. Then news department budgets and staff levels were themselves reduced. The problem, as many journalists saw it, was corporate greed. By the turn of the century a distinguished group of academic researchers into ethics and excellence chose journalism as a case study of a field where values and practice had fallen into discord.[2]

At the same time the most thoughtful within the profession were seeing other threats. In 1999 Bill Kovach and Tom Rosenstiel published a prophetic book in which they warned of a "new Mixed Media Culture" that had these characteristics:

- A Never-Ending News Cycle Makes Journalism Less Complete.
- Sources Are Gaining Power Over Journalists.
- There Are No More Gatekeepers.
- Argument Is Overwhelming Reporting.
- A Blockbuster Mentality Is Taking Over.[3]

It turned out that what alarmed them in 1999 was only the beginning.

Not until the first decade of the twenty-first century did the economic, social, historical, and technological forces all line up to throw the profession of journalism, particularly in newspapers, into such a severe crisis that it called the survival of any number of great news organizations into question. Advertising revenue moved from print to the Internet. So did readers. The problem with corporate leaders no longer seemed to be greed but their inability to make the business of news work. And the prophets became downright apocalyptic. In 2008 one Nostradamus got a fair amount of attention with a book predicting that distraction was pushing us toward "a new dark age."[4]

Even though throughout much of this history I worked in the newspaper business, struggling with these very forces, I came to this book project almost by chance. Like everyone in journalism, I was wracking my brain trying to understand what was happening, but I had no good idea how to approach the problem, let alone solve it.

Then, toward the end of my career at Tribune Company, the University of Illinois journalism program approached me to give a speech in Urbana. At the time, I was troubled and confused by the way serious journalists were dealing with celebrities. I decided to make this the subject of my talk.

To prepare for it, I began reading about fame and learned that a number of thoughtful writers on the subject believe that celebrity involves a surrogate emotional relationship between the audience and the image projected by and onto the famous individual. This led me to find out what I could learn about that emotional connection, and in the course of this I stumbled upon the rapidly advancing and increasingly influential field of affective neuroscience, the science of emotion.

In 1929 Walter Lippmann, the most important journalistic thinker of his time, wrote: "Scientific method and historical scholarship have enormously increased our competence in the whole field of physics and history. But for an understanding of human nature we are still largely dependent . . . upon introspection, general observation, and intuition. There has been no revolutionary advance here since the Hellenic philosophers."[5] Now we are seeing such an advance. As I began to read more neuroscience, I sensed that this growing body of knowledge had something to say, not just about the narrow question of how journalists do and should deal with celebrities, but also about why and how people have changed the way they take in news.

Lippmann will have a significant place in the pages of this book. Though he did not come close to solving the riddles of how to discipline human nature, more than any journalist of his time he struggled with them. His ideas about how journalists should behave in the interest of the public good influenced the profession, even as he himself became haunted by doubts about their efficacy. Though Lippmann was born in the nineteenth century, his professional and intellectual life embodied the yearning and the divided consciousness that still mark journalism in the twenty-first. There has never been anyone quite like him since, and for reasons I'll explore, there never will be again.

A mind like Lippmann's would surely have recognized the enormous implications of our changing understanding of human nature and human thought. I have no idea what he might have made of them, nor does it much matter. What is important is that smart, serious journalists bring this body of knowledge to bear on their work.

The discoveries of contemporary neuroscience provide insight into audience behavior that goes deeper than traditional approaches have gone. The trouble with opinion research is that people very often do not really know why they do and feel certain things, though their brains have a genius for offering up rationalizations. So when asked why they like a certain way a news story is presented better than another way, for example, most opinion research subjects will have an answer. Unfortunately for those of us trying to understand and predict their behavior, they often are quite wrong.

The human brain has been shaped by ancient evolutionary forces, and today it has to deal with an information environment inundating it with messages precisely aimed at pinning its attention. Understanding what scientists have learned about the structure and operation of the brain will help those attempting to find the right ways to do journalism in these radically new circumstances.

It turns out that the brain sciences also provide insight into a lot of older but still difficult questions. Tom Goldstein in his book *Journalism and Truth* lists seven that he developed with former *New York Times* executive editor Max Frankel when they taught a class together at Columbia University Journalism School. My reading of neuroscience research has provided direct answers to the following four of them:

- The crash of a commercial airliner is news. A safe landing is not, unless the plane was hijacked or otherwise crippled. Why does bad news crowd out the good?
- Why does the news of conflict crowd out the news of cooperation? Why do crime and sports get more attention than science and literature? Why do spectacle and photography so often take precedence over information? Or should we learn to understand spectacle as a kind of information? Why do our eyes and emotions define news more often than our intellect does?

- Why do we care where the famous eat and sleep? And why are they newsworthy in the first place?
- What happens to news as it ages, from the instantaneous to the daily, the weekly, the annually, the historic? What happens to news as it shifts from the neighborhood to the region, the natural environment, the globe, the universe? Should recent news trump previous news? Must news focus on "today" and "yesterday"? Should nearer news trump the distant?[6]

We cannot begin to answer these questions until we understand the psychology behind them. Nor can we realign our professional disciplines with the changed environment without understanding the effects the changes are having on our audience. In other words, we cannot possibly find our way before figuring out where we are. I hope this book helps us take our bearings.

: : :

I would like to thank the University of Illinois journalism program for giving me the invitation to speak that started me off on a remarkable journey. I would also like to thank John Cacioppo, John Carroll, John Crewdson, Jonathan Fanton, Michael Janeway, Bill Kovach, John Lavine, Ann Marie Lipinski, Debby Moskovits, John Puerner, Scott Smith, Wayne Smith, Howard Tyner, David Warsh, and Owen Youngman who were kind enough to read and comment on my work at various stages. My editor at University of Chicago Press, John Tryneski, has helped me sharpen ideas and expression at every step along the way.

: : :

Nobody has yet come up with a wholly satisfactory alternative to using the masculine pronoun when referring to someone or some people of no particular gender. Some writers have tried to create a new semi-word: "The journalist knows that s/he will offend someone." That seems to me worse than graceless. My solution here will be to use he in odd-numbered chapters and she in even-numbered ones, which I hope is not too distracting.

CHAPTER ONE

THE COLLAPSE OF THE OLD ORDER

In 1921 Walter Lippmann famously compared the press to "the beam of a searchlight that moves restlessly about, bringing one episode and then another out of darkness into vision." By the time he published those words, he had already laid out a program for the professionalization of journalism and was on his way to becoming the most influential American newspaperman of his era. Behind his searchlight simile lay the shadow of fundamental doubts about the press that darkened his thinking the rest of his life. "Men cannot do the work of the world," he wrote, "by this light alone."[1]

More than twenty years later in France, philosopher Maurice Merleau-Ponty used the searchlight simile to describe the way perception reaches out to the world. "The function which reveals . . . , as a searchlight shows up objects pre-existing in the darkness," he wrote, "is called attention."[2] Merleau-Ponty's work was as influential as Lippmann's, but within a much smaller compass. He insisted that the human mind was not a passive receiver of stimuli, to which it simply reacted. Behaviorism, centered on stimulus and response, was the prevailing psychological doctrine of the time, but he argued that the mind in important ways makes the world it finds. Modern neuroscience again and again is demonstrating the validity of the philosopher's insight. At the same time, the idea that the brain actively shapes the world it is trying to know raises questions about all claims of truth—whether in journalism, science, or anywhere else—and these questions have left a deep mark upon our times.

Though the two men used the same image, they were referring to quite different things. Lippmann was characterizing the economically driven behavior of the press—or as we would now call it, the media—the senders of messages. Merleau-Ponty was describing the singular activity of minds—the

1

receivers of messages. Lippmann saw the limitations of a quasi-public institution. Merleau-Ponty had an expansive view of the shaping, intensely
private power of the individual brain. Getting at what is happening today
requires us to look deeply into what is going on behind both searchlights.

: : :

Beginning in the late twentieth century and accelerating into the twenty-
first, the relationship between news media and audiences underwent a fundamental change. By the end of the first decade of the twenty-first century
it appeared that some of the central tenets of what I will call the Standard
Model of Professional Journalism, which was sketched out by Lippmann
and eventually almost universally accepted by serious journalists, were in
ragged retreat. While once they had offered reporters and editors a way of
disciplining their work so that it linked up with the public interest in a free,
self-governing society, in the twenty-first century much of the audience no
longer seemed to believe in them. The credibility of the established media
that tried to adhere to the Standard Model of Professional Journalism had
gone into a spiraling decline. Meantime, nakedly emotional approaches to
news, often involving intense expression of opinion and lacking verification
of factual assertions, gained both audience and credibility.

Journalists and others struggled to find explanations for the change: the
rise of the Internet, the decreasing attention span of a video-game generation, the increasing sophistication of image-makers in manipulating public
opinion. Some of the better thinkers in journalism and its academic institutions recorded shifts in the prevailing intellectual climate.[3] Others recognized the influence of trends in political and economic history.[4]

Of course, the leading factor reshaping the information environment, of
which the news is a small part, has been technology. In 1965 Gordon Moore,
cofounder of Intel Corporation, published a paper in *Electronics* magazine
predicting the rapid, continuous increase in the number of transistors that
can fit onto a square inch of silicon.[5] Though everyone including Moore
acknowledged a limit to the doubling and redoubling, in practical terms we
have not reached it yet. And so the speed and power of computing—and
therefore what computers can do—will continue to increase and the cost
will continue to decline for the foreseeable future.

Meanwhile, the cost of moving information is also declining precipitously as technological innovation and investment in communication infra-

structure rapidly increases the available bandwidth (a measure of how much information can move through a channel in a given amount of time). Text message boards on dial-up online services give way to static images over the Internet, then to music, then to full-motion video on demand. . . . Telephones connected to copper wires give way to cell phones that fit in your briefcase, to cell phones that fit in your shirt pocket, to cell phones with text messaging, with photographs, with Internet connection, with music, with video, with live TV, and on and on.

The continuous decline in the cost of computing and bandwidth means that for as long as it is worth trying to imagine, more and more information will be moving at a higher and higher rate of speed through and to more and more complex instruments. Exactly what products and services this will lead to is anybody's guess. But this much is not guesswork: There will be more messages for people to choose from—and more difficulty in avoiding the choice.

Newspapers have suffered catastrophic economic damage at the hands of the information revolution. This occurred, not in the first instance because the Internet took away newspapers' readers, though at some point it began to, but rather because it took away advertising, which had represented roughly three-quarters of the revenues of a newspaper and a larger proportion of its profits. The Internet delivered classified advertising (for jobs, homes, used cars, and so on) much more effectively than newspapers ever could. Since classified had been far and away newspapers' most profitable advertising, its deep decline was disastrous. Curiously, Marshall McLuhan foresaw the problem in his odd, oracular 1964 book *Understanding Media*. Writing of classified ads and stock market tables, he wrote, "Should an alternative source of easy access to such diverse daily information be found, the press will fold."[6] That did not quite happen, but as more and more classified advertising moved to the Internet, the financial pressure on newspapers ratcheted up.

The collapse of the old information order scourged journalism with a poisonous blend of doubt and defiance. As often happens, members of the old order—of whom I am one—lean toward denial while the pioneers of the new see the change as a means of improving everything, including human nature. French philosopher Paul Ricoeur caught the mood when he wrote, "The present is wholly a crisis when expectation takes refuge in utopia and when tradition becomes only a dead deposit of the past."[7]

We need to get beyond both nostalgia and utopianism by understanding what is happening at the most fundamental level, which is often hidden. Useful as the various explanations of the changes sweeping over journalism have sometimes been, deeper forces have been at work. There is more to it than the Internet.

WHERE I AM HEADED

Attention is the prize, which becomes more valuable as demand for it grows. For the institutions of the news media, the new information environment has meant a level of competition for a bit of people's time unimaginable during the 1960s through 1980s when the Standard Model of Professional Journalism rose to its zenith. People have become immersed in messages to a degree that the human mind has never before experienced. Their response to this onslaught has come from deep within the structure of their brains, a structure shaped much more by the evolutionary forces of *Homo sapiens'* prehistoric origins on the African savannah than by anything since. Within the individual human mind, the increased competition for attention calls into play an ancient mechanism that seizes and focuses the scarce information-processing resources of the brain. We call this mechanism emotion.

In the course of this book we will look closely at both the external competition for the attention of the audience (Lippmann's restless searchlight) and the internal competition within the brain (for control of Merleau-Ponty's searchlight). In the latter case, the young discipline of neuroscience has upended many of the prevailing views about how the mind relates to its world and is reshaping nearly every human-centered area of intellectual inquiry from psychology, sociology, and political science to philosophy, linguistics, and literary criticism. Strangely, the news of what neuroscience has discovered about how we think has so far had little effect on the discipline of journalism. A while back, a fine editor of one of the country's larger daily newspapers asked me what I'd been doing with myself. When I told him about my research, he said that when I was finished it might make for a good article for their science pages. That is where the gee-whiz discoveries of neuroscience have been relegated. Just one more passing curiosity. Not something that shakes journalism's world.

Neuroscience alone does not explain what is happening to the audience. It deals with only one of four separate forces that came together at the close of the twentieth century to reshape the way people take in news. A deep current in America's history made us ready to rebel against experts, including traditional journalists. A separate current in Western intellectual history promoted deep skepticism about how much humans could know reality and understand one another. Into these roiling waters dropped an information technology that facilitated the rebellion and embodied the skepticism. That technology also presented the human mind with unprecedented cognitive and attention challenges. We are in the midst of the turbulence created by the collision of these forces, and I will be dealing with each of them at some length, beginning with the last.

I will draw on the writings of scientists and philosophers (who, like Merleau-Ponty, were often well ahead of the scientists), as well of historians, political scientists, literary theorists, and many others who have worked at a considerable distance from journalism. One reason to go beyond the conventional and trusted tools of journalistic study (such as opinion research, content analysis, and close textual reading) is to get past the dead-end terms in which the question of the future of news easily becomes mired.

My primary goal is to describe the situation in a fresh and revealing light. From this description I will try to draw some implications about the way journalists will need to reshape their professional disciplines. I will have some concluding suggestions about how to connect with audiences in the new information environment, but I will present them with humility, in the full knowledge that new generations of journalists have to be the ones who experiment with the new methods of communicating with people. They will be the ones who discover a new rhetoric for the news.

I begin with a few premises that I don't examine deeply here.[8] First, a free and self-governing society requires sources of information other than the state in order to remain free and self-governing and to make good public decisions. Second, the quality of governance reflects the quality of the information available to the public. Third, it takes energy, skill, resourcefulness, and often courage to gather and disseminate information when powerful people and institutions do not want the information known. And finally, somehow the attention of people needs to be drawn to important matters, especially when the state and other institutions do not want people to believe they are important (think, for example, of the matter of racial injustice when it was officially countenanced).

Fulfilling these needs is the social mission of journalism. Though the means of accomplishing it are changing radically, the nature of the mission is not. Any arrangement for news in the future should be measured against it.

This is not an argument for the survival of the institutions, methods, rhetoric, or mechanisms of mainstream twentieth-century journalism. The fate of newspapers matters to me deeply because I invested my life in them. But the future does not depend on the persistence of ink on newsprint. What matters profoundly to our civic health, to the very way in which we live, is the fate of news itself, of public information about matters important to the commonweal.

One of the lessons of our new information environment is that you cannot entirely separate the message from the messenger. I will not try. I am a creature of the newspaper business, and along the way I will draw anecdotes from this experience and use examples mostly pulled from the newspaper I know best, the *Chicago Tribune*. I hope they will shed light not just on print journalism but on the challenges facing news in all forms. But I won't pretend to be a detached, disinterested observer. Nobody believes in them anymore anyway. I will be an "I" in this tale. So I guess I should introduce myself.

WHERE I'M COMING FROM

I started my newspaper career as a prep sports stringer and then copyboy with the *Chicago Tribune,* where my father spent his career as a reporter and copy editor. It is almost dream-like to recall how newspapers operated then. I suspect that when journalists starting out today look back forty years from now they will see that their careers spanned even more change.

When I began working at the *Chicago Tribune* in the early 1960s, reporters typed their stories on manual typewriters. A corps of copyboys, as both young men and women were then called, moved those stories and multiple carbon copies from desk to desk and finally to the composing room where linotype machine operators sat at oddly organized keyboards punching in the stories all over again to reproduce the stories in hot lead. There were four citywide, English-language daily newspapers in Chicago, three network television channels, one young public television station, and one independent television station owned by Tribune Company. Competition seemed fierce.

Tribune editors went over the rival newspapers, edition by edition, noting facts that they had and we didn't, and demanding to know why we didn't have them. But in fact the competition was circumscribed. To get into the newspaper game took an enormous printing plant and a fleet of trucks big enough to deliver papers to carriers who passed by everyone's house in the circulation area once a day. To broadcast required a federal license. News over the air was limited; even all-news radio had not yet arrived.

When I was a copyboy, the *Tribune* was one of the last holdouts against the elements of the Standard Model of Professional Journalism that required that opinion be kept out of news stories and that the news operation be run with indifference to the editorial position of the newspaper. The *Tribune* was conservative Republican from its first page to last and did not care who knew it.

The *Chicago Daily News,* where I went to work as a reporter a few years later while I was in college, was a different kind of paper, highly respected by news professionals, with nationally recognized correspondents such as Peter Lisagor, Keyes Beech, and Georgie Anne Geyer working in Washington and overseas and brilliant columnists, reporters, and critics—such as Mike Royko, Lois Wille, M. W. Neumann, and Richard Christiansen—working in Chicago. Nonetheless, some of the things we did at the *Daily News* in those days were inexcusable.

One night, for example, beset by a period utterly bereft of news, my editor assigned me to look into every crime reported on the city's Chicago Transit Authority (CTA) buses and elevated trains during my shift. I did and we put them together in a single big story for the front page. The next evening we did it again, and so did our competition. An attractive young woman improved the story by showing one of our photographers a big bruise high on her mini-skirted leg; she had suffered it when a mugger attacked her on an elevated train platform. By the following day the headlines were blaring about a "CTA crime wave," and that evening I was assigned to try to get myself mugged on the subway. (I failed miserably.) As the week came to a close, the mayor put a police officer on every train and many buses. Of course, there had been nothing out of the ordinary about the level of crime on the CTA. We had just shone the *Daily News*' searchlight on it to drum up excitement at the newsstands. Once the city took symbolic action, the story died, and crime on the buses, subways, and elevated trains once again went unnoticed. Later, when I heard journalists pine away for the journalism of that period, I always wondered whether they were thinking of things like the CTA crime wave.

By the time I returned to the *Tribune* in the early 1970s, the *Tribune* had professionalized. But the way a newspaper was produced remained fundamentally unchanged since early in the century. Then suddenly the typewriters vanished. Computer terminals replaced them. The linotype machines down in the composing room went away, too. No more hot lead. A new, quicker, cheaper paper and film process replaced it. The big, old presses disappeared from the basement pressroom in Tribune Tower. Modern ones began to roll at a new printing facility a couple miles away.

The changes went much deeper than the newspaper production process. I remember vividly one day when we were on deadline and I needed to decide quickly whether Anwar Sadat was dead or still alive, which was at that point not at all clear. If he was dead, we would go with an obituary editorial, which was already written. If alive, we needed to revise it quickly. To make the decision, I was able to summon up on the computer the very latest detail that either of the U.S. wire services, Reuters, and Agence France-Presse had reported about the shooting in Egypt. Having that kind of instantaneous access to information was a privilege of a very few of us in the news business. Our audience had to wait for us to decide what was accurate and important enough for them to know. They had no way around us.

When I became editor of the *Tribune*, another great change was on the way, and we were determined to prepare the paper and its journalists for it. In 1992 we teamed up with America Online to send the newspaper's contents to people through their computers. We knew that eventually the audience would be demanding and getting not only text but also photos and full-motion video in their news reports. So we set about creating an editorial operation that could handle multiple media. With the broadcasting side of Tribune we started an all-news local cable channel and put a small TV camera in the newsroom outside my office so our reporters could do live shots for it. Over the years we were as aggressive as any newspaper in pursuing electronic means of distributing the news. My successor, Howard Tyner, was particularly effective at overcoming professional conservatism among journalists. He rebuilt the whole newsroom around a sophisticated TV studio and pushed the paper onto the Internet.

But we were up against more than professional inertia and the need to learn new skills. Enormous national players like Microsoft began entering the field, along with a swarm of upstarts financed with money from the Internet bubble. It was in this context that, when I was president of Tribune Publishing Company, we began to think about acquiring Times Mirror Company, which owned the *Los Angeles Times*, *Newsday*, the *Baltimore Sun*, the *Hartford Courant*, and a few smaller papers. Tribune Company had television stations in Los Angeles, New York City, and Hartford, and jointly owned newspapers and TV stations in Chicago and South Florida. We felt we needed to get some kind of an edge to compete for audience on a national scale on the Internet, which knew no geographic boundaries. Gaining multiple media positions in the three biggest cities in the United States seemed an opportunity to get a better foothold in the new competitive environment.

Though we did acquire Times Mirror in 2000, the multimedia strategy struggled as the newspaper and broadcast cultures found it difficult to get comfortable with one another. Even if they had melded, it is clear in retrospect that this in itself would not have been enough to allow the company to steal the march on CNN.com, let alone Google, though the future to this day still belongs to those who use multiple and integrated ways to get through to people. Acquiring Times Mirror did help in one very important area: It allowed us to drive toward success in our national Internet classified businesses, CareerBuilder and Classified Ventures.

Meantime, the *Chicago Tribune* and the other original Tribune Company newspapers continued to do wonderful journalism, as did the acquired Times Mirror papers. For two years running, Tribune newspapers won five Pulitzer Prizes. A new publisher, editor, and managing editor at the *Los Angeles Times* (John Puerner, John Carroll, and Dean Baquet) were able to revive its journalism rapidly. The ten Pulitzer Prizes the paper won from 2003 through 2005 are some evidence of what they had achieved. At the same time the paper reduced its production and distribution costs even faster than we had planned.

I was extremely proud of the way Tribune Company's newspapers were serving the public, but I was frustrated by our lack of progress in finding a compelling and profitable way to publish news on the Internet. Then began a series of downturns in the economy—starting with the bursting of the Internet bubble. Meantime, the new media ground away at newspapers' advertising revenues and circulation. This bore down on the whole industry, and over time it took a toll. One manifestation was that editors and publishers began leaving rather than make the budget cuts their companies required of them. This happened at the *Los Angeles Times* with a vengeance. It lost three successive editors and publishers.

Along the way a number of news organizations came under the leadership of people who did not have much of a care for the social role journalism plays in a healthy, self-governing society. It was not just that they were not journalists. Most CEOs in the late twentieth century had come from the business side. I had served under three CEOs since returning to the *Chicago Tribune* as a journalist. The first was an engineer; the second came up through a newspaper finance department, and the third had joined Tribune from an investment bank. Though they were quite different from one another in many ways, they all appreciated the role a newspaper plays in the community and took delight in important journalism.

But as the financial pressure increased, companies began to lose sight of the societal aspects of what they were doing. Tribune Company was one of these. In 2003 a new CEO took over. He had come up on the advertising sales side of the broadcasting business, where news was a very small part of the enterprise. Not only did he not know much about journalism and its values, he made it clear to me that he did not care to learn. This did not inhibit him from inserting himself more and more in editorial matters in uncomfortable ways, often simply going around me when he could not get his way. And when the *Los Angeles Times* won its five Pulitzers in a single year, he took the occasion in a senior management meeting to tell the leaders of the company that the award did not measure anything of importance; it was just a journalistic self-indulgence. All I could do was to tell him he was wrong.

The great and profoundly important challenge of the news business is finding the sweet spot where both its financial and social missions can be fulfilled. This was not how the new CEO saw things. He simply wanted me to carry out his designs, with which I increasingly disagreed. I saw my choice as stark—to let myself be used or to leave. So I quit.

The sad thing is that the rapidly changing information environment then as now required *more* serious, high level discussion of journalism values, not *less*. Things clearly had to change, but the need for journalism was so important that some values had to be even more firmly rooted.

What has happened since I left haunts me. A CEO tone deaf to serious journalism did not help. But this just made a bad situation worse. Every newspaper company, even those led by people totally committed to striking a proper balance between the financial and social missions of journalism, has been beaten down. And all the efforts that I and so many others made to bring our papers through the information revolution did not make a decisive difference in their financial performance against other newspapers that had not been as aggressive. This is humbling, but it was useful to remember as I tried to puzzle out where journalism should go from here.

I am confident that I have identified some of the most important forces shaping the way news is evolving, but I don't know how anyone can be very confident about just what will work in the future. Nor about what the successful business strategy for serious journalism will be.

What I am sure about is that journalists and businesspeople will have to experiment boldly until they hit on the right answers. As they do, Lippmann's restless searchlight of the press and Merleau-Ponty's searchlight of the brain reach out to one another across the new information landscape, each seeking something from the other. Let's see how far we can navigate by them.

CHAPTER TWO

THE SCIENCE OF JOURNALISM

The Standard Model of Professional Journalism includes the disciplines of accuracy, disinterestedness in reporting, independence from the people and organizations reported upon or affected by the report, a mode of presentation sometimes called objective or neutral, and the clear labeling of what is fact and what is opinion. It grew out of a set of ideas concerning both the best way in general to come to know something about reality and what kind of information a free, self-governing society needs. Like all ideas, these reflected the historical moment in which they arose. Before examining the forces that have challenged the Standard Model, we need to go back in time in order to understand the forces that shaped it.

The nineteenth century began with the opening of vast new territories into which Americans could stretch and exercise their individuality. The landed but nontitled gentry east of the Appalachians lost power to westward-moving upstarts. Many aspects of the social world were changing dramatically, and the press was one of them. Where newspapers had once been owned and operated by the political parties, now new, independent papers began to surge in popularity by appealing to the masses that crowded into the cities that were sprouting across the face of the land. The manners of this new kind of newspaper were no better than those of their party-press predecessors, but they were rude in a different way. Rather than simply hurling calumny at the political opposition, the newspapers of the multitude splashed news of sensational crimes, the sexual escapades of the prominent, and heartbreaking tales of the victims of modern life, not so much to advance one party or another as to advance themselves.

Meanwhile, the old order mourned. Henry Adams wrote what was perhaps its most eloquent elegy in his *Education*. Born into a family of presidents, grandson of one and great-grandson of another, he watched as the power of Boston and New England waned and rustic upstarts like Lincoln and Grant from the edge of the nation took command. But more, he saw things grow increasingly democratic and complicated. "Of all the travels made by man since the voyages of Dante," he wrote, "this new exploration along the shores of Multiplicity and Complexity promised to be the longest."[1]

Toward the end of the century, the voices of Populism cried out against the economically powerful few who seemed to be responsible for crushing the many. At the same time a different part of the population was rising. More educated and middle class, it saw a way to tame both multiplicity and complexity, the way of science.

As often happens, philosophy got there first. The most important post–Civil War thinkers—among them William James, Charles Sanders Peirce, and Oliver Wendell Holmes, Jr.—were deeply affected by science's practical achievements. At least since the publication of Newton's great treatise on physics in 1687 science had been accelerating like an object pulled by gravity. Scientists pierced the mysteries of heat and chemical reactions and the circulation of blood. The periodicity of the properties of chemical elements, magnetism, the origin of nature's diversity, radioactivity, and the microbial basis of infectious disease stood revealed. These triumphs seemed all the proof anyone needed of the superiority of the scientific method and, by extension, the rational powers of the brain.

Moreover, they promised to provide an antidote to the human passions and fighting faiths that recently, as throughout history, had produced unutterable horror. Whether they had experienced battle firsthand, as Holmes had, or only its awful consequences, it had marked them all; their minds sought refuge. "To many of the men who had been through the [Civil] war," wrote Louis Menand of the intellectuals of Holmes's generation, "the values of professionalism and expertise were attractive; they implied impersonality, respect for institutions as effective organizers of enterprise, and a modern and scientific attitude."[2]

Peirce's arguments against metaphysical abstraction influenced the American philosophical movement known as pragmatism, which philosopher and psychologist William James described as "looking away from first things, principles, 'categories,' supposed necessities; and of looking toward last things, fruits, consequences, facts."[3] Pragmatism had affinities with the European philosophical movement known as logical positivism, which held that any statement that cannot be verified empirically is either meaningless or nothing but a definition. This was scientific method raised to a general theory of knowing. Eventually pragmatism's concentration on consequences and facts and positivism's insistence on verification became embodied in the celebrated Chicago journalistic maxim, "If your mother says she loves you, check it out." But first they passed through the mind of Walter Lippmann.

Born an only child in New York in 1889, Lippmann grew up in comfortable surroundings, graduated from Harvard full of promise, went to work for muckraker Lincoln Steffens, then helped found the *New Republic*. He began to publish his views in books when he was still quite young. His first was radical in mood, distrustful of reason, and sure of emotion. But Lippmann was only young briefly. Of his next book, biographer Ronald Steel wrote, "Gone was the exuberant celebration of experience for its own sake, the exaltation of intuition, the downgrading of reason. In their place was an emphasis on scientific management and rational blueprints for organizing society."[4] Lippmann had become an exemplar of the Progressive Era.

Central to the thinking of this time, observed Robert Wiebe, one of its leading historians, was the belief in the authority of experts. Progressive Era political theorists, he wrote, "were convinced that the process of becoming an expert, immersing oneself in the scientific method, eradicated petty passions and narrow ambitions, just as it removed flaws in reasoning. The product was a perfect bureaucrat."[5] Lippmann's important contribution was to include journalists among Progressive society's rational guardians; in Wiebe's less lofty terms, Lippmann imagined reporters and editors could be perfect bureaucrats, too.

Lippmann made this argument most unequivocally in his book *Liberty and the News*, written in 1919. There he proclaimed the columns of newspapers "common carriers," referring to a body of law limiting the power of railroads and other means of transport to refuse to carry things brought to them.[6] Lippmann's analogy was dramatic for its time; it suggested that newspapers had an obligation to print facts and ideas their owners did not like. Something very much like it persists in the Standard Model, an insistence that news media provide a forum for conflicting opinions and an expectation that media companies will publish even facts and opinions that sharply conflict with their business interests.

"There can be no higher law in journalism than to tell the truth and shame the devil," Lippmann wrote in *Liberty and the News*.[7] Though he did not give particular guidance about how to determine who or what was the devil, he did suggest a method for determining the truth and a program for getting journalists to use it. The program was professional training "in which the ideal of objective testimony is cardinal."[8] And as to the method: "It does not matter that the news is not susceptible of mathematical statement. In fact, just because news is complex and slippery, good reporting requires the exercise of the highest of the scientific virtues."[9]

I have a framed piece of paper that is a remnant of Lippmann's ideal. My degree from the Medill School of Journalism at Northwestern University, founded in 1921, not long after he wrote *Liberty and the News*, is a bachelor's of *science* in journalism, not a bachelor's of arts.

All of the central elements of the Standard Model can be found in one form or another in Lippmann's small book, but it would be an oversimplification to say that he was their only father. These ideas were in the Progressive Era air. Journalism was only one of the areas of activity trying to become professional and scientific.[10] Still, Lippmann's was the leading journalistic voice proclaiming a new methodology and a new set of obligations, and he projected it with an assurance bordering on arrogance. "They [journalists] need not be much concerned," he wrote, "if leathery-minded individuals ask What is Truth of all who plead for the effort of truth in modern journalism. Jesting Pilate asked the same question, and he also would not stay for an answer."[11]

Journalism professor Tom Goldstein noted the seeming disconnect between this jaunty assertion and the intellectual direction science was actually taking at the time. "While Lippmann was promoting greater objectivity for journalism, intellectuals and artists were moving away from objectivity . . . ," Goldstein wrote. "Lippmann's timing was off."[12]

Not by much. By the time he finished *Liberty and the News*, what he later called "the acids of modernity"[13] were already working on him, turning his own views leathery. This revealed itself in his next book, *Public Opinion*, published in 1922, which a communications scholar later called the "founding book" of American media studies.[14] Its skepticism undermined the professional aspirations of *Liberty and the News*. Not much in modernist or for that matter in late twentieth-century postmodern or critical theory goes deeper in its doubt than this: "There are no canons to direct [the journalist's] mind. . . . His version of the truth is only his version."[15]

In *Public Opinion* Lippmann concluded that the economic forces on newspapers are such that "public opinions must be organized for the press if they are to be sound, not by the press as is the case today."[16] In other words, journalists couldn't become wise bureaucrats after all. Real bureaucrats would have to show them the way.

His next book, *The Phantom Public*, published in 1927, took his skepticism even further, to the heart of the basic assumptions of American democracy. "In the cold light of experience," he wrote, "he [the citizen] knows that his sovereignty is a fiction. He reigns in theory, but in fact he does not govern."[17]

In the early part of the twentieth century, doubt about democracy was not the half of it. The theories of Einstein, and a little later Werner Heisenberg and Niels Bohr, seemed to attack our commonsense understanding of such basic things as space and time as well as the very possibility of certainty. Freud's writing called into question whether we even knew what drove us from inside, not to mention whether we could hope to reason well about the world outside. In a graduation speech in 1929 the great jurist Roscoe Pound complained: "In place of reason we have subconscious wishes, repressed desires, rooted behavior tendencies, habitual predispositions which are different for each individual economic unit. In place of enlightenment we have—well, glands."[18]

It would be mistaken to think that the Standard Model was naive about science. Sociologist of journalism Michael Schudson has argued that the journalistic ideal of objectivity arose "as a reaction against skepticism" and was "the assertion of a method designed for a world in which even facts could not be trusted."[19] Despite the corrosive modernity that ate away at Lippmann (or perhaps because of it), the Standard Model that he proposed took hold. First professional schools and organizations promoted it, and then, as competition declined in the second half of the twentieth century, most news businesses adopted it.

DISINTERESTEDNESS AS A DISCIPLINE

In his time Walter Lippmann was both a herald of professional journalism and a prophet of its philosophical weakness, while as a practitioner he built a huge following. His column appeared in more than two hundred newspapers at the height of his success.[20] Neither in theory nor in practice, did he ever abandon one aspect of the Standard Model, the distrust of emotion. This manifested itself in his belief in the discipline of disinterestedness as both a professional and personal imperative.

Lippmann sometimes behaved in ways that today might seem to conflict with this. He had relationships with political figures—even serving as an informal advisor—that now would face professional criticism. But he always seemed willing to follow his professional reasoning wherever it took him, even when this meant offending in print someone who might have thought him a friend and confidante. And when it came to financial conflicts of interest, Lippmann drew a much sharper line than most journalists of his day. In the 1920s while he was editorial page editor of the *New York World,* he overheard a contributor to his page talking on the phone with an official of a bank. The journalist appeared to be moonlighting, and Lippmann accused the man of providing the bank advance notice of what the *World* was going to publish. The man denied it, but Lippmann never let him appear on his page again. The man shortly thereafter left the *World* and joined the *New York Times.* His name was Arthur Krock, who went on to become Lippmann's greatest rival for political and journalistic influence.[21]

Even as he contended with the day-to-day management of an editorial page, Lippmann's mind drew him to philosophical concerns. The more profound his skepticism, the more strongly he held to the ideal of disinterestedness. In *Preface to Morals,* in which he struggled with the implications of human existence without God, he wrote: "To become detached from one's passions and to understand them consciously is to render them disinterested. A disinterested mind is harmonious with itself and with reality. This is the principle by which a humanistic culture becomes bearable."[22]

(One distinction worth making here: Detachment and disinterestedness can mean formal independence from the people and organizations one is reporting on. They can also mean holding at an emotional distance the matters one is writing about. When I use the words "detached" or "disinterested," it will be in the latter sense. I will use "independence" to describe the absence of conflict of interest. Another related concept is neutrality, by which I mean the discipline of withholding judgment among competing assertions or arguments. These days people have been using "disinterested" as a synonym for "uninterested." I promise that I will not use it that way.)

Though Lippmann understood that the press needed to touch people's emotions to get their attention,[23] he also believed that emotion got in the way of knowledge of the world. "In truly effective thinking," he wrote in *Public Opinion,* "the prime necessity is to liquidate judgments, regain an innocent eye, disentangle feelings, be curious and open-hearted."[24]

He did not think this was easy. "It is as exhilarating to think as it is to dance," he observed, "and just as natural."[25] Nevertheless, he believed that a person could actually live by this hard discipline, which provided the only true path to knowledge and spiritual health. Today there is reason to question all parts of his belief.

DANGEROUS FEELINGS

Distrust of emotion is implicit in the Standard Model of Professional Journalism, though this is not without ambiguities. Independence and neutrality can be threatened by the upheavals of emotion. Still, as Lippmann acknowledged, journalists need to connect with the audience, and communicators throughout recorded time have always known that the most powerful way to do that is through the audience's feelings. In practice the avoidance of emotion has never been complete. As Schudson wrote, "Journalists practice a more complex and more interesting journalism than they preach."[26]

When I started in journalism, a cliché of the trade, usually delivered with a sigh by a world-weary old hand to an apprentice, was that you had to "make 'em laugh or make 'em cry." I remember one day in 1974 in the old, precomputer *Tribune* newsroom, talking with another reporter about an interview she had been assigned. Simas Kudirka had just returned to the United States four years after having jumped ship from a Soviet naval vessel in U.S. waters, clambered aboard a U.S. Coast Guard cutter, only to be returned to the Soviets. When it was discovered that his mother was a U.S. citizen, the United States successfully demanded his release from Soviet prison.

The other reporter and I were sitting under the shadow left on the wall by the removal of the old *Tribune* watchwords, "The American Paper for Americans." She was telling me how Kudirka's supporters had bargained with U.S. news organizations vying for an interview with the sailor.

It was worth whatever we had to do to get it, she said. The story will tear at people's hearts.

Sounds like the real story is the Selling of Simas Kudirka, I said.

That's why you are never going to get ahead in this business, Fuller, she said.

But at that very moment the professionalization of newspapers was accelerating, and as it did, the reluctance to openly pluck at heartstrings in stories involving public policy increased. Schudson has written of how much the media since the 1960s matured and became "more professional, detached, and analytical."[27] By the late 1980s a study of public communications about politics concluded that news coverage by traditional media tended to be "dry" while audience reaction tended to be emotional.[28]

This certainly would not have been said of the journalism of Lippmann's time nor even of the journalism of my youth. But by the time I became editor in the late 1980s, the balance in the tension between reliance on and distrust of emotion had shifted so far toward the latter that I started to find myself stumbling on it.

One pratfall occurred in the course of the *Tribune*'s early efforts to adapt to the information revolution. As part of a two-day meeting of the paper's senior editors to discuss our digital future, I invited one of my predecessors to speak, the late Clayton Kirkpatrick, whom I revered. The changes he had made in the late 1960s had rapidly modernized the paper's approach to news and finally gotten it to follow the Standard Model's professional standards. It was he who had taken the grandiose motto, "The World's Greatest Newspaper," off the nameplate of the *Tribune* and "The American Paper for Americans" off the newsroom wall. I figured he would have something important to say about envisioning the future and getting a big institution like the *Tribune* to adapt to it.

He delivered a measured, thoughtful talk about good journalism and the challenges of change. But when someone asked him how the paper should think about using television to get its message out, his answer came instantly. Newspapers speak to people's reason, he said. Stay away from TV; it plays on the emotions.

Kirkpatrick's warning found a receptive audience among our editors, though it was anything but helpful to me, since I was trying to get the editorial department to embrace new forms of disseminating our messages, including TV. This was not the only time when I found myself wondering whether the Standard Model had become so severe that it was isolating us from the audience we were trying to reach. The editors who gathered every afternoon for the meeting to decide what should go on page one often seemed to shy away from playing up stories that they knew would fascinate readers. Sometimes I would ask for a show of hands who would read every word of such a story. Most would admit their curiosity but still would vote against page one play. My father used to have a phrase for this kind of story: "too good for our readers."

Nowhere did professional values and actual practice become as tangled up as they did in the way we dealt with celebrities.

THE CYCLE OF CELEBRITY

By the end of the first decade of the twenty-first century coverage of celebrities—entertainers, sports heroes, and high profile politicians and business leaders in their nonprofessional capacity—had become ubiquitous and largely unrestrained. So you may find it difficult to recall the time when newspapers and even television news did not overflow with gossip about the famous. But in the last decades of the twentieth century most good newspapers rarely stooped to report celebrity news, except perhaps on the sports or entertainment pages.

When celebrity news did slip out into the main news sections, it caused a professional stir. Kirkpatrick had been furious, for example, when one day in 1977 when he was away, his top editors had put the story of the death of Elvis at the top of the front page. Perhaps remembering this, my immediate predecessor as editor simply refused to put almost any obituary short of a president's or pope's on page one.

By the time I became editor, the immediate instinct of most serious journalists was to resist the audience's interest in celebrity, even when their stories had deep and meaningful social resonance. The very fact that huge numbers of people were powerfully drawn to such stories seemed to make serous journalists recoil, as if this embarrassed them.[29]

Take, for example, the 1997 death of Princess Diana. Her sudden, violent end was very big news everywhere. The outpouring of public sentiment was enormous. Newspapers rode the story heavily at first. Then the stern guardians of the Standard Model weighed in to complain that far too much attention was being paid.

Yet the story spoke powerfully to many women, reaching them emotionally in an important way. The storybook princess ended up living a nightmare. The prince had turned into a toad. Every woman whose expectations of happiness with a man had ever gone sour could empathize with Diana. Her death was the death of dreams, and the only reason anyone could say the story did not merit the attention it got was because its true significance had nothing to do with public policy.

Another curious aspect of our behavior is the cycle of fascination and revulsion about individual celebrities. First, we raise someone up to inhuman heights. Then we destroy her. Once the destructive part of the cycle takes hold, even decent journalists seem willing to say things about a celebrity that they would never think to say about anyone else. They all but forget the principle of verification, impute to a celebrity all manner of horrible motives, and delve into aspects of her family and sexual life that would generally deserve a respectful and total silence. The coverage of the royal follies in Great Britain was only one example. Even if you had no use for Prince Charles except as the best example of why Thomas Paine was right, think of all the awful things that were written about his second bride. Some years back a number of papers went so far as to publish the contents of a particularly graphic and repulsive love note Charles sent the unfortunate woman.

: : :

Historian Daniel Boorstin became something of a celebrity himself when he wrote that a celebrity "is a person who is known for his well-knownness."[30] That definition is good, as far as it goes, but what Boorstin did not begin to deal with was why. The simplest reason, of course, is that figures known to large numbers of people help the media attract the attention of a big audience. So nobody should be surprised that the media cooperate in creating such figures. This is not at all new. Even Homer needed heroes and knew how to fashion them from the messy stuff of history and myth, but the process has speeded up so much that it has degraded the very nature of fame. "True valor, true sainthood, true professionalism" wrote Leo Braudy in his magnificent history *The Frenzy of Renown*, "required no awards, no canonizations to affirm its conviction of accomplishment. But in a world characterized by the journalistic desire to find new stars every few seconds and then throw them aside, self approval was becoming more difficult for anyone whose profession, talent, genius, vocation, or mere occupation had anything to do with the approval of others."[31]

During a brief period away from the newspaper business, I worked as a lawyer on the staff of Attorney General Edward Levi during the Ford administration. One day a good friend of mine, who wrote for a distinguished magazine, sat down with Levi for an interview. After he finished, my friend walked down the hall to my office. I asked him how it had gone.

Like no interview I've ever had with a public official, he said.

How so? I asked.

At some point, my friend said, I told him that it sounded as though he was making his decisions for history. Without a moment's hesitation Levi said, "What else is there?"

Years later I went to the White House to talk to the Clintons. It was during the first half of the president's first term, and Hillary had invited a classmate of ours from Yale Law School and me to visit. I was editor of the *Tribune* by then, and the Clintons were troubled by the treatment they were receiving from the news media. We talked with Hillary first, and after listening to her complaints, I told her the story of what Ed Levi had said to my journalist friend about why he made decisions for history.

Do it that way, I said, and the media will take care of themselves.

It won't help us with the midterm elections, she said.

I tried the Levi anecdote again when we sat down with the president—with even less positive results.

A week or so later a photograph arrived in the mail of my friend and me with the president in the Oval Office. My children were very excited by this. I told them that one day the photo would be theirs.

Just remember, I said, that it is a picture of the president of the United States not listening to your daddy.

It is no surprise, of course, that the approval of others matters greatly to politicians, nor that what the media say makes a difference. Nor, for that matter, is it shocking that history can seem to politicians less important than midterm elections. The point is simply that the acceleration of events and the ubiquity of public performance and overnight ratings for everything and everybody have made it extremely difficult for people who are part of that world, including journalists, to think about assessments that transcend the immediate.

People who become celebrities are, in the words of a student of contemporary fame, "structured to be perpetually vulnerable."[32] Once the celebrity has become well known, journalists begin to compete with her. Again, this is not new. The competition between writers and their subjects goes all the way back to antiquity. Braudy wrote that "the greatest aspiration of writers is to be beyond the categories of social hierarchy."[33] Once that meant immortality; today the time horizon is probably even closer than the midterm elections. And so it does not take long for those who have shone their bright light upon a person to begin to see her blemishes, and in drawing attention to those blemishes attract attention to themselves.

This competition could explain why journalists tend to turn on the objects they've made fascinating. But why does the audience buy it? And people do buy it. Just go to a grocery store checkout counter, where the space is prime real estate for impulse purchases. Companies pay large amounts of money to have their products placed there; most are media companies. We have even given a name to a certain kind of hero-killing publication: supermarket tabloid. You will find magazines at the checkout counter that seem to specialize in extremely unflattering pictures of stars— bloodshot eyes, cellulite thighs, sagging bellies. You will also find, of course, the more balanced magazines like *People* that both build up celebrities and tear them down.

"There are two fame stories the public especially likes to hear," Braudy wrote. "In one, the triumph occurs only after the surmounting of overwhelming personal difficulties. Then, after fame is achieved, the second story appears. It is a story of retribution and revenge in which the hero or heroine falls, destroyed by fate, or chance, or just plain arrogance—because they mistakenly took their fame to be their own rather than a gift of the audience."[34]

The psychoanalytically inclined might say that the idealizing and subsequent destruction of idols repeats the basic family drama in which a child first thinks the world of his parents then needs to reject them in order to establish her own independent selfhood. Even if that seems farfetched, it is impossible to look deeply into the phenomenon of fame and celebrity without seeing it as a deeply emotional, triangular relationship among the famous individual, the people who depict her life, and the audience that drinks in all the details.

The emotional relationship between celebrity and audience, however distant in reality, can be intense. This is why, if you see a TV or movie star on the street or in a restaurant, you may feel an almost irresistible impulse to say hello. You know her so well that your mind whispers to you that she knows you as well.

As the information revolution broke down the fences that kept mass society together, the nature of a public person began to expand. Now celebrities can be created in many places, and the need to create them has increased. For example, when cable television opened more channels into people's homes, the price of original dramatic and comedy programming began to rise, as more competitors bid for scarce talent and ideas. Reality TV exploded on the scene not only because the audience liked seeing people just like them become celebrities of a sort but also because this kind of program was cheap to make. The same is true for semi-news shows like *Dateline, 20/20,* and *Entertainment Tonight.* The voraciousness of twenty-four-hour cable television and news on the Web drives a certain kind of tawdry crime story into an epic, usually with quite ordinary people at its center. They become celebrities whether they want to be or not; a surprising number want to be.

Thomas de Zengotita, a contributing editor of *Harper's Magazine,* has written provocatively about the democratization of fame. The profusion of media spaces in which to be noticed, he wrote, has permitted spectators to become "mini-celebrities . . . who dominate chat rooms and game sites, and the blogs, the intimate 'life journals.'"[35] As for the audience, the expansion of publicity venues has narrowed the distance between celebrity and public. "Identification. Self-recognition," de Zengotita wrote. "It may be fact, it may be fiction, it may be comedy or tragedy, but it's all aimed at eliciting responses that go, 'I'm exactly like that,' or 'Imagine how I would feel if . . .'

"It's all about you."[36]

Well, yes and no. It turns out that it is also all about your tribe.

OF GROOMING, GOSSIP, AND GETTING ALONG IN GROUPS

If the emotions provide an explanation for why people need heroes and celebrities, then what explains why human beings have this emotional need? Evolutionary psychologist Robin Dunbar provided an intriguing answer: It all started with our primate ancestors picking nits.[37]

When the terrestrial primates came down from the trees where their cousins spent most of their lives, they faced new predators. They had two ways of dealing with this—growing physically larger or living in larger groups, which increased the number of eyes looking out for trouble, deterred attack, and caused confusion in a predator by creating a chaos of individuals fleeing in all directions when an attack came. To increase group size, Dunbar wrote, they needed some way to keep individuals close enough to be useful but far enough away not to be a nuisance. The mechanism that developed through natural selection was grooming.

Touch promotes bonding. Think of a child at her mother's breast or lovers walking hand-in-hand. When an ape gets rid of little insects by combing its fingers through another's hair, it is accomplishing more than hygiene. It is establishing and reinforcing the feelings of mutual trust that hold the group together when, under threat, any single individual might do better on its own.

The time primates spend in social grooming, Dunbar argued, is directly related to group size. The more grooming, the bigger the group. But at some point the group could not get bigger, no matter how advantageous it might have been, because there was only so much time an individual could spend picking nits. After all, they had to eat and sleep and occasionally mate.

Dunbar proposed that natural selection favored a larger neocortex (roughly speaking, the part of the brain devoted to complex thought and behavior) because having bigger brains made it possible to hold together even larger social groups. Language, Dunbar argued, developed to replace the time-consuming practice of social grooming; an individual could only groom one other individual at a time, but she could gossip with quite a number of people at once.

Because people manage their direct relationships through conversation, most conversations are about social matters; a study Dunbar made in England showed that they accounted for about two-thirds of conversation time.[38] By talking about others, individuals not only learned information about whether the others were trustworthy, but also helped establish or enhance their own reputations by what they said and how they said it. To Dunbar, gossip is all about the management of reputation.

The size of the neocortex in humans seems to limit their social networks to about 150 people. As our society became more complicated, 150 relationships turned out to be not enough. The problem for humans usually is not avoidance of predators, of course. Or at least not of tigers and lions. The need for establishing trust has gone far beyond that. To whom will we entrust our children? With whom are we willing to do business? To whom are we willing to write a candid e-mail?

Not only do we need to know the reputation of many more than 150 people today; even among the people we do know, we may not have too many people in common to talk about. One way to solve this problem is to talk about a group of people that we all *do* have in common—celebrities. We don't, of course, need to evaluate their reputations in order to know whether to trust them, though when they act in disappointing ways it can seem like betrayal. It is just that by talking about them to others we can establish something about ourselves. We can manage our reputations by picking nits about them.

Meantime, as the size of the group of people with whom we need to have some relationship has increased to strain our capacity, the evidence suggests that the size of people's network of very close friends (rather than just those they converse with) has declined. In 1985 a study of a cross-section of Americans found that the average number of confidants reported by individuals was three. In 2004 the most common response—by 25 percent of those who answered—was none.[39] It is not much of a stretch to suggest that the rise of virtual social networks on the Internet relates directly to the deterioration of real social networks. But virtual networks provide impoverished communication: Ordinarily no facial expressions. No body language. Limited nuance in tone of voice. No touch. No smell. "The mind that seeks to connect is first about the body," wrote a leading neuroscientist, "and leaving the body behind can make human connections less satisfying."[40]

Toward the end of the era of mass communications, *New Yorker* writer George W. S. Trow argued that there are only two contexts in which people see the world. He called them "the intimate grid and the grid of two hundred million."[41] Celebrities connect the two. A star turns out to have a drug problem in her family. "Suddenly, the grids merge," Trow wrote. "You and me and baby and drugs together on the grid of two hundred million. It's so intimate. It's like waking up with a friend. But just for a minute."[42]

When mass media fragmented, the grids remained, as did the yearning for a connection between them. The free-for-all scramble for attention was on, and all the journalistic inhibition concerning celebrities seemed to vanish. The audience wants surrogate intimacy? You'd better give it intimacy, or someone else will. On television it became difficult to distinguish between celebrity pseudo-events and news of historical significance. Anchors spoke of U.S. relations with Britain and the tempestuous relationships of Britney Spears in the same breath. Even the most staid newspapers regularly reported the substance abuse problems and other indiscretions of actors and actresses. The Standard Model has not adapted to the challenge of celebrity; it simply has relegated these people to the same status as the comics and horoscope. Professionalism has not applied.

: : :

Celebrity is just one example of the way the Standard Model has failed to deal squarely with the tension between the need to reach people and the distrust of appeals to emotion. As the pressures to attract an audience grow, so does the need for some resolution of the tension. Finding the right balance must begin with an examination of the assumptions embedded in the Standard Model about the way the human mind works—how it knows and what gets in the way. Those assumptions have quite a pedigree. Plato shared them. So, in his own way, did Freud. But neuroscientists have come to see things differently. In order to appreciate how and why, we have to go back to the origins of the classical idea of the way people do and should think.

CHAPTER THREE

MODELS OF THE MIND

The human mind is a dazzling instrument. It is capable of producing everything from the poetry of Shakespeare and the music of Bach to the cruel obsessions of the Marquis de Sade, from the tenderness between parent and child to the savagery of war. It is also capable of great and rapid modulation. In the passing of an instant a person can break free of the deepest sorrow and embrace all the stars of the heavens. To borrow out of context one biologist's lovely phrase, the human brain is "a melody which sings itself."[1]

It is difficult to know with any precision when such human qualities as self-consciousness, spoken language, and awareness of one's own eventual death evolved. But at some point in the grand opera of our evolutionary line the hominid began to appreciate its ability to think, and since then our thinking about thinking has never stopped.

Long before we had scientific means to study the physical brain, philosophers and poets used their powers of observation, introspection, intuition, and reasoning to try to understand themselves. The philosophers in particular asked what we could truly know and how we could know it, a branch of philosophy that came to be known as epistemology. What resulted were various models of the mind, some of them remarkably prescient. The traces of these models live on in our contemporary habits of thinking about thought, even as neuroscience has rendered some of them obsolete.

The relation of emotion to human understanding has special importance as we consider how the ancient information processor in our skull is dealing with its rapidly evolving information environment and what this means for journalism. Classical philosophers observed a significant difference between the coolness of rational, logical thought and the heat of the passions. It was the difference between systematically working through the implications of the theorems of Euclidian geometry and the throb of love.

For Plato pure reason was the only way to reach the Truth. And living life in accordance with reason was more than a matter of epistemology. It was an ethical imperative. "The true moral ideal," he wrote, "whether self-control or integrity or courage, is really a kind of purgation from all these emotions, and wisdom itself is a sort of purification."[2] Aristotle's views had more nuance. While he agreed that when desire overcomes reason, a man is "incontinent,"[3] in another place he argued that in certain circumstances anger is appropriate; since it always results from the perception of an offense, it would be foolish not to get angry when the offense is real.[4]

The Stoics of Greece and Rome advanced the idea that emotion, like perception, could be a kind of knowing. Contemporary philosopher Martha Nussbaum described the Stoic view this way: "Emotions are forms of evaluative judgment that ascribe to certain things and persons outside a person's own control great importance for the person's own flourishing."[5] But the Stoics nonetheless made a sharp division between reason and emotion. They argued that in order for a human to live a good life, reason must control emotion and desire, which, as Epictetus wrote, brings "disturbances, tumults, misfortunes, bad fortunes, mournings, lamentations, envies."[6] Epictetus's solution was simple to state but impossible to follow: to let reason lead you not to desire anything but what is.

Walter Lippmann's distrust of emotion had its roots in the Stoic tradition. The mature man, he wrote, "would face pain with fortitude, for he would have put it away from the inner chambers of his soul. Fear would not haunt him, for he would be without compulsion to seize anything and without anxiety as to its fate. He would be strong, not with the strength of hard resolve, but because he was free of that tension which vain expectations beget."[7]

The model of the mind that most classical thinkers shared, whatever their differences, included two central elements: First, reason is an activity of the mind wholly distinct from emotion. And second, the two are hierarchically related, with reason supreme and emotions roiling below, always needing to be beaten back like an unruly mob.[8]

This philosophy and the related metaphor of the struggle between heart and head had remarkable power for more than a millennium. You can find their echoes in most of the great Western philosophies. Think of the enduring phrase of French theologian Blaise Pascal that "the heart has its reasons, which reason does not know."[9] Or political philosopher Thomas Jefferson's moving "Dialogue between My Head & My Heart."[10] You can even find its clear reflection in the work of Sigmund Freud. Ego and id are not precisely reason and emotion, but they are close. And Freud's goal for psychoanalysis—where id was, let ego be—could have been a translation of the classical philosophers' view of the hierarchy of the mind into a new idiom.

There have been very few dissenters along the way.[11] But now neuroscientists, using techniques that permit them to observe the functioning of the brain in real time, have disproved the classic model in both its aspects.

OUR MOST VEXING PROBLEM

The field of neuroscience began developing rapidly toward the end of the twentieth century. Competing theories always mark such times of rapid scientific discovery. Conclusions have to be more tentative than when a field has matured. When scientific change is occurring quickly, even explanations building on what seems to be scientific consensus need to be made with caution, clarity, and humility. That includes the ideas I will be offering here.

I will hew as closely as possible to what most experts in the field agree on. Where there is important disagreement, I will try to note it, sometimes in textual footnotes, which I will also occasionally use to provide more detail on a particular point. I will try to avoid being overly technical. Something will inevitably be lost in the effort. To compensate for this, I offer at the end of this book a bibliographic essay meant to help an interested reader go deeper into the science and philosophy.

Before I give a brief overview of the subject, readers who have not immersed themselves in the often difficult literature of neuroscience need to rid themselves of a few prevailing misconceptions.

First, whatever some teacher once told you, we do not use only 5 or 10 or 20 percent of our brainpower. Some parts of our brains function constantly—regulating our temperature, heartbeat, and other vital functions. Other parts flash into operation only briefly and occasionally. Think of the mathematical value of pi, if you can, or if you would rather, think of a few stanzas of a great poem or the melody of a song. The precise networks by which you store and recall these do not operate all the time. Most of the time they are dormant. But it would be wrong to think of them as part of an unused 80 percent. In fact, the brain's processing resources are limited, and mental tasks regularly have to compete with one another for access to them. The metaphor of economics applies. Just as scarcity is the rule in a full employment economy, scarcity is also the rule in the brain, which is why information overload causes stress.

Second, we must correct for our brains' natural binary bias, which manifests itself in the belief, for example, that behavior must be determined either by nature (genetics) or nurture (environment), that our thoughts and actions are either the product of fundamental and unchanging human nature or are socially constructed by our culture, that knowledge either comes hardwired as part of our brain's anatomy or is learned through interaction with the external world. Neuroscience pioneer Donald Hebb is credited with the canny observation that asking whether nature or nurture contributes more to human personality is like asking which contributes more to the area of a rectangle, its height or width.[12] Understanding the functioning of the brain requires that we appreciate the contributions to behavior of both nature and the environment, both the evolution of the human genome and the variety of human cultures, both anatomy and the brain's prodigious capacity to learn.

Third, though evolution has left many traces, our brains do not have a reptilian part, an early mammal part, and a later mammal part. Though structures that resemble those found in today's reptiles and nonprimate mammals can be found inside the human skull, the process of natural selection has significantly altered their functioning and made them human.

Fourth, though it is useful for some purposes to think of some of the more reflexive parts of our brains as a "limbic system," it is misleading to think of this system as being the part of the brain that processes emotion while the higher and more recently evolved neocortex executes reason. As we shall see, there is no clear boundary between reason and emotion, either conceptually or anatomically.

Fifth, though you can gain quite a bit of understanding about the human brain by thinking of it as a computer, the metaphor fails in important ways. As one prominent neuroscientist put it, "While computers obey a few rigid logical rules, biology carries out many subtle functions created by aeons of evolutionary selection."[13]

Sixth, as important and explanatory as the physiology and biochemistry of the brain are, what makes our brain human is its capacity to create and manipulate symbols in the face of profound uncertainty. Ambiguity, Maurice Merleau-Ponty observed, "is of the essence of human existence, and everything we live or think has several meanings. . . . Thus there is in human existence a principle of indeterminacy, and this indeterminacy . . . does not stem from some imperfection of our knowledge. . . . Existence is indeterminate in itself by reason of its fundamental structure."[14]

Science tends to deal with the subjectivity of lived experience by disregarding it.[15] As we go deeper into what neuroscience has discovered, we will find that there are truths that cannot be expressed in chemical equations or wiring diagrams but only through the creation of images or the telling of stories.

Today all but the most reductive thinkers would concur with Reinhold Niehbur that "man has always been his own most vexing problem."[16] And even the least reductive thinkers would probably agree that the brain is a special kind of information processor. But there is an abiding tension between the two ways of looking at the human mind. E. O. Wilson wrote that "the love of complexity without reductionism makes art; the love of complexity with reductionism makes science."[17] Only together do they make wisdom.

Finally, as we turn to the neuroscience, it is worth recalling this warning from a philosopher of technology: "The light of a new scientific theory blinds us for a while, and sometimes a long while, toward other things in our world. The greater and more spectacular the theory, the more likely it is to foster our indolent disposition to oversimplify, to twist all the ordinary matters of experience to fit into the new framework, and if they do not, to lop them off."[18] Some of that has been happening as the discoveries of neuroscience become available to the general public. At one time Freudian categories seized the popular imagination, giving rise to silly pseudo-explanations of nearly everything human. Today the rule of Oedipal Complex and the superego has given way to the rule of the amygdala and the dopamine reward system. Our minds are capable of being just as silly about those.

INFORMATION PROCESSORS OF FLESH AND BLOOD

Entry into the world of neuroscience can be daunting. We don't see or feel most of the anatomical structures of the brain; they don't have easy to understand names like collarbones or kneecaps or fingernails. They are called the aqueduct of Sylvius or the hippocampus or the anterior cingulate gyrus. We may have heard of some neurochemicals: dopamine because it has something to do with Parkinson's disease, serotonin because Prozac works on it some-how to alleviate depression, and of course endorphins because they give us natural highs. But these are only a few of the chemicals that work inside the brain, and each of them has multiple functions and malfunctions depending upon where, when, and in what quantity they appear.

Before approaching the aspects of brain functioning that have the great-est implications for understanding how humans are responding to the changes in their information environment, it is important to have at least a basic understanding of the way our information processor of flesh and blood works.

The brain is composed of nerve cells called neurons, which have projec-tions called axons and dendrites that reach out to make connections—axon to dendrite—with other neurons. Many people have tried to find words to express the astonishing complexity of the brain. One of my favorite descrip-tions is that every cubic millimeter (about the size of a pinhead) of the neo-cortex (the part of the brain where the most complex mental activity occurs) contains as many as one hundred thousand nerve cells, connected with one another by about a mile of fiber.[19] That means the six layers of the neocortex contain about 10 billion nerve cells and between one thousand and ten thou-sand times that many connections among them.[20] And the neocortex makes up only part of the brain. Here is another expert's way of approximating the sheer immensity of the brain's possibilities: if you factor in a conservative assumption about the various strengths with which nerve cells can influence one another, the different possible configurations of the brain come to ten to the trillionth power. The volume of the known universe, in cubic meters, by way of comparison, is only about ten to the eighty-seventh power.[21]

Neurons do their work by sending electrochemical impulses to other neurons. These impulses pass from a neuron's single transmission line (the axon) to one of another neuron's many receptors (the dendrites) at a point known as a synapse. Synapses are not simple plugs; their operation, even their number, changes depending on how often and when an electrochemi-cal charge passes through them.

How this happens provides a key to understanding how the brain learns. When a neuron fires an impulse across a synapse to another neuron, it changes the electrochemical condition of the second cell. If the change is great enough, the second cell will itself fire. But how much is great enough depends on what has happened before. In 1949 the Canadian psychologist Donald Hebb formulated what has come to be known as Hebb's rule:

Any two cells connected at a synapse that are repeatedly active at the same time will tend to become "associated" so that activity in one facilitates activity in the other.[22] In other words, it becomes easier for the first cell to get a rise out of the second if they both have previously fired at roughly the same time.

The real power of this process occurs when two neurons have synapses with a third, one of them strongly connected and the other weakly. If the first two fire together with a combined pulse strong enough to make the third fire, the next time it will take less of a combined pulse to get the third to fire. Moreover, the firing of the more weakly connected neuron will have as much effect as the firing of the strong one had before.

The behavioral implication of this is profound. Neuroscientist Joseph LeDoux put it this way: "This sort of thing happens all the time in daily life. If you are walking on the sidewalk in front of your neighbor's house (weak stimulus) and his dog bites you (strong stimulus), you will associate the sidewalk where you were bitten with the dog and be less inclined to walk that way."[23] Thus Hebb's rule helps explain the operant conditioning that occurred when Pavlov presented a dog with food and rang a bell at the same time. Soon the dog salivated whenever it heard the bell, even though no food was there.

The Hebb process applies not just to two- or three-neuron systems but to whole neuron networks as well. It is the reason learning takes place in all parts of the brain, not only the part that memorizes math facts or stanzas of poetry or that manipulates the grand abstractions of philosophy. Again, the connection between neurons strengthens through the coincidence of their mutual firing. As the neuroscience slogan has it, "Cells that fire together wire together." The more frequent the coincidence, the stronger the connection.

Thus, from the level of the neurons on up, the brain registers probability.[24] From probability it creates patterns. The pattern-making impulse is so powerful that the brain often thinks it has learned something about reality when it is simply registering pure coincidence.

Notice that even at the very basic, microscopic level, the brain experiences reality in a structurally biased way. In effect, it gives coincidence more than its due. Every neuron can learn, but structures sculpted by natural selection channel the learning process. The interplay between structure and learning is central to the way the brain works. And structural biasing occurs at all levels—from the activities of individual neurons right through the unconscious activities of the larger neuronal networks and on up to the conscious thought that humans have fancied to call rational.

CHAPTER FOUR

KNEES, NATURAL SELECTION, AND NEURON NETWORKS

Natural selection explains a great deal about why our brains came to have the structure they have today. It may be helpful to think of natural selection as a kind of tinkering. It does not build a structural feature that fits a particular purpose or ecological niche by starting from scratch. Instead, it takes what already exists and works from there. That is why our bodies contain features that trace directly back to quite differently functioning structures in earlier species. Or, as evolutionary biologist Neil Shubin cleverly put it, if we look hard enough into our own bodies, we can find our "inner fish."

Let's start somewhere—say the *Tiktaalik roseae,* whose fossilized remains Shubin and his team of researchers found on Ellesmere Island, Nunavik, Canada, in the Arctic Ocean. This creature lived about 375 million years ago when warm, shallow seas bathed the area. *Tiktaalik roseae* has many of the characteristics of a fish, such as gills. But its fins have a structure akin to a wrist and fingers, which allowed it to move about on land. It also had openings on the top of its head that suggested that it had begun to adapt to breathing air. So *Tiktaalik roseae* is a transitional animal—partway between fish and amphibian.

Its legacy also lives, somewhat unhappily, in our bodies. Shubin wrote: "Hurt your knee and you will almost certainly injure one or more of three structures. . . . So regular are injuries to these three parts of your knee that these three structures are known among doctors as the 'Unhappy Triad.' They are clear evidence of the pitfalls of having an inner fish. Fish do not walk on two legs."[1] Because our knees evolved from species that did not walk upright, because the tinkering of natural selection took what was given and made something new by changing it a little bit here and a little bit there, then a little more, then a little more, we do not have the knees that any reasonable designer would have given us for the purpose of running a marathon—or even walking downstairs.

The results of natural selection resemble New York City—with narrow cross-town streets that originated in the horse-drawn era—more than new communities like Columbia, Maryland, or Reston, Virginia, which were carefully planned for automobiles. In fact, what is so threatening to many people about Darwinism is that there is no master plan. Our brains are structured like handyman's gothic houses—except that there is no handyman.

Natural selection is an algorithmic process. That means it resembles the procedure by which you divide one four-digit number by another or the procedure by which a computer does the same thing. An algorithm is a routine for taking given inputs and producing a determinate output. (It is an intriguing antidote to fundamentalist atheism, by the way, to think about how the algorithm came into being.)

In the process of natural selection, chance occurrence—through mutation or otherwise—throws a change into the DNA of a single individual. If the change makes it more likely that she will pass on her genes, it will tend to spread in the population as generations succeed one another, child to grandchild to great-grandchild and so on down the centuries.

The survivors of the operation of the natural selection algorithm are the "fittest" only in a very specific sense. They have been likened to the winners of an elimination tournament in tennis. Twelve players begin. They play, two-by-two, with the winners playing one another two-by two in the next round until there is one winner. The winner is the best—not in some grand metaphysical sense, but only in the sense of having the qualities that allowed it to prevail in this particular game with these rules under these specific conditions.[2]

Unlike a tennis court, the playing field of the nature game does not remain fundamentally constant. Volcanoes erupt. Climate changes. Dry land floods. Continents collide and rupture. Moreover, the other organisms in the game—those with which one competes as well as those upon which one depends—also change. New predators arrive. Food withers on the vine. And, again, through the operation of chance, organisms' genes mutate, making slight differences in their physiognomies. Some of those differences give an individual a competitive advantage. Such an individual will have a greater chance of passing on her genes. To take the simplest case, her offspring have a 50 percent chance of inheriting those qualities.

After the next generation a quarter of her grandchildren will on average be advantaged. Even though the mathematical odds seem to decline, natural selection loads the dice. Eventually there will be more individuals with the mutated gene than without it because more of those without the mutation will die before reproducing or will have fewer offspring.

Under certain circumstances this can occur quickly. For example, any differential trait that made our European ancestors more likely to survive the plague would have fairly rapidly spread wherever the dread epidemic struck. Here the intensity of the environmental pressure would have driven selection more rapidly than usual. The ability of disease-causing bacteria to overcome antibiotics provides a simple, contemporary example of natural selection playing out within a relatively short period of time. A dangerous bacteria causes trouble for humans. Doctors develop medicine that kills the bacteria within the human body. But some of those bacteria will have mutated, giving them qualities (irrelevant before the introduction of the antibiotic) that make them a little more likely to survive the medical onslaught. They will reproduce more successfully. Some of their progeny will undergo more mutations, some of which will make them even more resistant to the antibiotic. They will have more reproductive success. And so on. Because the number of bacteria is enormous and reproduction is so rapid, slight increases in probability of success under intense selection pressure soon populate the environment with more resistant strains of the bacteria. Pretty soon the antibiotic doesn't work anymore, and doctors have to try to create a new one.

The evolution of bacteria can happen very quickly, but generally evolutionary change proceeds at a much slower pace. The time between generations in more complex organisms is typically longer, and advantages tend to be small and play themselves out over many, many generations. And so the human hand has not adapted to the typewriter, let alone the tiny cell phone keyboard. Our brains—our information processors—have not adapted to the overwhelming change in the information environment that began with the printing press and hurtles ahead at an ever-accelerating rate, since most of the genetic changes that affect social behavior occurred before the rise of civilization.[3]

Understanding the algorithmic process of natural selection helps us figure out how our brains got the way they are. One technique for doing so is analogous to the reverse engineering that businesses do with their competitors' products to understand the thinking behind their design. Knowing how the mind behaves today, theorists ask themselves how such behavior might have conferred an advantage in natural selection over time. Stephen Jay Gould scoffed at reverse engineering, calling its results "just so stories," after Rudyard Kipling's beguiling yarns; they may be intriguing but are incapable of scientific proof.[4] Gould's critique is a useful corrective; it is just not possible to be sure about the connection between today's human behavior and what life must have been like on the African savannah. But applied with eyes open to the risks, the technique of reverse engineering can offer intriguing hints about why we seem to have recurring habits of thought that get in the way of reliably knowing reality, which are as much a bane for journalists as for philosophers and scientists. "Our brains were shaped for fitness," wrote one psychologist, "not for truth."[5]

The brains we use to deal with today's message-saturated information environment are pretty much the same brains that our African ancestors used to outwit the big cats. Is it any wonder that we have lately been behaving kind of strangely toward the news?

THE ANATOMY OF THOUGHT

Neuroscientists and physicians use various terms to categorize the brain—rostral and caudal; forebrain, midbrain, and hindbrain; cortices and nuclei; frontal, occipital, parietal, and temporal lobes, and so on. In the interest of accessibility, whenever possible I will avoid using such terms. But mastering a few structural matters will help in understanding the way the brain relates to its information environment.

The brain is a system of systems, from the level of the single neuron with all its synaptic connections to neuronal networks that guide functions as basic as the beating of our hearts and as complex as the composition of a symphony. The normal human brain comes divided into two hemispheres. Though they seem in some ways anatomically and functionally symmetrical, with the right controlling activities on the left side of the body and the left controlling those on the right, in fact the hemispheres also display considerable specialization. In most right-handed people, for instance, the parts of the brain that control speech production and speech recognition are in the left hemisphere only.

The two hemispheres are connected so they can coordinate with one another. In professional musicians, who need intricate and precise collaboration of the two sides of their body, the structure that connects the hemispheres is larger than it is in the rest of us. This is one of the ways that, if presented with a brain from a person about whom they knew nothing, neuroanatomists could tell that it is a musician's—though they would not be able to recognize a painter's or writer's or mathematician's.[6]

In general the parts of the brain that form its core—and the parts lower down in the skull—emerged first in the evolutionary process, long predating the arrival of humans. They control such functions as respiration, heart rate, and blood pressure. As you can imagine, something very much like these structures must exist in all complex forms of animal life. They differ between bats and bards because of the tinkering of natural selection. But the basic structures are common to both.

Higher in the skull and farther forward are a series of structures involved in emotional response. These include, most prominently, the amygdala. Shaped something like an almond, the amygdala is centrally involved in human emotional response. It is particularly important in the emotion of fear and its cousin, anxiety.

The brain has the ability to send emotional messages via the amygdala through a quick route for immediate reaction and via a slower route for a more thoughtful response. So if we are sitting in a ballpark and a foul ball comes flying straight at our nose, our hands immediately fly up and our head drops down. We only think about it later.[7] The amygdala also connects in various ways to the hippocampus, which is involved in preparing memories to be stored elsewhere in the brain. Emotional arousal tends to make us more likely to remember something, like what we were doing the day the World Trade Center towers came down.

We share these structures with many of our ancestors. The similarity is especially close in mammals, which has allowed neuroscientists to learn a great deal that is applicable to humans by performing experiments on rats and monkeys that could not be performed on people.

At the top of the skull and wrapping around much of the rest of the brain is the neocortex. It consists of about two and a half square feet of neurons an eighth of an inch thick. If that seems awfully thin to be the thing that most makes us human, remember that it has about a million billion connections.

The neocortex receives information from the senses, through switching centers, such as the thalamus, that are deeper in the brain. In the neocortex the information begins to be readied for interpretation. For example, brain-imaging technology reveals that when simple figures are placed before the eyes, patterns appear in the visual part of the neocortex near the back of the skull, patterns that roughly resemble the figures.[8]

The neuron networks of the neocortex are interconnected with one another in such a way that what each network processes can be integrated with what the others process. The integration occurs in many places. For example, when our two eyes see something, the signals cross at a single point in the brain. There, half of the signal from each eye turns left and half turns right so that beyond it the binocular image is already beginning to be integrated into a single, three-dimensional whole. Systems such as the thalamus act as more than passive relay stations. They integrate signals from other centers, and this modulates the signals that are passed on ahead.[9] Moreover, integrating structures connect with other regions of the brain, broadening the context in which a moment is perceived. In addition to perceptions, long-term memories and other forms of learning can also enter the mix.

This is not the place to get deeply into the question of consciousness. Every aficionado of the mind from novelists to neuroscientists has weighed in, and still the nature of it remains a mystery. To some it will always be beyond human understanding, like the question why there is something rather than nothing. Others suggest that consciousness is just a question of the physical interactions of cells, chemicals, and the outside environment— like everything else we call biology.

There is no use our getting snared in this tangle, but one idea deserves mention, since it neatly contradicts the classical model of the mind as a hierarchy, with reason supreme and emotions subjugated. Philosopher Daniel Dennett and many others reject the idea, attributed to seventeenth-century philosopher René Descartes, that there is a single place in the brain where consciousness takes place. Instead, Dennett has argued that consciousness is distributed throughout the brain. The rods and cones of the eyes receive light and send a signal. As this proceeds through the thalamus, modified by other inputs, to the visual cortex and on from there, it meshes with memory, plans, moral judgments, all of which flash around the brain, sensing, contextualizing, interpreting, judging, in a continuous process. Dennett described it this way: "Contents arise, get revised, contribute to the interpretation of other contents or to the modulation of behavior . . . , and in the process leave their traces in memory, which then eventually decay or get incorporated into or overwritten by later contents, wholly or in part. . . . At any point in time there are multiple drafts of narrative fragments at various stages of editing in various places in the brain."[10]

Beyond the riddle of consciousness lies the mystery of the unconscious. We are only partly (perhaps minutely) aware of the information processing that goes on in our brains. There are many levels of the game. Are you conscious of what you do with the wheel of the car as you drive across country? Or does it arise in your mind only from time to time when the circumstances require attention to it? If you play the piano, are you thinking about the movement of each finger as you play a Bach fugue? (If you are, you won't get past a couple of notes.) Was Michael Jordan aware of the muscles he had to move as he found a way up through a moving mass of torsos, legs, and arms to fly to the net with the ball balanced in one hand for the stuff? More deeply, there are layers of hidden memory and habitual patterns that can color consciousness without entirely revealing the origin of the hue. Emotions have some of this quality.

With complexity of this sort attending every moment, you should doubt anyone who offers a simple, physical explanation of any mental activity such as a friend of mine's delighted repetition of what someone once told him—that everything we do will eventually be understood as the brain's effort to bathe itself in dopamine.

THE BRAIN'S RAM

If the classical philosophers had known brain anatomy, they might have identified as the seat of reason the lobes of the neocortex in the front part of the brain, particularly the prefrontal lobes (which lie under the forehead). This part of the brain plays the lead in controlling impulses, solving problems, making and carrying through with plans, interacting socially, and making ethical judgments.

One aspect of the frontal lobes has a central role in all conscious activity: working memory, which has been described as the brain's RAM, or random access memory.[11] Working memory holds small amounts of information briefly so that it can be used or integrated at a high level with other pieces of information. Everyone knows that nobody can hold very much information at the top of the mind at once. In fact, we can deal with much less than we probably realize. The prevailing view is that on average working memory can deal with only about seven pieces of information at a time. That happens to be the pre–area code number of digits in a phone number. Now even local phone numbers have gone to ten digits, and that is the least of the ways that life has gotten harder on the brain.

The size of working memory varies slightly from individual to individual. But it is never very large—not nearly as large as the working memory of other animals that need more because they lack the ability to symbolize, which increases how much our working memory can handle.

Working memory is perhaps the clearest example of a scarce resource in the brain. Overload it, and things go wrong. But if data come grouped together in chunks, then the working memory can be used to manipulate much larger concepts than a telephone number. Often area codes go into working memory as chunks. So do more complex pieces of information. The marketplace, for example, is a memory-conserving chunk that lumps together lots of things—economic theories, critiques of its assumptions of rationality, countercritiques, and so forth. As a concept, it can be held in working memory with other concepts, such as democracy or scarcity. There the brain can perform operations to solve problems, make plans, and so forth. The chunk can also be a metaphor—such as the marketplace of ideas.

It is a common mistake to think that the frontal lobes are in charge of learning. In fact, almost all parts of our brain learn, because that is what neurons do. This is as true in such regions as the amygdala as it is in the prefrontal lobe.

To demonstrate this, neuroscientist Antonio Damasio and his colleagues did an experiment in which subjects played a one-person card game (like solitaire). Unbeknownst to the subjects, some decks had a mix of cards that favored the player's success, and some decks were loaded toward failure. When a player won, she got a financial reward; when she failed, she received a financial penalty. Over time, players with normal brains began to favor the decks loaded for success and avoid the decks loaded for failure. When asked about their strategy, they did not consciously realize why they were doing what they were doing. But when tested for emotional response, they had shown arousal just before they picked a card from the bad deck.[12] Players with impaired emotional pathways did not pick the good decks more often than the bad. Damasio concluded that the normal players had learned a winning strategy with their emotional systems without consciously knowing that they had done so, let alone rationally thinking their way to it.

So some of what we sense as a gut feeling or intuition simply results from having confronted a situation before and learned from the experience. A biologist I know contends that she is not really smart—though she speaks multiple languages, finished her course work at one of the finest Ivy League colleges in three years, and got her Ph.D. at the University of Chicago in only four years. She's not smart, she says, because she does not think her way through problems. Answers just come to her, gut feelings. One thing her gut is wrong about is the nature of intelligence and learning. She does not understand that her intuition is the consequence of learning as surely as if she had gone to the library and looked up a bunch of treatises or taken out a yellow legal pad and listed the pluses and minuses of each answer.

Psychiatrist Heinz Kohut provided a good example of the way learning becomes intuition. Great diagnostic skill, he wrote, "may impress the observer as intuitive. In reality, however, the result is simply due to the fact that the trained mind of a great physician has, at great speed (and largely preconsciously), collected and sifted a large number of details and has, like a specialized computer, evaluated the various combinations."[13] I have noticed this in my own experience, though not at the level displayed by my scientist friend or Kohut's gifted physician. As a newspaper reporter and editor for most of my career, I became accustomed to the dynamics of large-group anger. What journalists do often irritates others, sometimes even sends them into a rage, and I'd been the object of a good bit of that over the years. I've also had many experiences with political protests and mob behavior. For the first years of my professional life I was a police reporter covering the turmoil of the late 1960s as it played itself out on the streets of Chicago. I covered the riots. I covered Martin Luther King, Jr.'s march through the white Southwest Side of the city. And during the Democratic National Convention of 1968 I stood on Balbo Drive as the police charged down it and attacked the demonstrators in front of the Conrad Hilton Hotel.

During the time I served as a senior editor at the *Tribune,* we occasionally touched off a firestorm. Perhaps it was a column that angered an ethnic group. Or it was the cartoon that so offended the Chicago cardinal that Catholic priests throughout our circulation area railed against the *Tribune* from the pulpit and refused to allow the paper to be sold to people leaving mass. Confronted with these situations, I did not have to do a lot of conscious reasoning about it, even when it came to mobs burning newspapers on the doorstep of Tribune Tower. The way to deal with the problem simply came to me as the situation unfolded—when to be firm, when conciliatory—as if I weren't thinking at all. It was the consequence, I now understand, of a lifetime of learning.

So just because you don't mull something over doesn't mean that learning isn't affecting your behavior. This, after all, is the key to psychoanalysis, which seeks to bring to the surface of consciousness certain events in a person's past—particularly childhood experiences—that still cause distress and dysfunction decades later. They are, as my wife likes to put it, like pieces of Velcro. When something occurs today that has some resemblance to a past experience—even trivially—the two stick together. Responses appropriate to the earlier event come into play in the present, even though the present circumstance may have nothing to do with the past experience and even though the person probably does not even realize what is causing her to act or feel the way she does.

The learning brain sometimes guides us well and sometimes guides us poorly, but it is always learning. In many important ways it is structured the same way it was when our ancestors walked the African savannah. But in other ways it shows great plasticity. As it develops in childhood, it shapes itself anatomically—neuron by neuron—in response both to the coding the genes provided and to the environment in which it finds itself. Take the fact that learning a second language in childhood is so much easier than doing so later in life. This occurs because a child's brain is rapidly developing. Neural networks are wiring themselves, a process that slows down greatly as the brain matures. In childhood, it simply wires itself to be bilingual. Again, Hebb's rule drives much of this process, which in some ways resembles natural selection.[14]

: : :

This brief description of brain anatomy and function should make it clear that classical philosophy's neat separation of the mind into reason and emotion does little justice to the complexity of the way the brain actually functions. But there is more. It turns out to be hard to distinguish which part of our brains—the frontal lobes, the emotional centers—are cognitive (knowledge producing) and which are not. The two are so interlinked—and so deeply involved together in judgment—that conceptually separating them usually impedes rather than enhances understanding.

Now we are ready to turn to the aspects of brain science that have the most direct and practical implications for journalism. In the chapters that follow we will see how message inundation increases general levels of emotional arousal. The more we are aroused the more we are attracted to emotionally charged stimuli. This suggests that the news will be driven to more and more emotional modes of presentation, regardless how much resistance the Standard Model puts up. But that is not necessarily all bad. We actually learn important things about reality through our emotions. In fact, they are a very good way of learning certain kinds of things and making judgments in the face of uncertainty. Sure, our emotions can lead us into error. But it turns out that the nonemotional ways of thinking can do that, too.

So the challenge for journalism is to reshape its news disciplines to the way our minds actually function and malfunction and how they are responding to today's information environment. The place to start is with a close look at what students of the brain now understand about the emotions.

CHAPTER FIVE

KNOWING WHAT YOU FEEL

Respect for the emotions did not begin with modern neuroscience nor was it confined to dazed romantics. One notable philosophical dissenter from the classic exaltation of reason over emotion was Scottish Enlightenment philosopher David Hume. In his 1740 book *A Treatise of Human Nature* he turned the classical idea on its head. "Reason is, and ought only to be the slave of the passions," he wrote, "and can never pretend to any other office than to serve and obey them."[1] Hume was as mistaken as the classical philosophers, but at least he was independent minded enough to be wrong in the opposite direction. We now know that reason and emotion are not neatly divided; they are inextricably interlaced.

Today you can still find some excellent neuroscientists who share enough of the classical outlook to view the control of the emotions by the reason as an unfinished evolutionary task.[2] But I know of no good one who would come close to supporting the classical model as a description of the way the mind actually works. In fact, given what we now know about the brain, it is a challenge even to define rational (or intellectual or cognitive) function as distinct from emotional (or affective) function.[3]

Why the difficulty? Two important reasons: First, those structures in the brain that we classify as emotional actually present important information that one philosopher has called "news of the world."[4] Second, the emotional structures are intricately wired not only to send messages to structures we might think of as seats of rationality but also to receive messages back. Though the amygdala and the prefrontal lobe are in different places and do different kinds of things, asking in which of them rational thought takes place is like asking whether digestion takes place in the stomach or the small intestine.

The impairment either of the (thinking) frontal lobes of the brain or of the (feeling) limbic system impairs reasoning. Antonio Damasio has been a pioneer in the neuroscience of emotion through his studies of patients who because of disease or injury have lost the use of part of their brains. His work has provided vivid examples of the way emotion helps us think straight. The strange case of Phineas Gage is one.

In 1848 Gage, at work on new tracks for the Rutland & Burlington Railroad in Vermont, suffered a grievous accident. An explosion meant to clear away rock sent an iron bar through his left cheek, into the base of his skull, and out the top of his head. Damasio's influential book *Descartes' Error* reconstructed the accident and its aftermath. Amazingly, Phineas Gage survived, but he was never the same. What Damasio found most revealing was the exact way the accident changed him. After it happened, Gage could no longer interact well with others. For example, he started using foul language in the presence of women, something that was just not done by men like him in the mid-nineteenth century. Other aspects of his behavior, in contrast, seemed unaffected. Though he could not keep a job, this was not because he had lost his working skills; he still had them. He just could not deal with ambiguous circumstances, particularly social situations.

Damasio and his team of researchers never had a chance to examine Gage, of course, but they were able to put together enough information about him to know that his case had similarities with patients they were working with. In his book Damasio called one of these Elliot. A tumor had destroyed parts of Elliot's brain just as the steel bar had injured Gage's. The damage was limited to the prefrontal lobe, which is ordinarily associated with rational thought, but its effect on Elliot was strange. Most of his cognitive abilities remained intact. But, like Gage, Elliott couldn't make decisions.[5]

It turned out that the tumor had destroyed Elliot's ability to feel emotion. Damasio's work with Elliot and other patients led him to conclude that lack of emotion actually led to poor reasoning. Damasio's summary in effect was a death certificate for the classical model: "I will not deny that uncontrolled or misdirected emotion can be a major source of irrational behavior. Nor will I deny that seemingly normal reason can be disturbed by subtle biases rooted in emotion. . . . Nevertheless, what the traditional account leaves out is a notion that emerges from the study of patients such as Elliot . . . : *Reduction in emotion may constitute an equally important source of irrational behavior.*"[6]

When required to make a human decision, even a simple one, people with severely impaired emotional systems stop cold. They are like the legendary donkey standing midway between two bales of hay and starving to death because it can't decide which to walk to.[7]

Damasio recalled encounters he had on successive days with one of his patients whose emotional responses were impaired. The anecdote illustrates both how emotion helps people make some kinds of decisions and how it can get in the way. The first encounter took place on a day of freezing rain with icy roads. When the patient arrived, Damasio asked him if he'd had difficulty with the dangerous conditions. He had seen cars and trucks skid off the road because, he said, they were not following "proper, rational procedures." In fact, a woman driving just ahead of him hit a patch of ice, skidded, then hit the brakes and went spinning into a ditch. Damasio's patient drove the same course "calmly and surely" and had no problem. He hadn't panicked, because he couldn't feel fear, and this kept him safe.

But the next day when Damasio talked with the same patient about scheduling a subsequent visit, the patient "enumerated reasons for and against each of the two dates: previous engagements, proximity to other engagements, possible meteorological conditions, virtually anything that one could reasonably think about concerning a simple date." Pure rationality did not permit him just to decide and get on with it.[8]

WHAT EMOTIONS DO FOR US

One useful way to understand emotions is to think of them as controlling attention, or at least the kind of attention that draws the mind to something perceived in the environment. Emotions are able to take command of the information processing power of the brain in the moment and focus it on something important.[9] Emotions also play the central role in determining what is important. They have been tuned by natural selection so that certain kinds of things always seem important: threats to survival, opportunities to procreate, the need to protect kin, and in social animals the need to get the most out of the group.[10] Of course, human beings have come to think of many more things as surpassingly important to them: the beauty of a sunrise or a painting by Miró, the thrill of discovery or creativity, the satisfaction of helping others whom one may not even know. But how individuals in the distant past handled the basics of survival, reproduction, kinship, and gathering in social groups made the difference between whether they passed on their genes or did not. In short, emotion helped our forebears become our forebears. As one neuroscientist observed, "Attempting to have sex with rather than defend against a predator would be costly."[11] Attention must be paid.

Scholars differ on what should be included in the list of basic emotions, experience's primary colors. One pioneering study of facial expressions across many cultures led to this list: surprise, happiness, anger, fear, disgust, and sadness. (By the way, the father of the study of facial expression and emotion was none other than Charles Darwin.) Other scholars use different methods and come up with slightly different lists.[12]

Which are basic emotions and which are blends is less important for our purposes than seeing the connection between the simplest emotional responses and evolutionary success. Disgust keeps us from ingesting something dangerous to our health or mating with a sibling. Anger mobilizes our internal systems for a fight. Happiness helps prepare for a human bond. Sadness can be a powerful nonverbal plea for help. As these descriptions suggest, facial expressions indicate more than an individual's emotional state. They communicate to others what an individual is likely to do next and invite particular kinds of responses from others, for example, sympathy in the presence of distress, fear in the presence of anger.[13] Neuroscientists think they have identified specialized cells they call "mirror neurons" that fire both when we perform an act (like speaking or making a face) and when we see the same act performed by another.[14] This could help explain how we are able to read others' minds and how we feel empathy.

Emotions may well up or they may burst upon us in an instant. In fact, they operate on two separate time scales at once. We have already briefly encountered this insight, but it is worth elaboration.

By carefully dissecting brains and by physically manipulating the brains of lab animals, Joseph LeDoux showed that the amygdala (which is central to the emotion of fear) receives information from the senses through two separate pathways. One goes from the sense organs to the thalamus switching station and then directly to the amygdala. The other goes from the thalamus first to the neocortex (the part of the brain we usually think of as rational) and then on to the amygdala. The "low" road, bypassing the neocortex, allows the amygdala to marshal other parts of the brain to direct the body quickly to respond to the perceived danger. The "high" road permits the neocortex to analyze the danger signal along with lots of other information and alter the initial strategy: That snake is too close for you to survive by freezing in place. Back up![15] This dual pathway must have provided a powerful advantage in the process of natural selection. In the face of some dangers, if a person waits to figure things out he dies. Avoiding other dangers requires a much more holistic understanding of the situation and a more flexible response.

The neuron networks along both the "high" road and the "low" road paths are capable of learning, as we know from Hebb's rule. (Synapses that fire together wire together.) On the high side, if the water in the bathroom sink of an individual's workplace sometimes is scalding but the water in his home never is, he knows to be careful, not of all sinks, only of those at work. He knows this in a quite conscious way. If someone new joins the workforce, he might even tell the rookie to be careful of the water temperature. But from the low road path he might feel a vague sense of discomfort just approaching an unfamiliar sink of the same general sort as those in the office bathroom. He may not have any conscious idea why he feels this way. This is because his neocortex didn't make the connection, but his amygdala did. It may be, as LeDoux has written, that our emotions are actually "more easily influenced when we are not aware that the influence is occurring."[16] This stands to reason, simply because when we are not aware the influence is occurring, reason is not standing in the way.

LeDoux's discovery of the dual fear pathways points to one important way that the classical model of the mind got it wrong. Reason is not better than emotion in knowing the world. Our ancestors would not have had the good fortune to have us as progeny if they had needed to wait until their neocortex thought things through before reacting to a charging lion.

JUMP-STARTING DECISIONS

The way the emotions evaluate some situations seems programmed at birth. But the emotional brain is also plastic. It learns. It comes to understand that there are dangers beyond the ones the amygdala seems hardwired to appreciate—snakes, spiders, fast-moving objects coming toward the head. There are guns. There are drunken drivers. There is malicious e-mail gossip.

The brain is also plastic in the way it establishes higher-level goals— a career, a special friend, even an inanimate object. As I write this, my beloved Steinway B grand piano sits lifeless in the living room, destroyed by a gusher of water that poured into it from a frozen pipe six floors up in the apartment building in which my wife and I live. The day we returned from exercising to see the water cascading into the piano, I felt a sadness as deep as mourning. I knew that the piano was just a material object, at some level replaceable. And yet, through countless hours of practice it had revealed to me its complexity; we had adapted to one another. At one point, after the technician who had for fifteen years helped me keep it in good condition told me that it would never recover, I said to my wife, "I want my friend back." Emotions relate to whatever has become important in our lives, however it has come to be important.

It is fairly easy to see the natural selection advantage of a mental tool that permitted a complex organism to recognize that which is important to its well-being and focus on it amid the welter of things impinging on its mind.[17] Imagine a distant relative on the African savannah, surrounded by a landscape teeming with wildlife in motion. Wildebeests, ibises, zebras, spoonbills—and that lion.

It also makes sense that at lower levels of intensity the emotions play what has been called "a largely 'advisory' role," while at higher levels the emotions overwhelm other ways of thinking and monopolize the economy of the brain.[18] The more direct, extreme, and immediate a situation is to one's well-being, the more the emotions take over.

This helps explain why Damasio's patients with impaired emotional systems had trouble making certain kinds of decisions: They didn't have the instrument the rest of us have for making a connection between the choices before them and an important personal priority or goal. They could not appraise the situation.

Beyond this straightforward role of emotion in decision making, there is something deeper and even more intriguing. Philosopher Paul Ricoeur described the mind locked in rational calculation as stuck "in the motionless march of reflection and its melancholy."[19] But why is reflection motionless?

To find the answer it is useful to think of the brain for a moment as a computer (though we know it is a very different kind of computer than the one on which I am writing these words). Computers need to be programmed to do every step of an algorithm. If any step is left out, the program fails. This is a fundamental problem for the brain. Something has to establish the program's ultimate objective. Since there is no sentient programmer to establish what the program is trying to attain, the mindless algorithm of natural selection has provided it in the form of emotion.

"No rational creature can consult rules all the way down; that way infinite regress lies," wrote brain scientist Steven Pinker. "At some point a thinker must *execute* a rule because he just can't help it."[20] This kind of reasoning is as old as Aristotle. When an object moves, he observed, some force does the moving. And something moves that force to act on the object. And something moves the force that moves the force. And so on to infinity. For Aristotle this was proof of God, because there simply had to be a mover that was not itself moved, or else nothing would ever get moving at all.

Aristotle's understanding of the problem of infinite regress comes together with the limited information processing resources in the human brain in what cognitive theorists call the Philosopher's Frame Problem. In order to think, we need to retrieve information from the memory and, for that matter, pay selective attention to some things presented by the senses. The problem is how we know what *not* to retrieve, what *not* to pay attention to *before* we have retrieved or paid attention to it.

Philosopher Daniel Dennett proposed the following thought experiment. An artificial intelligence–empowered robot in an airplane hangar is informed that a bomb is about to go off in the hangar. First, it decides to leave the hangar in order to survive the blast. But the bomb is on the robot's wagon, so the robot is destroyed. The next time around, a new robot is programmed to infer the consequences of everything it knows. It sits there computing. When the bomb goes off it has just determined that pulling the wagon out of the room wouldn't change the price of tea in China.

For the next try, another robot is programmed to ignore irrelevant implications. It ends up sitting there "Hamlet-like" as the bomb ticks away. The programmers send the robot an urgent message:

"Do something!"

"I am," it replies, "I'm busily ignoring some thousands of implications I have determined to be irrelevant."

At which point the bomb goes off again.[21]

Emotion solves the Philosopher's Frame Problem. It allocates the scarce information processing resources of the brain by focusing attention on something it has either been pre-wired by natural selection to recognize or has learned, through the operation of Hebb's rule, is important to well-being. This allows the brain to avoid the "motionless march of reflection."

Except in extreme or instantaneous situations, emotion does not rule out rational calculation; it makes it possible. "There is still room for using a cost/benefit analysis . . . ," wrote Damasio, "but only *after* the automated step drastically reduces the number of options."[22]

MATTERS OF DEBATE

Students of the mind do not all agree about the relationship between reason and emotion. LeDoux, for example, has questioned the breadth of the theory that holds that emotion is a kind of cognition, arguing that this blurs an important distinction.[23] De Sousa, a philosopher, cleverly put the opposing camps together to draw a single picture of the mind: "There is a deadly opposition between emotion and reason: it's just that 'reason' can't set its own goals or do anything much about them without the connivance of its adversary."[24]

There are other disagreements. Damasio argued that consciously feeling an emotion constitutes a "somatic marker," a signal from the brain through the body that helps a person make a decision.[25] An eerie sensation of danger can lead one to move down a forest trail with more care, for example, even if he does not know exactly what has caused the sensation. It could in fact be produced by a subtle, otherwise unnoticed hint in the air that a mountain lion has been in the area. LeDoux, on the other hand, would just as soon disregard conscious feelings. He called them "red herrings, detours, in the scientific study of emotion."[26]

And finally there are some scholars who reject the very idea that the specific emotions are universal elements of human nature, rooted in the physiology of the human brain. These are the social constructionists. "Emotions are responses," wrote one of them, "that have been institutionalized by society as a means of resolving conflicts which exist within the social system."[27] This view owes a great deal to the deeply skeptical intellectual milieu of the latter part of the twentieth century and has drawn intense criticism.[28]

We will come back to this bitter debate later because it sheds light on why people are not responding to disciplined professional journalism as they once did. For now, though, suffice it to say that while neuroscientists engage in plenty of spirited disagreement, all would agree that the classical model of the mind is inaccurate in its assertion that the rational and emotional are neatly and completely divided, one from the other. And all recognize that both play a role in good decision making.

THE END OF HIERARCHY

The classical idea that reason and emotion stand in a hierarchy, with reason supreme, has also fallen to the discoveries of neuroscience. We have already encountered one such discovery: the amygdala receives messages both via the neocortex and through a "quick and dirty" pathway that bypasses the neocortex. This nonhierarchical structure makes for better decision making.

Many functions in the brain involve multiple pathways. As just one example, the neurons of the neocortex that control movement connect both with the brainstem where the motor reflexes are produced and, bypassing the brainstem, directly with the spine. The prevalence of multiple pathways has led to an emerging view that the brain is organized, not hierarchically, but heterarchically.[29]

Think of it this way: information comes together at various points in the brain—from the senses, from the memory, and so on. The lower the level of the information gathering, the fewer inputs feed into the response. At one level, for example, you could imagine that only visual information is available. Another integrates audio. Another touch. Still another integrates those with smell. Then memory. At the highest level of integration in the neocortex the most information comes into play. Decisions can be executed at all levels, but they can also be modified by higher levels that integrate more information. This is what is meant by a heterarchical brain.

Speed of response was probably one reason natural selection produced this kind of decentralized organizational structure. Another likely reason was to allocate the limited information processing resources of the brain efficiently. More information brought to bear on a situation means more flexibility of response. But flexibility comes at a cost: It requires more processing power. And there is no Moore's law operating in the brain; its capacity does not expand significantly over time. If anything, after maturation, its capacity declines.

Through study of the mental functioning of many species Hebb came up with the intriguing and counterintuitive thought that the more sophisticated the central nervous system, the greater part emotions play in it.

Building on this, another scholar asked himself what behaviors in the more advanced species might benefit from emotional input. He identified the following: the ability to process more inputs from the environment, multiple goals and motivations, great flexibility in behavior, and social behavior based on social organization.[30] If their view is right, man is both the most rational and the most emotional animal.

This is all a far cry from the classical model that formed the intellectual foundation of professional journalism's guiding principles. But don't think this is simply a matter of abstract philosophizing; its implications are practical and immediate. To be effective, journalism needs to communicate with people as they are, and their minds turn out to be more complicated than we once thought. Today our message-immersed environment summons their emotional side with greater and greater intensity. Our next step is to understand how and why this is the case.

CHAPTER SIX

THE TWO SEARCHLIGHTS

We are getting close to a neuroscience-based answer to the question why professionally undisciplined purveyors of news are gaining while adherents to the Standard Model of Professional Journalism decline. There are many surface explanations, the most mechanical of which is that mass media had only one way to go in the face of upstart competitors—down. But the change in the way people take in news has been so dramatic that something more powerful must be at work. Neuroscience points us toward such a force: The effect of message immersion on human brains that evolved in response to a very different information environment.

Not that the information environment for our ancient ancestors was without challenges. Their world teemed with activity, some of which provided an opportunity for sustenance and some of which threatened death. At some point in our species' history, conversation began, of course, but personal messages did not fly in constantly from the ether, disembodied from social interaction and face-to-face indicators of trust, coming from anybody or nobody. None of our ancestors, not even those as recent as our World War II generation parents or grandparents, came of age inundated by messages the way nearly every American child is today. And it isn't only the children. Gahan Wilson captured the sense of our time in a cartoon in the *New Yorker*. It depicted a group of commuters grimacing with terminal annoyance as one man looks out the window at a billboard advertising sofas and says excitedly on his cell phone, "Now we're passing by a great big sign urging us to buy sofas!"[1]

We are not the first era to sense that distraction has altered our ability to think. Here is Lippmann from 1921: "If the beat of a metronome will depress intelligence [a conclusion of a psychological experiment of that time], what do eight or twelve hours of noise, odor, and heat in a factory, or day upon day among chattering typewriters and telephone bells and slamming doors, do to the political judgments formed on the basis of newspapers read in streetcars and subways?"[2]

Today's distraction is not heedless of us, like noise in a factory. Today it calls our name. This makes today's messages very difficult to tune out. We carry instruments that allow anyone who knows our telephone number or e-mail address to beckon us. Whether by choice or inadvertence, we tell computers what interests us, and they shoot answers our way, barbed with this knowledge.

Here's a day in the life in the first decade of the twenty-first century. The subject is a middle-aged business professional who cannot keep up with her children's electronic literacy, though her work has pushed her into the digital world deeper than she would ever have imagined:

Wake up to clock radio blaring the latest weather report. Radio in bathroom continues with the latest news. Bundle children into the car pool. Finish the first cup of coffee while taking a quick look at the newspaper as the television on the counter delivers the morning weather and traffic reports. Walk to the garage and turn on car radio tuned to National Public Radio—voices talking, talking, talking, talking. Leave car at railroad station and wait for train. Put iPod earbuds in and listen to an audiobook on becoming a better manager. Idly stare at the billboards on the platform until the train rolls up. In the train, look over at seatmate's paper. The man in the next seat is talking so loudly on his cell phone that it bleeds right through the earbuds and into the audiobook. Blackberry vibrates. First e-mail of the day. Pulling the device from its holster, notice that fifty e-mails have backed up overnight from satellite offices abroad. Spend commute going through them and answering the ones that require it. Blackberry plays electronic version of Bach, signaling that someone is calling. The number of the incoming call is unfamiliar, but it might be important. Remove earbuds and take the call, which turns out to be from a computer, trying to sell an extended auto warranty. Hang up, irritated. On the bus ride to the office write and send several e-mails. Eyes barely light on the ads on the cards above the windows.

In the office, piles of documents to review. Pink "While You Were Out" slips with telephone calls to return. But not as many as there once would have been. Now people just send you a message whenever they please and expect you to respond immediately. They don't even have to get past the secretary. Blackberry plays Bach, disregarded this time. Let them leave a voice-mail message. More incoming e-mail rings a chime on the computer. Front screen arrays the latest news. The top item is from two minutes ago, an earthquake on an island in Indonesia. Read first sentence. Another item tells of a leadership change at a customer company Google is programmed to track. Read all three paragraphs. Make mental note to call contact at the company to get the latest gossip about what it all means.

The day proceeds: e-mail, documents, phone calls; phone calls, documents, e-mails. And meetings, meetings, meetings, some with people she knows, some with people she has never seen before and will probably never see again. During conference calls, put phone on mute, click on Amazon, which suggests several new releases. Buy one of them. Jump to Google News, where the newest news again is at the top, only a few minutes old, ten dead in a fire in an apartment building in another state. E-mail arrives announcing the touring schedule of favorite singer. Click over to calendar to check the date then buy a pair of tickets online. Meeting drones on. Hear own name and, disoriented, fumble way out of mute.

At the end of the day, ride down in the elevator looking at the screen that alternates bits of information on the markets with advertisements. Running behind, hail taxi. Screen on the back of the front seat is talking. Touch it to make it stop, without success.

Train is late, so stop in a friendly place for a glass of wine. Two televisions are on, each tuned to a different all-news station. Anchors seem very angry. Train finally arrives. Sit down, and within minutes the man in the next seat begins speaking into a cell phone with a voice as sharp as a blade.

On the way home from the train station, gas up the car as the screen above the pump greets you and plays some ads. Stop by the grocery store where a screen at the checkout line features cooking tips and more ads.

Home at last. Find note from son saying he has gone to hockey practice with a friend. Daughter's ride to dance lessons was already arranged. Husband has dinner meeting downtown. They'll all be gone at least until nine. Finally a little peace. Radio on, cook a microwave dinner, then go to the family room. Turn on flat-panel High Def TV. National Geographic Channel. An ad. Fire up laptop with its WiFi connection to the router the kids set up. Look at Google News again as the flat-panel TV screen cuts to an arresting image of lions tearing apart a wildebeest on the African savannah.

THE INUNDATED BRAIN

In his 1964 book *Understanding Media* Marshall McLuhan famously proclaimed that the medium is the message. Though McLuhan said a lot of preposterous things in his time, he was right about this: The nature of the medium can be a more powerful force in the world than the content of the messages that pass through it.

Today it is not only the medium that is the message; it is the media altogether, the ways that messages from everywhere pound away at the senses, trying to force their way into our ancient brains. A former executive of Microsoft and Apple called ours an era of "continuous partial attention."[3] One critic described the condition in which this leaves us as a "state of distracted absorption."[4]

There are actually three types of attention: First, the kind that is driven by conscious, high-level concentration guided by the executive systems of the brain. If you are still with me, it is probably because you are engaged in this kind of attention. Second, stimulus-driven attention of the sort that occurs when a snake slithers out of the grass in front of you. The third type of attention is arousal, which is different from the other two types because it does not focus on anything in particular. It is a general heightening of perception and the feeling of awareness. It can change from moment to moment or stay stable for long periods.[5] When it reaches a certain level, we call arousal stress.

The principal way our brains sort out, find a focus, and make initial sense of the bombardment is through our emotional systems. This happens continuously. As one student of the brain put it, even before we become conscious of a sense perception, "the amygdala has already branded it with a raw emotional valence somewhere along the continuum from mildly interesting to 'oh my God!'"[6]

The greater the bombardment, the more that emotion comes into play. A fancier way of saying this is that certain kinds of cognitive challenge produce emotional response. Not only are reason and emotion not separated, but challenges to our reasoning brain make us more emotionally aroused. It certainly would have seemed odd to Plato that the more one is called upon to exercise the parts of the mind that he believed should dominate, the more the parts he feared kick into action.

Even before it is given special cognitive challenges, our limited capacity brain has a daunting job to do. Here is one scholar's vivid description: "The

brain's task is to guide the body it controls through a world of shifting conditions and sudden surprises, so it must gather information from the world
and use it *swiftly* . . . to stay one step ahead of disaster. . . . The processes
responsible for executing this are spatially distributed in a large brain with
no central node, and the communication between regions of this brain is
relatively slow; electrochemical nerve impulses travel thousands of times
slower than . . . electric signals through wires."[7] Who was it who told you
that you only use 10 percent of your brainpower?

When the mind working on a problem encounters distraction, time
pressure, or too much information, the brain's daunting task becomes
much harder. It needs a referee to sort out the demands on its capacity.
Emotions come to the fore. The more brain processing a task requires, the
more likely emotion will affect judgment.[8] The greater the challenge, the
greater the emotional arousal.[9] Interruption, which has become a way of
life, can cause arousal all by itself.[10] Wait. There's your Blackberry buzzing
again!

Time pressure alone also increases cognitive challenge and emotional
response. Some studies have shown that when given tasks under severe
deadlines, people use more negative information—which suggests that negative emotions are in play—than when doing the same task without being
time pressured.[11] Multitasking and information overload, too, increase the
challenge to the brain's processing resources.[12] And when a person's information processing capacity is stressed through information overload or
multitasking, she is more likely to rely on emotional cues and use social
stereotypes in making decisions about another person.[13]

So predictable is emotional response to cognitive challenge that one of
the ways brain researchers induce emotions in their subjects is to give them
demanding thinking tasks.[14] The tasks can be such things as bedeviling anagrams. Even better are anagrams that have no solutions. The latter combine
cognitive challenge with powerlessness to deal with the situation, which is
another strong producer of emotional response.[15] (Think of an e-mail that
comes in from your boss requiring an immediate response, just before your
wireless network goes dead.)

There actually have been video games specially designed to induce emotion through cognitive challenge. One of these is called the Geneva Appraisal
Manipulation Environment (GAME, naturally). In it a player's agent has
to fight or flee from enemies through a series of mazes. Researchers using

GAME can program it to ratchet up and down the amount of cognitive processing under time pressure a subject needs to deploy.[16]

The linkage between cognition and emotion shows up in experiments using what is called the Stroop task.[17] When an experimenter flashed before the eyes of subjects with anxiety problems different colored words, some of whose meanings were anxiety laden and others neutral, the subjects were slower to name the color of the emotional words. The meaning of an emotional word seemed to pull the subject's attention away from her task, which was simply to identify the colors. Another experiment using something similar to the Stroop task with normal subjects indicated that emotional words seemed similarly to draw attention away from the cognitive work at hand.[18]

I know of no empirical research that goes directly to the question of the effect message inundation has on the way people take in news today, so the explanation of audience behavior I am offering here is in the nature of inference and hypothesis. But the more you immerse yourself in the world of GAME and Stroop tasks, difficult anagrams, multiple reasoning tasks, and distraction, the more it feels like the world we now inhabit.

Consider the day I was taking notes on one of the neuroscience pieces I just referred to. The external hard drive holding all the music I had fed into it for my iPod had crashed, and so I was copying CDs to a new hard drive. As I was sitting at my desk trying to make sure every word and comma in a quotation I was writing down on a note card was correct, the computer periodically made noises that told me the transfer of one CD was finished and it was time to put in another. (Yes, I was taking notes by hand and listening to music on CDs. I confess.) Oh, and then my wife called from Ecuador where she was trying to get a flight home after an airplane (fortunately not hers) slid to an emergency stop on the Quito airport runway and got stuck there. She was calling me on a cell phone as she rode in a van from Quito to Guayaquil, where the airport was open. Earlier she had called while scrambling for a ride to Guayaquil to ask that I check with American Airlines to see about her alternatives. I relayed what I had learned then went back to the note taking and music transfer. Most of this could not have occurred even a decade previous. Of course, back then I would have been writing longhand on note cards just as I was doing that day. But my wife would not have been able to call from a van in Ecuador on a cell phone. I would not have been loading CDs into my computer for transfer to my iPod.

We have gotten so used to distraction that I don't think I would even have noticed it if I hadn't been thinking about the brain under stress. In fact, it is simply the way we live. A few days later I saw a woman exercising on a step machine, consulting MSNBC on a muted TV with closed captioning while writing checks and talking on a cell phone. Lying under her checkbook was a magazine open to some article or another.

Scarcity of information processing resources in the working memory makes us particularly vulnerable to distraction. Working memory, again, is like random access memory on a computer, and in the human brain it is very limited, which is why trying to remember for a short period of time much more than a telephone number is very difficult. When a person performs tasks that load up the working memory, she is more easily distracted.[19] That explains why multitaskers are more likely to be emotionally aroused.

Swedish neuroscientist Torkel Klingberg has focused on the question whether humans can increase the capacity of their working memory and make themselves less subject to distraction. After all, we know that the brain is plastic. Most parts of it can and do learn. This would be the only real basis for the hopeful conjecture that young people who have grown up message immersed actually can do multiple tasks better than their elders, really can watch television while text messaging their friends and using the Web as a research tool for a homework assignment they are writing on their laptop.

Klingberg's research suggests, however, that with a lot of effort and proper pedagogy, working memory can improve by only about 20 percent. That seven-digit telephone number can expand to perhaps eight or nine before it becomes hard to remember. This learning does not occur spontaneously. It requires the right teaching method plus time, practice, and mental discipline. Meanwhile, the demands on working memory are increasing faster than the mind, even under the best conditions, can adapt.

"You are very possibly 10 per cent better at talking on the phone while erasing spam today than you were three years ago," Klingberg wrote, "On the other hand, the number of e-mails you receive per day has probably shot up 200 per cent."[20]

I have heard some people suggest that through natural selection our brains will evolve the capacity to handle the demands we are now putting on them. Maybe, but not in any time period worth imagining. Remember that natural selection happens over multiple generations and only when an adaptation confers an advantage in the spreading of one's genes. So even if a fortuitous mutation comes along that expands working memory and this somehow helps those who possess it survive and procreate, a child of today would have to pass it on to her children, who would pass it on to their children, who would pass it on to their children, who would pass it on to their children. . . . This is no way to meet journalism's current crisis.

Stimulus-driven attention will pull at us more and more as the information environment gets richer. This means that we will be more and more attentive to emotionally charged messages, which are particularly effective for the purpose. One group of brain researchers put it this way, "Humans have an evolutionarily determined readiness to let their attention be captured automatically by emotionally significant stimuli lurking in the psychological darkness outside the spotlight of conscious attention."[21]

There is that searchlight again, the internal one that Merleau-Ponty said sent its beam outward through the sense organs. As we have seen, there is a lot of competition inside the brain for use of that searchlight. And at any moment the emotions have the power to take control.

THE OTHER SEARCHLIGHT

Concerned folks both inside and outside journalism have engaged in quite a lot of discussion about the economic challenge the radically changing information environment has created for traditional news media, particularly newspapers. There have been numerous examinations of ways the existing advertising and reader revenue-based business model could be fixed or replaced with some form of philanthropic or government subsidy. But with audience attitudes and behavior changing as dramatically as they are, getting funding to support the production of serious journalism is only part of the problem.

Journalism is a very practical affair. For one thing, it plays an important role in keeping those most actively engaged in public policy informed about things that are pertinent to the effort. In this regard, a journalism that appeals to a relatively small, elite audience can be important. But journalism is also the way the wider public learns of the world outside its ken. The news shapes public opinion, which ultimately shapes public decision making. It does this, that is, if the public pays attention to it. So if journalism is to serve its fundamental social mission—through whatever medium—it needs not only to be available but to *get through to* a large portion of the public. Changing the business model without changing the way journalism presents itself will not accomplish the mission.

A 2009 article in the *Guardian* (U.K.) by law professors Bruce Ackerman and Ian Ayres is a useful example of the kind of ideas serious people put forward for saving journalism.[22] It proposed that democracies around the world create national endowments for journalism to give financial support for investigative reporting. The authors recognized the double nature of the challenge. Without the profit motive, they wrote, "the endowments will pursue their own agendas without paying much attention to the issues that the public really cares about." To get around this, while avoiding the obvious danger of government deciding what investigations to fund, money from the national endowments would be allocated "on a strict mathematical formula based on the number of citizens who actually read their reports on news sites."

They recognized that readers "may flock to sensationalist tabloids that will also qualify for grants for their 'investigations.'" But they did not seem to realize how very difficult it is to get people to read investigative reports about complex subjects, especially the kind that a news organization has to unravel over time, as the *Washington Post* did with Watergate. I'm afraid that even Watergate, let alone less epic investigations, might have died aborning for insufficient national endowment funding under the Ackerman-Ayres rules.

Ever since newspapers gave up being supported by political parties about two centuries ago, the need to attract and hold an audience has been the hand on Lippmann's searchlight of the press as it chooses what to illuminate and what to leave in shadows. "It is a problem of provoking feeling in the reader," Lippmann wrote, "of inducing him to feel a sense of personal identification with the stories he is reading. News which does not offer this opportunity cannot appeal to a wide audience."[23] The more the competition, the harder the problem.

As the number of competing newspapers declined in the second half of the twentieth century, before the explosion of choice that cable television offered, the Standard Model of Professional Journalism rose to the apex of its influence. This was the Golden Age that many journalists later looked back to longingly. In even the largest cities of the United States the sources of general news consisted of, at most, a few daily newspapers, a few television stations, and a little news on the radio. In most medium-sized cities there was only one newspaper. Moreover, in-home entertainment choices were also limited to only a few television stations, radio that was increasingly turning to popular music, and of course the now extinct phonograph.

The emergence of cable TV changed everything. In the beginning cable was known as Community Antenna Television (CATV). It offered remote rural communities access to broadcast signals that otherwise would not have reached it. In 1972 the business model of CATV started to evolve, thanks to a change in government regulation. Cable began to offer programming that was not already being broadcast. In 1975 HBO debuted. In 1976 Ted Turner's superstation went up on satellite for national delivery via cable. His brainchild CNN debuted in 1980. This all happened at a time when total newspaper daily circulation remained for a period at a high plateau. Ten years later, as cable penetration soared, daily circulation began a decline from which it never recovered.[24]

Cable did not change everything by increasing competition in news. It did so by offering alternatives to news. Political scientist Markus Prior has offered strong evidence that when TV viewers could only watch broadcast television and when the networks all programmed news in the same time slots, a lot of people watched the news simply because their only alternative was to watch nothing at all. Then cable came along, offering these marginal news consumers entertainment programming during the news hours. The broadcast news audience quickly began to drop as the proportion of homes with cable rose. "Ironically," Prior wrote, "the share of politically uninformed people has risen since we entered the so-called 'information age.'"[25]

At the *Tribune* we struggled to understand why single copy sales of the paper (on newsstands, in convenience stores and train stations, and so forth) had gone on a long decline even as home delivery sales were holding up. The whole newspaper industry was suffering the same thing. Occasionally the trend would reverse itself sharply, such as during the Persian Gulf War or whenever Michael Jordan was leading the Bulls through the playoffs to an NBA championship. The reason for this seemed obvious. News sells newspapers. But why news that everyone had already watched on television?

I recall a meeting in which one of our senior executives noted that the single copy decline seemed to have occurred as household penetration of cable TV rose. Could this have been the X factor that explained our problem?

I could not see it. CNN's regular audience in our circulation area was tiny. I did not believe it could possibly have been making a significant difference in our sales.

Now I think that senior executive was onto something, and Prior's work shows why. In the pre-cable era, Prior argued, large numbers of people got exposure to news, just because it was on. They came to know about public affairs through by-product learning; they learned without meaning to. Other researchers' work tends to support this. One useful study found television more successful in communicating information that the audience is not already interested in, while newspapers and magazines are better at communicating information about subjects the audience is interested in.[26] The by-product learning effect changed the political behavior of people with marginal interest in news, Prior argued. By-product learning probably also engaged them with the news enough to pick up the paper from time to time at the newsstand. But as cable television's reach grew, so did the alternatives to watching the news, thus the by-product learning declined, and with it their inclination to buy a newspaper.

In Prior's view there was nothing journalists and news organizations could do about this.[27] Many have tried. Long form documentary narratives of true crime stories became a staple on television. Some have included dramatic re-creations of events with actors in the roles of real people. When *USA Today* had its debut, it quite obviously aimed to ape television in its approach. News about popular entertainment increased dramatically on television and in newspapers. Comedians began delivering the news on cable's Comedy Channel. Then cable news channels hired their own comedians.

What we have seen is the restless searchlight flitting around trying to find whatever it can to attract the folks who just aren't interested in news and now have lots of alternatives. According to Prior, it is getting harder. The rise of the Internet offers "plentiful distraction to those who want to avoid the news, thereby contributing to an increasing knowledge gap."[28]

COMPETITION'S DARKER SIDE

In 1947 a distinguished commission chaired by University of Chicago President Robert Maynard Hutchins and including First Amendment scholar Zechariah Chaffee, Jr.; poet, lawyer, and former Assistant Secretary of State Archibald MacLeish; theologian Reinhold Niebuhr; and historian Arthur M. Schlesinger issued a report entitled *A Free and Responsible Press*. It examined the question: Is the freedom of the press in danger? Its answer:

Yes, because the press is too concentrated and its behavior has been so bad that it invites government regulation.[29]

Though the Hutchins Commission report is largely unread today, its focus on concentration of media power has been a staple ever since, both among professional journalists and nonjournalists worried about the relationship between the news media and our system of government. Even as the Internet began to offer people both instantaneous access to news reports from all over the planet and the ability to make their contribution available to everyone with a computer and a modem, people still talked about news media concentration. I don't know how many times—at dinner parties, receptions, during the question-and-answer period after speeches—I was asked how seriously I viewed the problem of news media power. I always explained that from my point of view, it looked as though whatever power traditional news media once had was being shattered into a million shards. I doubt that I ever persuaded a single person. I'm sure most thought that I was just saying this because I was part of the problem.

At one point I testified before a committee of Congress in favor of the repeal of the Federal Communications Commission rule preventing newspapers and broadcast channels in the same community from being owned by the same person or corporation. My argument referred to independent evaluations showing that local television news on cross-ownership stations (that had been grandfathered when the ban went into effect) was generally better than the news on other stations. I noted that nobody had offered any evidence that the newspaper-owned television stations had adopted the editorial opinions of the newspapers. (After all, the news department of most newspapers, true to the Standard Model, did not even themselves adopt the paper's editorial page position). And I asked why, with the whole media world in turmoil and newspapers under economic threat, only newspapers were hobbled by a rule that inhibited their ability to find cost and revenue advantages. Many years later, after newspaper economics collapsed and papers began going out of business, the cross-ownership ban remained on the books.

It has become clearer and clearer that the Hutchins Commission's concern, whatever merit it may have had in 1947, is the least of our problems in the twenty-first century. Perhaps people inside and outside of journalism are ready now to recognize that rapidly increasing competition has been the enemy of disinterested, unemotional, Standard Model journalism.

Two academic economists have built a sophisticated mathematical model of the behavior of rational readers and used it to predict how rational news businesses would respond under various competitive conditions. It showed that in a competitive market, news media would all slant in the same direction when the audience shared common beliefs but slant toward specific segments of public opinion when public beliefs diverged significantly. "Generally speaking," they wrote, "competition forces newspapers to cater to the prejudices of their readers, and greater competition typically results in more aggressive catering to such prejudices."[30]

In a provocative front page article in the *New York Times Book Review*, U.S. Court of Appeals Judge Richard Posner, a leader of the law and economics movement, made a similar argument. Political polarization in news reporting, he wrote, is "a consequence of changes not in underlying political opinions but in costs, specifically the falling costs of new entrants" to the news market. He called an increase in sensationalism in reporting "a parallel phenomenon."[31]

This would not have had as much bite, had not critics from within journalism's professional ranks been complaining more and more loudly about just the phenomena that Posner was explaining. The judge had a painful message for those critics as well: "Journalists express dismay that bottom-line pressures are reducing the quality of news coverage. What this actually means is that when competition is intense, providers of a service are forced to give the consumer what he or she wants, not what they, as proud professionals, think the consumer should want, or more bluntly, what *they* want."[32]

This might have been easier to take had there not been evidence on mainstream media's own Web sites of what consumers really seemed to want. A particularly extreme example: on the *Los Angeles Times'* Web site, a story about the world's ugliest dog ranked among the top ten most looked-at items for all of 2005.[33]

If a Hutchins Commission were beginning its work in the second decade of the twenty-first century, it would have to ask how a "free and responsible press" is possible in a radically fragmented, message-immersed information environment. The commission members would be forced to conclude that the "responsible" part has become much harder, that some of the news disciplines in the Standard Model can thrive only in conditions of relatively low competition, and that the news media not only have to figure out new ways to get important information through to people who are increasingly difficult to reach but also to find new ways to discipline themselves as they try.

WHERE THE LIGHTS CONVERGE

So the two searchlights restlessly play across the landscape. One is the searchlight of the media looking for anything that will attract the attention of an audience. The other is the searchlight of the audience members scanning a cluttered and intrusive environment for something that seems important enough to attend to. The interplay of these two processes explains a good deal of what has been happening in the way news is presented and received.

There is nothing new about people trying to get attention by appealing to the emotions. Read Greek tragedy. Read the turn of the twentieth century's yellow press, of which Lippmann complained, "Can anything be heard in the hubbub that does not shriek, or be seen in the general glare that does not flash like an electric sign?"[34]

When I was a boy in the mid-1950s and we finally got a television, I used to watch a show called *The Best of MGM*. One of the movies that I've never forgotten, for reasons that will soon become apparent, was *The Hucksters* with Clark Gable and Deborah Kerr. Here is one of the opening scenes, as narrated in the book on which the movie was based. It is set in the plush boardroom of a New York advertising agency:

> In the expressive silence, Mr. Evans raised his straw-covered head once more, hawked and spit on the mahogany board table.
>
> No one spoke. Very deliberately, he took the handkerchief out of his sleeve, wiped the spit off the table, and threw the handkerchief into a wastebasket. . . .
>
> "Mr. Norman," he said, shouting in a deep bass. "You have just seen me do a disgusting thing. Ugly word, spit. But you know, you'll always remember what I just did."
>
> Taut silence.
>
> Then Mr. Evans leaned forward and whispered hoarsely, "Mr. Norman, if nobody remembers your brand, then you ain't gonna sell any soap."[35]

Intense emotion, in this case disgust, drives a moment deeply, often indelibly into the memory. I remember exactly where I was when I learned that President John F. Kennedy had been shot. But I do not remember where I was the day I heard that President Obama's economic stimulus plan passed. Emotion makes you pay attention. "Taut silence." Emotion makes you remember. "If nobody remembers your brand, then you ain't gonna sell any soap."

The increase in competition for people's attention has caused competitors to become more and more intense in their pursuit of the vivid. It is an emotional arms race out there. Meanwhile, inside our heads distraction, information overload, time pressure, and multitasking cause emotional arousal. An emotionally aroused brain is more likely to be drawn to emotionally charged stimuli. The aroused brain might be drawn to a neo-populist commentator railing about illegal immigration, a film clip of an explosion ripping, or—turning to humor to regulate a surfeit of emotion[36]—a comedian delivering a satire on the day's news.

Arousal comes and goes. If you have ever watched the way a baby, when presented with a familiar brightly colored object, rather quickly loses interest in it, you have seen in its most basic form the mechanism sometimes known as habituation.[37] Similarly, you probably have experienced the way food loses its flavor as you eat more of it in the course of a meal.[38]

This simply intensifies the arms race. Visual media have more weapons at their disposal than print. Not all of them are obvious. For example, notice how little time each shot in most movies lasts today. A few seconds. Compare this with films made even a decade or two ago. You often hear this described as a response to our shortened attention span. A better explanation is that rapid cutting takes advantage of our brain's reflex to orient toward movement.[39] Film and TV makers, faced with increased competition, are simply making use of our ancient attention systems.[40] Count on the inner fish to go for a darting lure.

Let's go back to the competition metaphor. Inside the brain there is competition for scarce information processing resources. When the competition gets fierce, the emotions take control and direct resources to matters that are important to a person's goals—from the basic biological goals of survival and procreation right on up to her highest aspirations, such as the desire to do work of value or to be brave or loving.

Out in the external environment in which the brain functions, there is intense competition, too, for the very same thing—the brain's information processing resources. The competition produces a torrent of messages—from advertisers, media, family and friends, and business associates sending e-mail, messaging, tweeting, or just calling on the cell phone. There is competition among music producers, among movie studios, among video game makers, among news organizations. Everybody wants a piece of you.

Worse, the two dimensions of competition—inside and outside the brain—feed on one another: At the same time that the increasing demands on our old brains make us more vulnerable to emotional presentation, the increasing competition among media leads them to ratchet up the emotion. Television featuring nature programming, such as the National Geographic Channel and the Discovery Channel, provide a good example of this. One would expect them to appeal to a more thoughtful viewer, a viewer deeply and broadly interested in the diversity of the natural world. But the mix of nature shows on even those channels disproportionately features predators, especially those that threaten humans.

Again, not everyone is equally vulnerable to the use of emotion as an attention-getter. Some people seem almost immune, or at least are immune with respect to some kinds of information. A clinical neurologist is not likely to be deeply engaged by a TV show weeping over the sorrows of Alzheimer's disease. An economist is probably not going to read news stories about the effect of free trade on workers with the same anger and fear that a factory worker does, because she is not personally threatened and because she understands the larger economic context of the policy. Nor is anybody equally vulnerable to emotional appeals at all times. If I have had a bad day or am very tired, I'm more likely to be drawn deeply into a television show that on a better day might strike me as melodramatic.

Some people appear drawn to emotional arousal the way certain folks are drawn to danger, and perhaps for the same reason. People like roller coasters just as they like horror movies, because under certain circumstances intense emotion can be pleasurable. The intensity of overload-driven arousal—as in a video game—can become addictive, as most teenage boys will be glad to explain.

It is all a matter of averages. If you imagine the population's emotional arousal level and thus responsiveness to emotional stimuli to be represented by a bell curve distribution, it is not that all audience members who are unresponsive to emotional presentation have disappeared. What has happened is that the center of the curve is shifting in the direction of more responsiveness. Michael Schudson observed that during much of the twentieth century newspapers roughly divided between what he called a "story" model and an "information" model.[41] The *New York Times* exemplified the information model—with quite strict adherence to the standard journal-istic disciplines. The *New York Daily News* exemplified the story model, with its emotional blare and emphasis on human interest. In the past the story model was identified with the middle and working classes while the information model was identified with the more educated class.[42] Today this class identification has broken down. People of all educational attain-ment levels watch (and admit to watching) cable news shows that follow the story model with a vengeance. Emotional presentation succeeds across all class lines and has attained wide legitimacy. The curve has shifted toward emotional presentation. As bandwidth increases and the cost of computing drops, message immersion will continue to increase, and with it a further shift of the curve. We may only be at the beginning of the process.

The fact that you can't find a new Walter Cronkite on television today is no fluke. The dispassionate approach embedded in the Standard Model of Professional Journalism and embodied by Cronkite does not attract the audience that it used to. Walter Cronkite was lucky to have worked when he did. (And we are lucky, too, for he helped the country through some very difficult times.) Today he would be cancelled. So, by the way, would Walter Lippmann.

CHAPTER SEVEN

TRICKED BY OUR MINDS

The healthy mind has many predictable habits that lead it into error. Understanding them is of special importance to journalists, both so that they can avoid error themselves and counteract erroneous thinking in their audience.

One systematic bias in the brain is so ubiquitous that it is almost impossible to recognize—the overwhelming impulse to find patterns. And among all patterns, our brains seem particularly biased toward one that leads us to see the world in terms of opposites—good or evil, free or fated, nature or nurture. The most problematic pair is "us" and "them."

For our human and primate ancestors, the ability to distinguish between members of their own social group and others had enormous survival advantages as rival bands competed bloodily for territory and food and mates. This capacity persists in such behavior as people's intense loyalty to a local sports team, even though it may be made up of athletes recruited from all over the world. The us-and-them pattern also produces savage rivalries between nation-states, tribes, and religious groups, as well as the full range of bigotry from exclusion to extermination. Psychologists have shown that they can produce hostility among groups established by nothing more than a flip of a coin.[1] Later in the chapter we will see how this biasing mechanism can team up with the way the brain learns and end up producing racial prejudice even in an atmosphere of racial tolerance.

The systematic biases that most often muddle us in our everyday life originate in the difference between what gave a person an advantage in the prehistoric struggle for survival and what the brain needs to meet today's challenges—how to invest retirements savings, what news provider to believe, whether that nagging headache needs an aspirin or a brain surgeon. Because the basic structure of our brains has not changed very much, we often automatically respond to current circumstances as if the circumstances of the ancient past still prevail.[2] To conserve the brain's limited resources and provide quick responses, *Homo sapiens* developed shortcuts that led them, not to the best answers their brains could possibly provide, but to answers that were usually good enough. A simple way to think of systematic errors is this: Answers that were good enough then may not be good enough now.

One systematic bias results from our brain's reluctance to be wrong. F. Scott Fitzgerald thought that the test of first-rate intelligence was the ability to hold two opposed ideas in mind at the same time and still function. The eons shaped our brains in the opposite direction. Confirmation bias is a term for the way the mind systematically avoids confronting contradiction. It does this by overvaluing evidence that confirms what we already think or feel and undervaluing or simply disregarding evidence that refutes it.[3]

Testimony from members of the Crow tribe about the destruction of their culture provides an extreme and tragic example of this. A man named Plenty Coups reported that "when the buffalo went away the hearts of my people fell to the ground and they could not lift them up again. After this *nothing happened.*"[4] He was not alone in describing the depth of despair as the end of history. "Nothing happened after that," another Crow warrior said. "We just lived."[5] The emotion was so strong that the brain rejected evidence of the continued existence of normal, everyday life that might have ameliorated it.

Just as our brains bias us because they reflect circumstances that were extremely important in prehistoric times, the capacity of our emotions to learn through individual experience also can lead to profoundly skewed responses. This was one of Sigmund Freud's most profound insights. Adult psychological problems very often originate in the events of early childhood, events that haunt everything after. As Freud showed, we have powerful ways of protecting ourselves from conscious recognition of the most painful memories that shape our behavior.

Of course, little children can mislearn all kinds of things. But there is a difference between conscious and unconscious learning. If someone rejects the concept of natural selection because his parents pounded away at the lesson, he usually at least recognizes that they taught him. Later, others may teach him that what he had learned from his parents was erroneous. But if he reacts badly to a person with red hair because when he was little a red-headed caregiver abused him, the current feeling of revulsion

overwhelming him may seem to come from nowhere. Emotional learning is especially potent and durable simply because we may not even realize that we have learned anything.[6] In fact, because the pattern-making,
contradiction-avoiding brain has a gift for rationalizing, it will usually
make up a reason for any feeling it has and believe it, at least consciously. It
can take years of skilled professional help and extraordinary personal effort
to bring the real origin of the feeling to light.

MATTERS OF MISATTRIBUTION

Richard Nisbett and Lee Ross, social psychologists who did pioneering work
on how ordinary human inference differs from logical inference, emphasized
the special importance of one kind of error. They called it the fundamental
attribution error, which they defined as "the tendency to attribute behavior
exclusively to someone's dispositions and ignore" other causes beyond their
control.[7] Lippmann noticed this phenomenon a century ago but did not
have any context in which to understand it: "To many simple and frightened
minds there was no political reverse, no strike, no obstruction, no mysterious death or mysterious conflagration anywhere in the world of which the
causes did not wind back to . . . personal sources of evil."[8]

A related basic error of attribution Nisbett and Ross called "misguided
parsimony," the tendency to see things as having only a single cause. Journalists have been easy prey for this kind of bias as well as the fundamental misattribution error. News reports rarely have the patience to describe
the complex causes of events or conditions. Did greedy bankers or reck-
less home buyers cause the mortgage meltdown of 2008? Or was it Federal
Reserve chairman Alan Greenspan? Don't expect a lot of news attention to
the general and repeating misapprehension of the historical cycles of asset
prices. If a particular human can be blamed, journalists in most cases will
focus on him. How much easier it was immediately after 9/11 to concentrate on Osama bin Laden than on popular resentment at the decline of
Islam's power in the world and rejection of the modern culture that seemed
to have brought about the decline. Of course it is an oversimplification to
ascribe this kind of oversimplification to all journalism. The point is that
these deeply ingrained habits of mind play a role in the way journalists—
and everyone else—see and describe the world.

Emotions play an important role in most misattribution. This is why people who want to sell things—whether automobiles or stories—find it an especially useful way to manipulate others. Misattribution explains the effectiveness of sports celebrities' endorsements of products that have nothing to do with their respective sports and of images of beautiful females in selling products like cars to male customers.

Many people over the years have noted the misattribution effect in political discourse. Perhaps it is a high-minded speech by a candidate invoking the memory of iconic presidents of the past or a giant American flag as the backdrop of a presidential appearance. Or it is an attack ad picturing a candidate in an unappealing setting. Remember the repeated image of presidential candidate Michael Dukakis's riding a tank wearing a ridiculous looking helmet?

The tricks of the mind always become the tricks of the manipulators.

WHY IS NOVELTY NEWS?

At first glance that question may seem silly. But you could imagine a world, or a science fiction writer could, in which things that happened recently would have an advantage in the competition for attention over things that happened a day ago or a week ago or a year ago.

Not long after I left the newspaper business, a student group at the University of Chicago asked me to come and speak about the future of news. At one point I asked the students how many of them used the Internet to keep up with current events. Most people raised their hands. I asked how often they checked out the news site. A remarkable proportion of the audience did it many times each day.

Those sites are strongly biased toward displaying the most recent information most prominently, I said. They even indicate precisely how much time has elapsed since the item appeared. Why do you care how recently something happened? Why would the recent have particular significance to you? Wouldn't you rather have news ranked in terms of its importance?

Ordinarily the significance of a piece of information and the time of its revelation bear little relationship to one another. A decision in the Kremlin days ago to move back into some of the territory it lost when Communism fell may reverberate throughout the West for a year. Or a decade. A report five minutes ago that an earthquake rocked rural China will be forgotten within days, if not minutes, by most people not immediately affected.

Why does it matter to you that something just happened? I asked the students again.

They looked at one another. Then they looked at me as if I were from the planet that science fiction writer might have been describing. What these extraordinarily smart, well-read young people could not do was give a good account of their behavior.

If there had been budding neuroscientists in the audience, they might have done better. They might have known that the attraction to novelty is one of the most powerful forces in the human mind.[9]

You don't have to work too hard to reverse-engineer this through the evolutionary process. We give attention to the new because it may either be a threat to survival or an opportunity for advantage. Things of the past we may have already assessed and usually can be safely attended to in due time. The new could be anything . . . anything! It could be prey. It could be a potential mate. It could be a lion.

The first thing an organism does when it detects something new is to orient its senses toward the novelty.[10] The attention that novelty attracts actually builds upon itself, up to a point.[11] That point occurs when the organism has figured out that the change isn't important to it, and then novelty wears off. Time for the local news anchor to cut to a different live report.

ACCENTUATING THE NEGATIVE

People from every line of work must face certain annoying, persistent questions whenever they go to cocktail parties. One that used to drive me to distraction was, "Why do the media always pay so much attention to negative things? Aren't there positive things you could write about?" When I was in the business I didn't have a very good answer. Now I do.

It is this simple: Negative events are more emotionally powerful than positive events.[12] Little children engage in the most sophisticated storytelling when they are talking about emotionally negative experiences.[13] They are also drawn to fairy tales full of witches and frightening beasts. Negative events powerfully attract the attention of adults, too.[14] Negative emotions narrow a person's focus.[15] Common sense offers an explanation for this. In situations that present a person with a serious problem, it very useful to concentrate.[16]

It is pretty easy to imagine why natural selection may have yielded a bias toward negativity. Usually animals have more than one chance at finding food or a mate. But fail to spot a stalking lion and it's the end of the line.

The next time anybody asks me the annoying question, he had better be ready for an extended answer. Of course, just because people have a tropism to negative information doesn't end the discussion about how serious journalism should deal with this aspect of human nature. Later chapters will return to the question. For now, though, suffice it to say that the increasing competition for attention and the increasing emotional arousal levels in the audience push purveyors of news even more strongly than before in the direction of satisfying people's curiosity about bad news.

Even though I have seen vastly more apartment fires in my reporting life than I care to have, when the nine o'clock local news comes on television and a live report showing the dome lights of the hook and ladders flashing and flames flicking out an upstairs window, I do not turn the channel. Nor when the anchor cuts to a three-car pileup on an expressway killing one person who has no relationship to me or to anyone I know. The local news features such items simply because it is so hard for us to look away from them. In the live shot, if you look closely, the traffic going the other direction on that expressway has slowed to a crawl.

THE BRAIN'S RULES OF THUMB

Even in simpler times, the mind had too much to figure out. So it developed rules of thumb. The technical term for them is heuristics. These rules of thumb sacrifice a certain amount of accuracy for speed and efficiency in the use of the brain's information processing resources.[17] Fortunately, when they lead us astray, they do so in predictable ways. In this sense they are like optical illusions.[18] Unfortunately, some of the unmediated ways that the Internet has provided for us to locate information can magnify the systematic individual errors and produce large societal effects. Journalists need to understand and figure out how to combat this.

Various writers have categorized the mind's shortcuts in various ways. Drawing from their work, I have found it most useful to think of the list this way:

- The availability rule of thumb, in which matters that are front of mind are taken to be most important.
- Framing biases, in which the starting point for thinking has undue influence on the outcome.
- The representativeness rule of thumb, in which resemblance is taken to imply something about probability.
- Other probability biases.
- Failures in forecasting future emotions.[19]

AVAILABILITY

Emotions play a central role in many manifestations of the availability rule of thumb. The purpose of emotion is to drive something to the front of the mind, so such emotionally based biases as novelty and negativity can lead to erroneous judgments about what is probable or otherwise important. The newest or most negative information, being most available to the mind, is often taken to be the most significant, when in fact it may be trivial or beside the point. News reporting very often is led astray by the availability rule of thumb. During the financial crisis of 2008, for example, cable news focused initially on the plunge of the stock markets (many people had money invested there, which made them very top of mind), while the real threats to the economy were in the banks and obscure credit derivatives markets.

Cass Sunstein has written extensively on the subject of brain biases and ways to compensate for them. In his book *Laws of Fear* he reported on experiments demonstrating that in highly emotional situations people take probability into account less than in less emotional situations. In one experiment, researchers asked four groups of law students how much they would be willing to pay to reduce arsenic levels in drinking water. Experimenters asked the first group how much they would pay to reduce the risk of arsenic-induced cancer by one in a million, the second group one in a hundred thousand. The third group got the same question as the first but was given a vivid description of the "very gruesome and intensely painful" way the cancer "eats away at the internal organs of the body." The fourth got the same question as the second but also got the vivid description.

It turned out that without the emotional description, the tenfold difference in the reduction of cancer risk produced a significant difference in the amount the subjects were willing to pay to avoid it. But with the vivid description, the difference in risk avoidance had a much weaker effect. Both groups that were told how awful the cancer death was were willing to pay much more than the other groups to avoid it, but a tenfold increase in avoided cancer risk produced a willingness to pay little more than twice as much.[20] In short, the groups provided with a vivid picture of cancer death caused by arsenic levels didn't care much about probabilities. They wanted to avoid the risk and that was that. The description had turned the dry, abstract probability figures into front-of-mind images. The availability rule of thumb did the rest.

Availability helps explain two problems that have intrigued moral philosophers. Why would society be unwilling to pay $x to reduce the risk of coal miners being trapped in collapsed mines while it is willing to pay $10x or $100x, almost any amount to rescue one individual miner who actually becomes trapped? The answer is that "coal miners" is an abstraction, while the individual miner crying out in the darkness of the shaft has a name and a history and a family. We see pictures of his wife and children weeping. We come to know him. He is, as the scientists like to say, emotionally salient to us. With his life seemingly in our hands, cost is not an object.

Philosophers state the second problem this way: Imagine two situations. In the first a trolley car is racing down a track toward five unsuspecting workers, who will die when it strikes them. You can flip a switch that will send the trolley down another track. On that track there is only one workman; so only he would die. The second situation is just a little bit different. In order to keep the trolley from killing the five workers, you have to throw one worker off a bridge into the trolley's path to stop it.

Tragic as the first choice may be, in empirical studies most people say flipping the switch is acceptable. As to the second choice, even though it results in the same human toll, one dead and five saved, most people say it is morally unacceptable to throw the worker off the bridge.

One can argue endlessly from philosophical principle about whether there is a moral difference between the two cases, but neuroscientists approached the problem by using MRI technology to watch the way the brain actually processed the differing scenarios. It turned out that the deliberative centers of the brain became active in people presented with the first kind of scenario, while the emotional centers lighted up in people presented with the second, which required them to think about actually grabbing and violently throwing a human being to his death.[21] Another way of describing this is that the second situation is more emotionally vivid than the first, so the brain's availability rule of thumb assesses it differently than by logically summing the number of dead and saved.

A piece of information need not be emotional to affect thinking through the availability rule of thumb: You have an interesting conversation with someone and afterward notice a book he is carrying. Then you happen to go into a bookstore. Rationally, the fact that an interesting friend has a particular book says very little about the chance that you will like it. For all you know, the friend might be hating the book. But when faced with the overwhelming blare of unfamiliar titles in the bookstore, the one recently mentioned to you is top of mind. You are more likely to buy it than some other book. I believe that online stores like Amazon that offer up suggestions of books you might like based on what others like you have liked actually get a boost to sales just because of the availability rule of thumb. Whether or not the algorithm making the suggestion is reliable, the seemingly personal suggestion is there as you shop, top of mind.

FRAMING

To continue the old-fashioned, printed-word examples, say somebody tells you that most used hardbound books now sell for about $10 dollars. Shortly thereafter you find in an Internet auction an obscure, out-of-print book you have been looking for (which happened to have been signed by an author nobody ever heard of). Your bid will very probably be lower than if you were first told that signed copies of out-of-print books usually sell for $100. This makes no rational sense. The variance around the market prices of both used books and out-of-print signed books is much too great to make even an accurate statement of average price meaningful. So why the difference in the bid? The framing of an issue influences the way you think about it. This is why if a potential boss ever asks for your thoughts about salary, don't start too low. Get him to anchor on a higher number at the start, and even if he ultimately decides you were too high, he'll probably not go down as far as he would have if your opening suggestion had been too low and he decided he should go up.

Availability plays a role here. The suggestion that begins the process is, by definition, front of mind. Unless something else is even more vividly present (the fact that the boss has just taken the painful step of freezing everyone's pay for a year), the suggestion will affect the assessment.[22]

People are pushing frames on journalists all the time. Contenders in controversies fight to get the media to call something what they would like it called. Terrorist or freedom-fighter. Pro-choice or pro-life. I have often wondered whether we should call the two sides of the abortion debate anti-choice and pro-death for a time, just to cleanse the public mind.

A further turn in the game of spin is to create low expectations (for the outcome of a political debate or primary election, for example) so that exceeding those lower expectations seems a victory. This may at first seem the exact opposite of the way framing worked in price bargaining. But that is because the game is different. In negotiation, a manipulator wants to frame the situation close to where he wants the bargaining to end up. But since the outcome of an expectation game is a judgment about how some-one has done, the manipulator's trick is to frame the situation in such a way as to set the brain up for a positive surprise.

Whatever the game, using the mind's rules of thumb to manipulate is the essence of every spin doctor's job.

REPRESENTATIVENESS

Consider the following problem: John has a friend who is a journalist. He played football in college, coaches his daughter's soccer team, and sub-scribes to *Sports Illustrated*. Is John's friend a sports columnist or a local reporter?[23]

If you decided he is a sports columnist, you have been misled by the rep-resentativeness rule of thumb. You had a stereotype of what a representative sports columnist is like, and the facts I gave you about John's friend made him resemble it. But far more journalists are local reporters than sports columnists. The disproportion is so great that it would overwhelm almost any other factor. What you have done is to disregard the base rate in guess-ing probability. This is only one of the persistent ways that the human mind makes mistaken guesses about the odds.

OTHER PROBABILITY BIASES

Our mental rules of thumb make human minds terrible at figuring probabili-ties. This may seem odd, since thinkers as disparate as David Hume and Don-ald Hebb have persuasively argued that all the brain *can* know is probability.

The rules of thumb permit us to make rapid guesses about the odds, using as little of the brain's processing power as possible. When people consider gambles, they ordinarily don't think long term (if they did, they would never play against the house) but rather about how much they will gain or lose with each roll of the dice.[24] People typically overweight small probabilities, don't pay much attention to probabilities in the middle range, and underweight high probabilities.[25] They have a devil of a time determining how well one thing is correlated with another.[26]

The laws of chance predict that when things start happening much more or less than they usually do, eventually they will return to the normal level of occurrence. But people don't expect this, which is why they buy stocks during market bubbles. Journalists should remember "regression to the mean," as this notion in probability theory is known, whenever there is a spike in crime or disease or death rates. Politicians who announce strong measures are making a pretty good bet, because usually such crises will pass on their own as the rates regress to the mean.[27] Beware in doling out blame for the crisis or credit for its amelioration.

Memory plays probabilities tricks on us, too. You probably take it for granted when your memory comes up with a piece of information at the very moment it is useful. But ask yourself this: How can it know what information will be useful before it has put it to use? One theory is that instead of estimating the probability that a piece of information will be useful, the brain employs rules of thumb, such as how many times a piece of information has been retrieved in the past and how recently it has been retrieved.[28] Sometimes this works, but sometimes it gets tripped up by errors produced by some other of the brain's rules of thumb. The negativity bias, for example, would lead a brain to retrieve the memory of bad experiences more than good ones. Emotional vividness would have an effect as well.

The trouble the brain has estimating the odds is so great that it seems as if, in the words of brain scientist Steven Pinker, it "was not designed to grasp the laws of probability, even though the laws rule the universe."[29] But minds were not designed to grasp relativity or quantum mechanics, either, though they can learn to do so. And with a lot of practice, some individuals can even learn to calculate the odds so well against blackjack dealers that when casinos detect them, they throw them out. The fact that we can overcome the systematic biases in our brains is the principal reason journalists should study them.[30]

FORECASTING FUTURE EMOTIONS

The human mind is lousy at forecasting how something will feel. Emotions have their effect in the immediate moment, and this can easily overwhelm any sense of how an action now will make a person feel later.[31] This has been the death of many diets and other New Year's resolutions. A related matter is the tendency to exaggerate the future emotional impact of anything a person happens to be focusing on.[32] When you think of getting a big raise, you will probably spend it five times over in your mind without even realizing it, just because it feels so good to think about now.

One reason people usually get predictions about their future emotions wrong is that they don't recognize how much they can adapt emotionally to positive or negative events.[33] This explains why anticipation can make cowards of us all. That operation you are facing? You will probably quickly get used to the discomfort, and even if the recovery is arduous, it is likely that you will quickly be perceiving good and bad days within it more than the badness of the whole process.

LEARNING TO BE PREJUDICED

Neuroscientists John Cacioppo and Gary Berntson have described a way a person living in an egalitarian society can inadvertently learn to be racially prejudiced.[34] They begin by assuming a society that has racial equality as a genuine aspiration, which children learn from parents and others. But in this society people from a given race still, for the most part, know and interact with people of their own race. This egalitarian value system and actual social separation seems fairly close to the life a lot of people live in the United States.

A child in such a society will be exposed secondhand through news media to people of their own and the other race. Most of those exposures will be negative (because news is usually about bad situations, because people's curiosity has a strong bias in that direction). This is so even if the media carry an absolutely equal number of bad stories about people of each race. Since the children don't have much actual contact with people of the other race, most of their exposure to them will be through the negative secondhand depictions. On the other hand, most of their exposure to people of their own race will be neutral or positive based on the interactions of everyday life.

Time-tested psychological models of learning (or conditioning as it is sometimes called) suggest that the exposure to predominantly negative images of people of the other race will leave children negatively biased against them. This effect will be most pronounced when the negative images are in one way or another fearful. The learning will happen outside of consciousness; the children will not even know what is happening to them. Because they are at the same time being socialized to believe consciously that all races are equal, this will leave them quite literally of two minds.

: : :

From time to time as I worked through books and articles about the many ways in which the mind can lead us into error, I found myself doubting my own thinking. Once I saw the possibility that information overload, multitasking, and distraction could be raising overall rates of emotional arousal, did I fall prey to the confirmation bias, overlooking contrary evidence and giving undue weight to evidence supporting the hypothesis? Have my personal experiences in the news business misled me in my general conclusions through the power of the availability rule of thumb? In what way has the crisis in the newspaper business established a frame that influences my thinking without my even knowing it?

Recognizing the mind's rules of thumb and how they can trick us into error actually helps avoid those errors. Critical self-examination and logical reasoning in most instances can have the final say if you want them to. Simply knowing the brain is fallible should not lead to the profoundly skeptical conclusion that it can't really know anything about reality.

Yet that was an extremely influential idea throughout the twentieth century, growing in importance over the years since Walter Lippmann struggled with the skeptical "acids of modernity." It still has a certain hold on some parts of the intellectual world. And its effects have gone deep into the general public's way of thinking, lingering there and shaping attitudes and behavior in the twenty-first century concerning many things, including traditional news media.

CHAPTER EIGHT

THE ACIDS
OF POSTMODERNITY

It is one thing to explain why emotional presentations of the news attract and hold people's attention. It is another to understand why people seem to base their assessments of credibility less and less on whether journalism is professionally disciplined.

Public confidence in the press, measured by the National Opinion Research Center, fell from about 85 percent in 1973 to a low point of 56 percent in 2004, after which it went back up slightly to 59 percent in 2006.[1] Most of the decline occurred since 1991, generally coinciding with the rise of the Internet, where larger and larger audiences, especially among young people, are going to nontraditional sites to get their news. One study has shown that when people believe news stories on an online service are selected by professional editors, they consider them to be significantly *lower* in quality and attractiveness than when the same people believe the same stories are served up by a computer on the basis of what other users have chosen.[2]

The loss of trust in traditional media is part of a much more widespread decline in trust in experts of all sorts. Traditional media's credibility problem may be particularly pronounced, but it arises out of general historical forces that have been gathering for a long time and that promise to last a long time, too.

When I was a boy my father, who had never been to college, would often draw my attention to a person in the news or someone giving a talk on television. "He is a highly educated man," my father would say. "He graduated from Yale" . . . or Princeton or got a Ph.D. from Harvard or was trained in economics at the University of Chicago. I am sure this spurred me to go as far with higher education as I could. But it also imparted to me a deep sense that these individuals had some special claim to my attention. What they said mattered, just because of who said it.

In 2008, by way of contrast, a presidential candidate born of a Kenyan father and an eighteen-year-old white woman, a man who by dint of his intelligence and hard work and courage rose to become editor of the *Harvard Law Review*, was seriously attacked by opponents as "elitist." My father would have wondered what in the world they were talking about.

Many factors have come together to cause the decline in belief in the authority of experts. Violent changes in the main currents of intellectual life eroded the status of such institutions as the established news media, Congress, and the Catholic Church. So have the longer, larger waves in American political and social history, not to mention the choppy waters of the recent past.

The easiest to see, of course, is the chop: unpopular, unvictorious wars in Vietnam and Iraq; the Watergate scandal; revelations about what our intelligence agencies have done in secret; the tawdry sexual and financial corruption of government leaders and the cynical political response to it; the Catholic Church's problem of pederast priests; corporate scandals, and of course, the disclosures of instances of gross journalistic malpractice at leading newspapers. Add to this a series of assassinations and close-call assassination attempts, the Great Society exploding in urban riots, political parties declining in power, and globalization radically reshaping the American economy, and you have some sense of the tumult we have been through.[3]

In light of the sheer number of extraordinary forces that came to bear on the United States in a short period of time it is no wonder that acute observers have seen them as more than enough to explain the breakdown in trust in expert authority. But even if somehow suddenly the turbulence ended and our history calmed, more durable historical forces would continue to move us in the same direction.

THE ORTHODOXY OF DOUBT

"The acids of modernity," Walter Lippmann wrote in 1921, "are so powerful that they do not tolerate a crystallization of ideas which will serve as the new orthodoxy into which men can retreat."[4] It turned out that later in the century the acids became the orthodoxy.

By the late twentieth century the optimism of a hundred years earlier about the capacity of the human mind to master its world had given way to a powerful current of thought that held that we cannot really know much of anything. One former newspaper editor called dubbed this "what-the-hell postmodernism."[5] Literary theory tortured texts to demonstrate their impenetrability. In law the aspiration to principled decision making stood accused of being nothing more than an assertion of class power. For story-tellers who hoped to approach truth in the telling, the room the skeptics built for them had no exit. Neutral narrative was an oxymoron.

Up to a certain point, no one can deny some of this. A story is not the reality it depicts. And, of course, it reflects the workings of the mind of the teller. Simply to write someone's name is an evaluation—after all, the writer has some reason to choose that very name. Even if the choice were random, the writing makes the evaluative statement, in effect, that "this is gratuitous." The more complicated the statement, the more value laden it will be. To illustrate I will pick just a couple of articles from the front page of the *New York Times* of a random date.

The first begins in a typical expository mode known as a straight news lead:

> Barely a year after Congress enacted an energy law meant to foster a
> huge national enterprise capable of converting plants and agricultural
> wastes into automotive fuel, the goals lawmakers set for the ethanol indus-
> try are in serious jeopardy.[6]

Let's speed through the most obviously loaded phrases: Barely a year. Huge national enterprise. Serious jeopardy. Of course they are evaluative. But what about the statement that Congress meant to foster a national ethanol enterprise? How does anyone know the intention of 535 legislators on Capitol Hill? Scholars and judges still ardently debate the intentions of just fifty-five men who gathered in Philadelphia to write our Constitution. When lawyers and law professors turn to legislative history to discover what Congress's words meant when written, they usually find a hopeless muddle.

When Congress passed the ethanol legislation some members surely meant nothing by their votes than to make farmers happy. Perhaps they cared not a whit whether the enterprise succeeded or failed, so long as they could be seen to be doing something to reduce consumption of oil. Or per-haps they were just trying to get the bill out of the way because they had better things to do. The *New York Times* article is replete with judgments.

Here is the opening of another piece that approaches its subject with what is known as a feature lead:

MONTEBELLO, Calif.—Pictures of children, his trophies, decorate Dr. Tien C. Chieu's office.[7]

What could be more straightforward, right? Of course, even such a simple description falls prey to the skeptic's question: Why this rather than all the other things the journalist might have chosen to report? Isn't that evaluative? But passing this favorite skeptic's trick, a noun and a verb in the one-sentence lead paragraph of the article quite directly betray something about the judgment the writer is rendering. The photos are "trophies," not mementoes or keepsakes. They must represent to the doctor his triumphs, at least as the writer sees it. And they "decorate" the office. They don't simply hang on the walls. Again the writer is suggesting something not only about the way the office looks but why it looks that way and what it says about the office's inhabitant.

You can do this kind of analysis endlessly, tediously, and some scholars have. In the end it tells you that whenever a person says something that has meaning, she renders a value judgment.

Skeptics argue that reading is loaded too. "The interpretation we offer, whether historical or literary, or judicial, is always normative," wrote psychologist Jerome Bruner. "You cannot argue any of these interpretations without taking a moral stance."[8] Again, at one level this has to be the case. Any writer who has not spent her life holed up in a cave knows it. An environmentalist, worried that increasing ethanol production will lead to deforestation, might take the word "jeopardy" in the ethanol story as showing bias in favor of the ethanol project. Another person might read between the lines and discover the influence of the big oil companies. The project was doomed, they might think, because it was designed not to work in the first place. The master narrative within the mind of each reader will profoundly color the meaning she perceives.

Likewise the in-vitro clinic description. For the reader concerned about population growth, those trophies may represent dark victories. For the deeply pro-life, they are worth more than gold.

For a long time journalists simply disregarded such matters as sophistries of little practical consequence. But without even realizing it, they were themselves increasingly coming under the influence of the acids of skepticism: Perception is reality. Everything is spin. As one journalism scholar described it, "We're all post-modern now."[9]

SLAVES OF DEFUNCT IDEAS

Few people have read the work or heard the lectures of the proponents of acidic intellectual skepticism. Nonetheless, the situation is like what John Maynard Keynes famously observed about economic theories: "Practical men, who believe themselves to be quite exempt from any intellectual influences, are usually the slaves of some defunct economist."[10]

Even people who have utterly no direct acquaintance with the canonic works of skepticism still breathe their vapors. This is not the least because more than a generation of college students spent four or more formative years immersed in an intellectual climate in which these works held sway. And so it has become commonplace in conversation to hear folks say things like, "it all depends on your point of view," or "you are where you sit," or "it is all relative," or in the case of media, "you only published that to sell newspapers." I once had a reader complain about a complex *Chicago Tribune* article that filled a full section of a Sunday paper debunking claims by a scientist that he had been first to isolate the AIDS virus. The reader told me that we were just interested in a sensational story to sell papers. The article was so dense that, though I had edited it myself, I wondered whether anyone but specialists in human retrovirology would be able to understand it. If we published that story to increase single copy sales, we should have been fired, not for venality but for stupidity.

As we have seen, at some level the skeptics were onto something. Value judgment and subjectivity cannot be excluded through journalistic discipline; they are in the very structure of narrative. Increasingly wise to this, people doubt professional journalists even more than opinionated bloggers *because* of the journalists' claim to neutrality. A lot of people seem to think that Standard Model journalism is more dangerous than obviously partisan voices because, as Reinhold Niebuhr wrote about courts, its partiality "is obscured by its prestige of impartiality."[11]

Postmodernist skepticism in its extreme form has declined in the academic world.[12] But in society at large the information revolution has breathed power into it. "Computers," wrote sociologist Sherry Turkle, "embody postmodern theory and bring it down to earth."[13] On the Internet there is no master narrative, no definitive reading. Authority means next to nothing.

WHAT IS RESPONSIBLE FOR REALITY?

That kind of question leads most journalists to start making wisecracks to one another under their breath. Such abstract matters seem to have nothing to do with the world of immediate facts and disputes they live in and report about. Yet our children have learned not to scoff at the question. In fact, it strongly influences how they prefer to get their news.

Postmodern skepticism has mixed with utopian yearning and our growing understanding of how the searchlight of the mind shapes what we perceive. The result is a thesis generally known as constructivism. One believer in it described it as the idea "that contrary to common sense there is no unique 'real world' that preexists and is independent of human mental activity and human symbolic language, that what we call the world is a product of some mind whose symbolic procedures construct a world."[14] Moreover, in this constructivist's view, culture rather than biology shapes the human mind "by imposing the patterns inherent in the culture's symbolic systems."[15] Put the two thoughts together and you have a radically skeptical theory that holds that meaning, even reality itself, is entirely created through social interaction.[16]

When applied to news, this easily slides into political ideology. A movement called critical theory draws on Marxist thought and argues that, in the words of Brian McNair, a British media studies scholar, "journalism's function is essentially one of social reproduction, in the service not of society as a whole, but of its dominant groups or classes."[17] It does this by "constructing the world for us in terms of categories, such as 'normal' versus 'deviant,' or 'militant' versus 'moderate,' which are then used to police society."[18]

Disregarding the Marxist tone for a moment, critical theory's focus on in-groups and outsiders does draw our attention to the powerful pattern-seeking impulse of the brain and its bias toward binary categories, one with good vibrations and the other with bad, us and them. These categories are passed from one person and one generation to another. As the old joke goes, people are divided into two types, those who divide things into two types and those who don't. Biology and culture. External reality and human construction.

But you can't disregard ideology for long, because the social constructivists so often throw it in your face. One English professor, for example, explained that the postmodern approach seeks to "problematize" the telling and interpretation of story because "traditional narrative structures are perceived as part of a system of psycho-social dependencies that inhibit both individual human growth and significant social change. To challenge and lay bare these structures is thus a necessary prelude to any improvement in the human situation."[19] McNair provided a revealing example of social constructionism. In the United Kingdom and the United States and other liberal democracies, he wrote, "news tends to be about conflict and negativity. . . . In the Soviet Union, on the other hand, journalists were taught an alternative conception of news values, which emphasized positive social phenomena."[20]

Not too long before the fall of communism in Poland a delegation from the doomed government of Wojciech Jaruzelski paid a visit to the *Chicago Tribune*'s editorial board. Since in Poland there was already considerable pressure against the system of political repression, our conversation at some point turned to protest and freedom of expression.

In that day's paper our political cartoonist, Jeff MacNelly, had depicted President Ronald Reagan in a less than flattering light. One of the Polish officials pointed to it and said, In our country people would not stand for such ridicule of its leader.

Someone suggested that they try it once just to see. The members of the delegation simply shook their heads at our ignorance of their culture.

Of course, when the communist government fell, Poles were delighted to ridicule their former oppressors as well as their democratic leaders, just as in Romania the people broke out in religious songs that had been forbidden but never for an instant forgotten.

News in the West leans toward conflict and negativity because extraordinary curiosity about negative things is in the basic structure of the brain. News in the Soviet Union leaned toward the positive, not because a different culture there had shaped brains differently. There never was a New Soviet Man. The news in the Soviet Union was always positive because the government would not permit it to be otherwise.

NOT ONE THING OR ANOTHER BUT BOTH

The debate over whether reality exists apart from human minds and the debate over whether nature or culture shapes the mind both come down to false dichotomies. Both sides have some useful insights, but as orthodoxy, both fall apart under the other's assault.

We know that some structures in the human brain resist being reshaped even by the most powerful experiences. There is such a thing as human nature. But we also know brains learn through culture and social interaction as well as from other experiences.[21] So yes, cultures do shape how and when individuals express emotions. What produced blushing in the parlors of Victorian England would probably produce a lusty laugh in polite company today. But cultures do not shape the anatomy of the amygdala or how it functions. Nor by any stretch of academic abstraction are they entirely responsible for reality. As one psychologist neatly put it, "Death is socially constructed by every culture, but bodies die without consulting these constructions."[22] As for the news, Michael Schudson got it right: "News is socially constructed, but it is constructed out of Something, not out of whole cloth."[23]

Similarly, despite the radical skeptics, communication is no more inscrutable than people are. We have means of knowing what people mean by what they are saying, just as we have ways of discerning what they are thinking even when they don't say a word. These means are not perfect, but they have worked well enough to let our ancestors traverse complex social situations down the millennia. Thanks to their general success, we were born and can use the interpretive skills we inherited from them.

More generally, dealing with corrosive intellectual skepticism is not too different from dealing with the knowledge that our brains' shortcuts can mislead us. The question is whether knowing of our imperfection leads to "what-the-hell" nihilism or to an effort to do better: Better at knowing when shortcut answers are good enough and when they aren't. Better at depicting reality in ways that reality will not rise up and refute. Better at expressing what we mean—and interpreting what people mean when they express things to us. In fact, a useful counterargument to radical skepticism grows from the very process of natural selection: Humans must be able to know something; after all, we have survived.[24]

The antidote to the acids of postmodernism is to recognize that even though absolute truth forever eludes us, some statements about reality are truer than others, some interpretations of a text more valid than others. "We know that some methods of inquiry are better than others," wrote John Dewey, "in just the same way which we know that some methods of surgery, farming, road-making, navigating or what-not are better than others."[25] Paradoxically, it is only the insistence on certainty that leads to the proposition that we can know nothing.

Karl Popper, the great philosopher of science, described the human struggle for knowledge eloquently:

> Here we are, with the immensely difficult task before us of getting to know the beautiful world we live in, and ourselves; and fallible though we are, we nevertheless find that our powers of understanding, surprisingly, are almost adequate for the task—more so than we ever dreamt in our wildest dreams. We really do learn from our mistakes, by trial and error. . . .
>
> We can *learn,* we can *grow* in knowledge, even if we can never *know*— that is, know for certain. Since we can learn, there is no reason for despair of reason; and since we can never know, there are no grounds here for smugness.[26]

There are ample pressures on journalism to adapt to the changes in its environment, to rethink its basic disciplines. But let's never let the skepticism of our times tempt us to say what the hell to the task of finding ways to use the tools available to us, which are almost adequate for the task, to express accurate, important things about the world in a way that gets through to readers.

THE CYCLES OF DEMOCRACY

A single word sums up the current era in the cultural history of our democracy: antielitist. Elitism summons up images of ill-gotten wealth, aristocracy, unearned power, and exclusion. Elitism suggests authority that is unworthy of respect. It is a very unpleasant word.

Though the postmodern corrosion of belief in our capacity to know has played a role in the decline of expert authority, so powerful is the antielitism of our times that it is shared even by those who react against skepticism with absolutist faith. Antielitism unites radical left and radical right, fundamentalist and atheist. It is driven by more than the force of intellectual history. It has the whole surge of American past behind it.

The history of the role of elites in U.S. society is the history of the rise and decline of the democratic impulse. Robert Wiebe has been the best teller of that tale. The story does not much resemble the one children learn in school. Yes, the revolution gave birth to constitutional democracy, but in its first years it was a democracy organized as a hierarchy. Land and position ordained its leaders. The French Revolution came and went without upending the established social order on this side of the Atlantic. Only a relative few had a real voice in public affairs. It took nothing less than the opening of the land stretching from the Appalachian Mountains to the Pacific Ocean to bring on the first great cycle of profound democratization. As people pushed westward, where anyone could have land who cleared it, authority diffused.[27] "Centrifugal politics," Wiebe wrote, "produced leaders with an ordinary look about them, men who were comfortable mixing with their constituents, not standing above them."[28]

This period of democratization persisted, occasionally punctuated by countervailing impulses, until the late nineteenth century. By then railroads and the telegraph had tied the vast land together, linking it to great centers of commerce and industry. Businesses that once might have managed to isolate themselves in a single locality now needed regional and even national organization to support them. The Progressive Era, with its belief in scientific management and the professions, gave the new cycle not only a name but also an ideology. The Standard Model of Professional Journalism was part of it.

Soon the experts were everywhere. "Without expert guidance," wrote Wiebe, "who could prepare a balanced meal, evaluate candidates for the local judiciary, understand one's children, relieve headaches, enjoy sex?"[29]

Then came the U.S. entry into World War I and with it a model of hierarchical discipline that won the day.[30] Though the Depression shook the nation's confidence, a group of intellectual elites led by the patrician Franklin Delano Roosevelt brought the country through. World War II exposed a large proportion of the male population to military discipline, and a remarkable proportion of the female population to industrial organization.

The men who served in the military were still independent-minded Americans; as the Cold War began, it was said that the average American sergeant was ready to take more individual initiative than the average Soviet colonel. These citizen-soldiers bridled under regimentation and found ingenious ways of subverting it. But when the veterans returned home, they were used to saluting their officers, generally obeying orders, and getting things done. Formal organization, planning, and hierarchical execution won the war, and everyone knew it.

But something was stirring. George W. S. Trow identified the rise of television as a market-driven democratizing force that eroded deference to authority. Dwight Eisenhower, the former commanding general who had vanquished Hitler, found himself presiding over the transformation. History, Trow wrote, "was turning into demography, in which judgment—and Ike possessed judgment with a capital J—was being drained out of every powerful situation, and marketing considerations were being pumped in."[31]

Television usage turned out to bear a strong negative relationship to social trust.[32] Perhaps this helps explain why confidence in the press began to slide steeply as cable television took hold. It did so again with the rise of interactive media,[33] which made it easy for people to seize control from information elites such as traditional news media.

Back in the 1960s youthful rebellion had seemed on the verge of upending the existing order. This included a challenge to the Standard Model of Professional Journalism as young people poured into newsrooms. But the revolution did not materialize. The institutions of authority, including the Standard Model, bent but did not break. Nonetheless, many of the young people most swept up in the 1960s critique of the existing order became the teachers of the next generation. The forces of a new era of profound democratization quietly gathered strength.

Then came the digital revolution. Wiebe wrote his book *Self-Rule* at the earliest stage of this revolution. In it he mentioned in passing the possibility that "electronic bulletin boards" might provide an opportunity for democratic action.[34] More prophetically he argued that the cycle of history might be ready to turn toward the centrifugal forces of democracy again. What would it take to bring about the change? Such moments, he wrote, "rise only out of systemic breakdowns, not out of an accretion of many small adjustments."[35]

The Internet, with its ability to put readers and viewers in apparent control and its capacity to provide interaction, sometimes human, sometimes machine simulated, gave the democratic restiveness stirring in the country a means of bringing on a systemic breakdown. Lest anyone imagine that the antielitist cycle of our history—with its rejection of expert authority such as offered by traditional journalism—will soon reverse itself, remember that each of the past cycles lasted about a century.

SOLVING THE CREDIBILITY CONUNDRUM

A couple more points will enrich our understanding of why people increasingly trust undisciplined sources while continuing to lose confidence in journalists who try to follow the disciplines of the Standard Model of Professional Journalism.

The first comes from philosopher Russell Hardin. Trust, he argued, consists in "encapsulated interest." By that he meant that I trust you because I believe it is in your interest to take my interests seriously.[36] This occurs most strongly, he argued, in ongoing relationships between people. Trust in government (and by extension trust in other impersonal institutions like the news media), he wrote, "may in fact be something short of trust as we experience it in interpersonal relations."[37]

The other is an intriguing study by three neuroeconomists. Researchers had subjects play a "trust game" in which people were given $10 then assigned to two groups. A computer asked individuals in the first group how much of the $10 they would transfer to a counterpart in the other group, who would actually receive triple the amount sent and would be asked by the computer how much of the bounty to send back to the donor. As the game was played, some of the members of the second group were told that a person in the first group had chosen to send the money to them (which the game tripled). Others were told that the computer itself took a random amount of their counterpart's money, tripled that, and transferred it. Soon after the game everyone gave a blood sample, which was tested.

Two important things turned up. First, when members of the second group believed that a human being had sent them the money, they had a significantly higher level of oxytocin in their blood afterward than those who thought the computer had sent the money. Oxytocin is a neurotransmitter associated with human bonding (for example, between lovers or between mother and child). So a specific brain chemical seems related to trust. The second striking result is that people who think a human counterpart decided how much to send them sent back significantly more money than those who thought the computer sent the money.[38]

It comes as no surprise that brain chemistry relates to something as intimate, social, and emotionally important as trust. But what is particularly interesting is that it can happen at a distance, electronically, and between people who have not met.

So there is reason to think that in addition to the democratic historical moment and deeply skeptical intellectual climate, the very interactivity of the new information environment can stimulate trust—perhaps greater than traditional media ever can—even between people who don't know one another's name.

CHAPTER NINE

TULIPS AND THE HIVE

It took a couple of decades before traditional journalists acknowledged that the future of news belonged to digital interactive media. The dead weight of tradition, as well as the commercial difficulty of moving away from a highly profitable product, made mainstream news organizations slow in adapting to the information revolution until disaster was upon them.

The task is still unfinished, despite the many brilliant, usually younger journalists who have thrown themselves against the inertia of the profession and pioneered new ways of presenting news with the new tools at hand. The health of our self-governing society urgently depends on their continued efforts.

Our two searchlights can help illuminate the way. The first involves the economic marketplace, the second the marketplace of ideas and the brain's shortcuts in processing what it finds there. We will consider them in turn, but first it is useful to clear away the utopian dreams of the original information revolutionaries, dreams that obscure some of the special challenges journalists face in trying to fulfill their social mission in the new environment.

The ideological origins of the information revolution trace back to the counterculture and commune movement of the 1960s. In revolt against everything hierarchical—or even organized, for that matter—its followers did not feel the need to have a coherent philosophy. They lived somewhere between Rousseau and Ayn Rand, with dollops of Timothy Leary and Thoreau, acid rock, and the *I Ching* folded in.

Utopian from the start, the information revolution drew strength from the intellectual currency of the times. Skeptical of conventional ideas about how to know reality, it was constructivist in its belief in the malleability of the human mind. But then, every utopian has to believe either in genetic engineering or the social construction of human behavior. How else could people and societies be made perfect?

In his useful history of the period, *From Counterculture to Cyberculture,* Fred Turner identified Stewart Brand's *Whole Earth Catalog* as the defining icon of a movement that defied any other kind of definition. It was, Turner wrote, "something new in American publishing, and no one at the time could say quite what." The catalog was a hodgepodge of items that might be useful in living off the land or transforming one's head. "Home weaving kits and potters' wheels banged up against reports on the science of plastics," wrote Turner. "Bamboo flutes shared space with books on computer-generated music."[1] By 1971 the *Whole Earth Catalog* had won the National Book Award, which seemed to signify that it was a book that would last. However, it did not turn out to be a volume for the ages so much as a quaint artifact, like a pair of bell-bottoms appliquéd with flowers and butterflies.

The counterculture movement aspired not only to sweep away hierarchies and the institutions that supported them, but also to eliminate competition, jealousy, and possessiveness, among other human traits. Trouble was that when people actually tried to live these aspirations, whether in rural communes or Haight-Ashbury, human nature showed its resilience. The Summer of Love turned into a festival of use and being used. Communities without leaders either dissolved into dictatorships of the charismatic or simply dissolved. Meantime, the Vietnam War ended, which drained a great deal of fear and moral outrage that had fueled the youth movements of the late 1960s and early 1970s. The Baby Boom cohort grew older. Dreams of a utopian future faded into the regularity of a job, a car, a spouse, and children—and a nostalgia for the time when it seemed as if all ideals could become real.

Still, a few continued to dream. And others, working with silicon and binary math, gave them something to dream about, something that turned out much more influential than turning on, tuning in, and dropping out. The public embraced computer technology as thoroughly as it had rejected the call to turn its back on modern life and scratch out a subsistence livelihood from the land. The development of intuitive graphic user interfaces and the Web browser made computers easier and easier to use. Even navigating from an individual computer into the wilds of the Internet began to seem an adventure rather than an ordeal. Eventually the World Wide Web followed people wherever they went via wireless telephones.

Nobody can fail to see the liberating power of these developments. While there are still parts of the world where people have not yet been touched by the information revolution, in many places it has leaped over rickety older technology. The cost of getting access to the Internet is becoming less prohibitive by the day. In developed economies virtually no technical barrier stands in the way of full participation by everyone in the great debates of our time. It simply takes a computer or cellular phone and an Internet connection to make your words, photos, or video available virtually everywhere on the planet.

While it is possible for governments to censor the Internet, it is difficult, and the costs are extremely high. On a trip to Cuba during the late Fidel Castro era, I heard government officials explain that the country was making a great investment in training people in information and communication technology, hoping to build on the proven scientific acumen of the Cuban people to make this an engine of economic growth. Unfortunately Cuba strictly controlled what it permitted anyone, even information and communication technologists, to see on the Internet. This doomed its plan to win in the economic market; the people it was training simply could not be relevant if they were unable to follow in real time the accelerating development of technology. Any country that wants to participate fully in the economic life of the planet today must eventually open itself to what to some regimes must feel is dangerously free expression.

Though repressive governments like China's might try to keep the opening small, human ingenuity has proven quite capable of frustrating government control—just as it has been able to frustrate security systems that protect us against fraud and other abuses. While privacy advocates shudder at the pervasive information about people that the Internet distributes, the same technology has permitted us to peer inside societies as ruthlessly closed as Myanmar and see with our own eyes the evidence refuting government lies.

The potential for just this kind of power quite naturally led early visionaries to imagine transformations in society at a much deeper level. A 1996 statement, entitled "Declaration of the Independence of Cyberspace," captures the flavor. It was written by John Perry Barlow, a former lyricist for the Grateful Dead who became an influential voice in the making of the ideology of the Web:

> Your legal concepts of property, expression, identity, movement, and context do not apply to us. They are all based on matter, and there is no matter here.

Our identities have no bodies, so, unlike you, we cannot obtain order by physical coercion. We believe that from ethics, enlightened self-interest, and the commonweal, our governance will emerge.[2]

But matter wasn't the only thing the Web utopians thought to overturn. Kevin Kelly was the editor of Brand's *Whole Earth Review* who went on to become executive editor of *Wired Magazine,* the tribune of information utopianism. In 1998 he wrote that "thinking is a type of computation, DNA is software, evolution is an algorithmic process."[3] With this, Kelly turned all biology into a supercomputer. Tom Wolfe, with characteristically savage wit, captured the goofiness of such pronouncements: "A computer is a computer, and the human brain is a computer. Therefore, a computer is a brain, too, and if we get a sufficient number of them, millions, billions, operating all over the world, in a single, seamless Web, we will have a superbrain that converges on a plane above such old-fashioned concerns as nationalism and racial and ethnic competition."[4]

This wasn't the first time Americans soared into the kind of rhapsodies over technology that one communications scholar described as "nostalgia for the future."[5] At the outset of the Industrial Revolution people published essays with titles like "The Moral Influence of Steam," and in 1838 Samuel Morse, inventor of the telegraph, wrote that it would not be long before "the whole surface of this country would be channeled for those nerves which are to diffuse with the speed of thought, a knowledge of all that is occurring throughout the land; making in fact one neighborhood of the whole country."[6] Of course, the telegraph got its first big workout, not by creating a national neighborhood, but rather as the nation tore itself apart in the Civil War.

For the silicon utopians the dream took an unprecedented turn— beyond machines, beyond electricity. If biology was computation, then maybe computation allowed humans to be, well, more biological. The penetration of computing and the Internet offered the possibility of a different and less complicated kind of human social interaction. This would take us back way beyond Rousseau's primitive ideal. The silicon utopians believed that networked systems would lead to, in Turner's words, "an ability to run with the bees."[7]

Like bees, individuals would achieve selfless social purposes guided only by information freely provided by others, without hierarchy or commands. The image of the hive mind lies behind much of the success of

Wikipedia—which, by the way, was often helpful as I wrote this work. It also has become a kind of unspoken article of faith among vast numbers of Web users that what the hive produces is right—is wisdom even. Meantime, more and more academics, from biologists to researchers in robotics, seemed to be focusing on swarm behavior. In 2007 *National Geographic* completed the circle of popular and scientific interest with a major article entitled "Swarm Theory: Ants, Bees, and Birds Teach Us How to Cope with a Complex World."[8]

There are differences between bees and humans, of course, not the least of which is the nature of their social brains. Bees and ants are not symbolizing creatures. They cannot read one another's facial expressions or body language to determine whether they are telling the truth. But then, again, within the colony they do not lie. Moreover, as the *National Geographic* article reminded, "Crowds tend to be wise only if individual members act responsibly and make their own decisions."[9] History offers little hope that humans will ever be able to live up to those two conditions. In this vein a provocative essay entitled "Digital Maoism: The Hazards of the New Online Collectivism" by computer scientist Jaron Lanier reminded his enthusiastic colleagues that the "collective can be stupid, too. Witness tulip crazes and stock bubbles."[10] He might also have mentioned real estate.

Or, for that matter, newspapers.

SOMETHING FOR NOTHING

Though there is some dispute about it,[11] Stewart Brand usually gets credit for coining the phrase, "Information wants to be free." Here is what Brand said during a 1984 panel discussion: "On the one hand information wants to be expensive, because it is so valuable. The right information in the right place just changes your life. On the other hand, information wants to be free, because the cost of getting it out is getting lower and lower all the time. So you have these two fighting against each other."[12] (One day a museum designer friend of mine patiently explained to me his discovery that information wants to be free. I told him museum design wants to be free, too.)

Today most information delivered on the Internet, including almost all news, costs the user not a penny. Free information on the Web naturally seems like a very good deal to the hive. But it has a potentially high social cost.

Economic markets bring together buyers and sellers to do transactions. All other things being equal, better access to information makes for more efficient markets. Perfect markets maximize the total satisfaction of everyone who participates. That does not mean the effects of perfect markets are perfect in any way other than producing the greatest possible aggregate satisfaction for those participating. A perfectly efficient market in nuclear materials will not necessarily reduce the danger they pose to generations yet unborn. And it is not necessary that individual buyers or sellers in a market know what is good for them; all they need to know is what they desire. This is why there can be a perfect market in tobacco.

We do not have to engage in the debate about whether that abstract being, Economic Man, is perfectly rational. We have seen from the sciences of the brain that he is not, at least in the sense that classic philosophers imagined he could be. The growing fields of behavioral economics and neuroeconomics are at work refining the assumptions about the way he thinks.

Still, so long as people know what they think they want, the economic market is a way to give as many of them as much of it as possible. What markets need in order efficiently to maximize aggregate satisfaction are large numbers of buyers and sellers with access to information pertinent to transactions between them. In fact, in one sense economic markets are fundamentally information markets. The most important thing they do is to induce people to reveal what they know, starting with information about what they really want, how much they want it, and what they can really provide.

Efficient markets not only sum individual desires but also allocate scarce resources among competing uses to maximize overall satisfaction. Imagine a simplified world in which manufacturers can produce only needles or spears with the iron available to them. Buyers need both goods in order to clothe themselves and to hunt. The relationship of the price of needles and spears will tell manufacturers how much of each to produce so that the buyers will get the greatest satisfaction from the mix. If needle manufacturers produce too many needles, the price of needles will fall and the price of spears will go up (because less iron is available to make them and people will bid up the price in order to get the spears they need for obtaining food). The needle manufacturer's profits will decline and the spear manufacturer's will rise. The needle manufacturer will reduce production to avoid the expense of making unsold needles, and the spear manufacturer will produce more spears to chase the higher price. This will ultimately bring the price of spears down and the price of needles up to the point at which iron is allocated in a way that optimizes overall satisfaction.

But what about the folks who live downwind of the factories, breathing the unhealthy pollution they generate? This is an example of what economists call an externality. Externalities lead markets to fail to maximize overall satisfaction. They occur when someone bears the cost of an economic activity without getting the benefit of it. Pollution is a classic case. A firm puts dangerous chemical wastes into a river and gets paid for the products whose manufacture generates the waste, but people downriver who drink the water pay the price. Consequently for the whole system—that includes the seller, all the buyers, and the people who drink the river water—the result does not maximize satisfaction. Too many of the products whose byproduct is pollution are produced. Another way of putting it is that if the seller had to pay the price of providing the people downriver with pure water, he would have to charge more for his products and would therefore sell less.

The rapid expansion of our capacity to communicate facilitates efficient markets by bringing more buyers and sellers together faster and getting them to reveal more of what they know. The information revolution has made some kinds of economic markets more perfect, with more competition, which produces lower prices. You can see how this works by going on the Internet and pricing a specific product from multiple sellers. It is almost effortless to make comparisons that without the Internet would require lots of telephoning or even physical visits to accomplish. The airline industry, among many others, has had to adapt to the ease of comparison shopping. It developed elaborate methods to adjust prices minute by minute to fill planes and get the maximum revenue in the process. The increased ease of searching the globe for products and comparing their prices has caused some prices to plunge precipitously—the price of news, for example.

On the Internet every organization offering news is available to everyone in the world with access to the Web. So the supply of general news—about national policy and politics, foreign affairs, movies, travel—increased dramatically from the perspective of any given news-seeker. But that was only the first step. News organizations that tried to charge consumers on the Web quickly lost audience, and the Internet price locked in at zero (with a few very isolated and specialized exceptions).

At Tribune Company I often tiptoed toward pulling most of our newspaper content from the open Web and charging for it. I always lost my nerve because for this strategy to succeed, other news organizations—all significant news organizations really—would have had to do the same thing. Antitrust laws—which are aimed at avoiding another kind of market failure—prevented me from going to other companies and seeking with them to raise the price of our work from zero.[13] Of course, I might have taken the step unilaterally and hoped to lead without collusion. Even though Tribune included a number of the most important newspapers in the United States, I had no confidence that if we led, others would follow.

As the price of news on the Web went to zero, services such as Google grew rapidly by offering an easy way for Internet users to find what they wanted amid an overabundance of information. The key to the search engines' success in gaining an audience were algorithms (computerized routines) that sorted through everything on the Web and then conveniently offered up to users the information they seemed most likely to find useful. The search engines made their money by using content on the Web as bait to get individual Web users to identify their precise interests. This allowed Google and others to offer advertisers an extremely efficient way to reach the very people most likely to be interested in their goods and services.

The consequence of all this has been the kind of externality that economists call a "free rider" problem. Original producers of news spent a lot of money collecting, verifying, sorting, prioritizing, and presenting the information of the day. But they did not get the benefit of the advertising the search engines were selling. When a producer of a good does not get the full economic benefit of producing it, eventually it will produce less than people want. The free rider (Google) is happy, but the total satisfaction of the system is not maximized. In other words the market fails.

In the case of news production, late in the twenty-first century's first decade the established news media faced severe economic pressures and began to reduce output sharply. The few newspapers that still had national and foreign correspondents were under pressure to reduce these staffs. But as important as foreign correspondents are, much more was being lost. Most of the basic information the public gets about everything from property tax rate proposals in city councils to education bills in state legislatures, from danger prowling the streets of a neighborhood to criminal charges brought against public officials, originated with newspaper reporters. They provided the data of democracy. The rapid decline of the print press caused a great deal of alarm, both inside and outside the newspaper business.

To replace what was lost some people have put their hopes on decentralized, nonprofessional, unorganized contributors on the Web. These citizen-journalists have from time to time come up with some very useful things, but even in the aggregate they do not do much in the way of original reporting.[14] They do not provide the data of democracy. The hive may provide some bits, but until it is hooked up to the economic market, it won't in the long term be able to give people what and how much they want.

When newspapers plunged into economic crisis late in the first decade of the twenty-first century, the push to find a lawful way to get together and exact payment for news on the Web grew strong.[15] Short of this, if the output of news shrunk enough, the dynamic in the marketplace would itself change. Most people believe there is still strong consumer demand for news, though increasingly for news presented very differently from the way traditional media provided it. We know that people have been willing to pay for news whenever it was unavailable for free. The question is where and when a new economic model will establish itself and what will happen to us in the interim.

A MARKETPLACE OF THOUGHT?

So striking are the similarities between a system of free expression and the marketplace of goods and services that "marketplace of ideas" hardly seems a metaphor anymore. Audience members become speakers and speakers become audience members in a dynamic process, just as buyers become sellers and vice versa in the stock market. In a system of free expression each person is sovereign over his own views just as in an economic marketplace the actors are sovereign over their own wants and the disposition of their disposable resources. Opinion shifts the way prices do. The central marketplace metaphor looms so large that it has spun off many satellites: "I'm not buying it" for I don't agree. "A bill of goods" for deception. "His stock is up" for reputation. And so on.

Metaphors are one way the human mind enriches its understanding of and control over the world. Some think it is the most important way that people create new modes of understanding. But as beautifully expressive and mind expanding as metaphors can be, their very power can also obscure important dissimilarities.

This is precisely what occurred as the information revolution accelerated. If ideas operate in a marketplace, and the market is becoming more and more efficient (more participants, more competition), shouldn't an Invisible Hand be bringing us closer to the truth?

The economic marketplace does maximize. Not everything and not flawlessly, as we have seen, but perfect markets do maximize the aggregate satisfaction of those who trade on them and allocate resources efficiently toward that end. But what exactly does the marketplace of ideas maximize?

It has long been a commonplace among free expression enthusiasts that the truth will prevail in a free marketplace of ideas. The origin of this thought usually is attributed to Milton's *Areopagitica,* which forcefully argued against government licensing of books—except those that advocated Catholicism: "Let [Truth] and Falsehood grapple; who ever knew Truth put to the worse, in a free and open encounter?"[16]

The idea made its way into American constitutional jurisprudence, beginning with Supreme Court Justice Oliver Wendell Holmes's 1919 dissenting opinion in the case of *Abrams v. United States,*[17] where he wrote that "the best test of truth is the power of the thought to get itself accepted in the competition of the market."

But is acceptance in the market a good test of truth? While it may be the case that other tests—especially its ability to win government approval—are vastly inferior to the competition of free expression, this does not mean that the marketplace of ideas maximizes truth the way the economic marketplace maximizes aggregate satisfaction. The free exchange of information and opinion results not so much in truth as in something like a summing of the balance of opinion among the participants in the forum. The balance of opinion does not even lead to the efficient allocation of the information processing resources of the human brain toward the determination of truth. These are allocated in large part by emotional structures of the human brain carried down from prehistory. The best one can say of the free marketplace of ideas is what Holmes said in *Abrams,* that over time it has a greater capacity to correct itself than other systems because it involves no enforced orthodoxy.

When the participants in a forum by and large share a dedication to the pursuit of truth and a disciplined methodology for reaching it (scientific method among scientists, for example, or verification of facts among journalists), the outcome of discussion and debate within the forum may be an ongoing, improving approximation of something like truth with a very small *t*: tentative truth, Karl Popper's kind of truth. Even then there is always the chance that the shared methodology or other common assumptions obscures something important, which is why revolutionary ideas in science and elsewhere so often meet heavy resistance at first.

I don't mean to raise doubts about a system of free expression as an alternative to institutions of established truth. Government monopoly over information makes popular sovereignty impossible, leads to tyranny, and often hides barbaric inhumanity. Moreover, a decent humility about what human beings can know for sure makes a regime of free expression the only way we can hope to increase knowledge. We need to be free because we can never be certain.

But it is wrong to expect the marketplace of ideas to maximize truth moment by moment the way the economic marketplace maximizes satisfaction. We need to keep this in mind as we examine the freest, most open marketplace of ideas and information ever devised by humans.

THE DEMOCRATIZATION OF JUDGMENT

The intellectual and historical situation at the turn of the twenty-first century strongly favored decentralized judgment rather than the informal authority of experts. The information revolution magnified a tendency inherent in the cycle between egalitarianism and hierarchy that originated deep in America's past. De Tocqueville wrote about it during the first period of democratization in America as people fanned out across the wilderness: "In times of equality, because of their similarity, men have no faith in one another; but this same similarity gives them an almost unlimited trust in the judgment of the public; for it does not seem plausible to them that when all have the same enlightenment, truth is not found on the side of the greatest number."[18]

We live in such times again. The information revolution empowered users to decide for themselves what is important, what is credible, not entrust the decision to some faceless editor in the pay of a conglomerate. But notice that this is not just any kind of democracy; it is direct democracy in which preferences are summed moment by moment. Imagine government by national referendum, with everyone having a device upon which they can cast binding votes on every issue as it arises. That is what the democracy of information is like. In fact, some utopians hope that Internet democracy will supplant the representative republic as our fundamental form of public governance.

Voting has become a way of life on the Web. Authors torment themselves by regularly checking out where their books' sales rank on Amazon.com or looking to see how many stars their reader-reviewers have given them. Countless sites invite us to review electronic devices, musical instruments, books, CDs, films, restaurants, hotels. Of course, where there is voting, there is vote fraud. Sometimes authors and other sellers try to rig the system by voting early and often themselves. And sometimes they are caught. Short of fraud, businesses and individuals learn how to game the system. There are even get-out-the-vote campaigns, which can be relentless.

Beyond the ubiquitous polling on the question of what's good, interesting, useful, and so forth, the very priority of presentation on the Web results from an extreme version of democracy. Its purveyors have marketed it as such. Here is how Google, at least as recently as 2008, described its system for determining what pages on the Web appear first in answer to a query: "Page-Rank relies on the uniquely democratic nature of the web by using its vast link structure as an indicator of an individual page's value."[19] Note that it said Web links indicate value, not popularity or usage or audience share. Value.

Set against all this is a strong tradition in political philosophy of distrust of unfettered, direct democracy as a means of arriving at sound political judgments. Lanier, in his insider's criticism of digital utopianism, drew attention to this: "The balancing of influence between people and collectives is at the heart of the design of democracies, scientific communities, and many other long-standing projects. . . . A few of these old ideas provide interesting new ways to approach the question of how best to use the hive mind."[20]

It is intriguing to read the work of Greek writers from the time of the humans' first great experiments with democracy. Plato. Thucydides. Aristotle. They all had deep reservations. Among them Aristotle took the most constructive approach, looking for institutional ways to cure some of the problems of direct democracy. In *Politics*, for example, he observed that democracy "will not last long unless well regulated by laws and customs."[21] The idea that to function well democracy must be mediated through mechanisms that restrain and channel majority whim is a recurrent theme among thoughtful believers in this form of government.

The men who established the American constitutional republic drew from the ancient critiques of democracy as well as from more contemporary writers such as Montesquieu. They had experienced the ill effects of the Articles of Confederation period, during which state legislatures ran roughshod over the interests of political minorities, cancelled private debts, and changed policies so rapidly and often that it was impossible to rely on any constancy in the law. As historian Gordon Wood wrote: "An excess of power in the people was leading not simply to licentiousness but to a new kind of tyranny, not by the traditional rulers, but by the people themselves—what John Adams in 1776 had called a theoretical contradiction, a democratic despotism."[22]

The Constitution that emerged to replace the Articles was democratic, but various mediating devices held the power of popular will in check, dividing the institutions of government against themselves, for example, and having each of them—president, members of the House of Representatives, senators, Supreme Court justices, and so on—chosen by a different method. It also made it extremely difficult for majorities to intrude into certain matters—expression, for example. The Bill of Rights is the most blatant expression of distrust of democracy in the Constitution. It says no majority can do certain things to people unless it is large and durable enough to succeed at the difficult, multilayered, highly mediated process of amending the basic document itself. While the notion that the only solution to the problems of democracy is more democracy has an appealing ring, the mediation of institutions not directly democratic remains the only antidote for democratic excess that does not kill the patient.

Our understanding of human nature today is quite different from what it was in the late eighteenth century when the U.S. Constitution was written. But the challenge remains the same: to find ways to allow our brains sovereignty but at the same time mediate the effects of the fundamental imperfections in them.

Recall for a moment the metaphor that Tom Wolfe ridiculed of the Web as a giant brain, linking all the human brains that use it in a kind of massively parallel processor. Take away the grandiosity, and it suggests a serious question. What happens when those giant computer brains reflect the systematic biases shared by all of our individual brains? What does the democratization of judgment produce then?

HOW INFORMATION MARKETS FAIL

Immediately after proclaiming that "the medium is the message," Marshall McLuhan went on to assert that the social and personal consequences of a medium "result from the new scale that is introduced into our affairs by each extension of ourselves, or by any new technology."[23] Though he became in the public mind the utopian guru of the global village, McLuhan actually warned sternly against failing to recognize the distorting effects of the "extensions of ourselves" through information media, the worst effect being what he called a "Narcissus trance." Any medium, he wrote, "has the power of imposing its own assumption on the unwary." The best way of avoiding this "is simply in knowing that the spell can occur immediately on contact, as in the first bars of a melody."[24] An excellent antidote to the Narcissus trance in our information revolutionary times is to examine how the systematic biases in our thinking work their way into the electronic marketplace of ideas.

A number of devices for the democratic summing of preferences have taken hold on the Internet. One is collaborative filtering algorithms, which compare your choices with others' and make suggestions to you based on what others with patterns of preference like yours have chosen. Amazon, Netflix, and others offering goods for sale or rent use this method heavily. Another device is the wiki, in which the hive produces and repairs statements of fact, plans, arguments, even fictions. The two most important devices for our purposes are prediction markets and search engine algorithms.

In prediction markets people make monetary bets about future events such as the outcome of an election. Prediction markets have worked fairly well. They are really no different than financial markets where people bet on the future price of stocks, bonds, and commodities. They are also similar to pari-mutuel wagering, where people's betting pattern establishes the odds (which is another way of saying prices). The power of prediction markets is that, like purely financial markets, they give people an incentive to disclose the information they hold.[25] Individuals don't make the disclosure by writing a blog, of course. They do it by the very act of making a bet, which says that everything they know leads them to believe that X will occur. Providing an incentive to disclose is why strong prediction markets require people to stake money on their guesses.

This leads us to something called the Condorcet Jury Theorem, which holds that the probability of a majority vote in favor of the correct answer to a question approaches 100 percent as the size of the group increases, but only if each person is at least slightly more likely than not to be right. With sufficiently large voting groups in which most people answer randomly—not having any notion of what is the right answer nor any bias in favor of the wrong answer—their vote will be split 50–50, so that even a few more accurate answers will be enough to tilt the balance. (The theorem also assumes that each voter will act with complete independence of the others, which avoids groupthink and related sources of error.) In prediction markets where people stake money on their answers, a few participants believing intensely in the right answer and betting big as a result can carry the day.[26] An open political system, by the way, has its own ways of registering intensity. Civil disobedience is one of them. A person who commits it says, I believe this so much that I am willing to risk jail for it.[27]

The Condorcet Jury Theorem (and by extension prediction markets) has a dark side, which shows itself when because of widespread bias each individual is a little more likely to be wrong than right. In that case the larger the group, the more wrong it will be.[28]

Oddly, discussion can end up promoting a "dark side" bias. The Condorcet Theorem recognized this by assuming that people not be affected by other people's votes.[29] Deliberation among people who think similarly drives them to more extreme views.[30] One reason for this is the tendency to seize upon that which confirms one's preexisting ideas. Another is the desire to be part of the group (the "us") rather than at odds with it (the "them"). There is evidence that the more people communicate among themselves in an influential way, the more likely the group will reach a consensus—a poor one. Some intuition that this might be the case was probably what led to procedures that isolate certain kinds of decision makers from one another, such as the rule against jurors discussing a case until all the evidence is in.[31] Strangely enough, in this respect the vastly increased interpersonal communication available today may invite vast error. It has even been suggested that this helps explain the economic meltdown of 2008.[32]

: : :

Search engines provide most people their way into the profusion of information on the Web. The algorithms that establish what Web pages are displayed first in answer to a query operate by a kind of voting. Google, whose algorithms propelled it into a commanding leadership position as Internet usage soared, counts votes this way: First, it scans the entire Web to see how many Web sites link to a given page, how many in effect have voted for it. Then Google determines how much to weight each Web link vote by seeing how many Web sites link to each voter. And so on. All of this is summed up in a number from 1 to 10.[33]

When Google moved into news, the links-only approach did not work very well. Though it could measure how well people thought of various *sources* for news on the Web, it did not quickly take into account how many people were attracted to *a given breaking news item*. Nor did it grow smarter with use as it did with more durable pieces of information.[34]

Though search engines guard their algorithms like state secrets, it is pretty clear that Google solved its news problem by counting clicks on its own site in real time as well as Web links. Most people assume that all search engines, including Google, do some form of this as part of all their calculations of what to serve up. The search engines' algorithms make them, according to one critic, an "electronic mirror of ourselves."[35] This is precisely the Narcissus trance that McLuhan warned about.

The methodology of the search engines, democratic though it may be, amplifies any general and systematic bias in our thinking. Of course, we know that systematic bias promotes coverage in traditional media that tilts sharply toward bad news. But how much more quickly and pervasively this happens with search algorithms, which involve no human being trained at least to distinguish between important frightening things and unimportant ones.

Two researchers at Microsoft have published on the Web a study of "cyberchondria,"[36] the way people who look up a symptom on search engines tend to be drawn to grave diagnoses of that symptom. Using Microsoft Network's enormous database, they examined how this can lead alarming information to be ranked high on the page delivering search results. Because availability is one of the brain's rules of thumb, the fact that information about a serious condition shows up high on the list will tend to make people believe that the probability that the symptom is caused by the grave condition is higher than it really is. Hence "cyberchondria."

While researching this book, I heard from someone close to me that he had come down with a cancer he thought might have been caused by exposure to Agent Orange in Vietnam. I went to Google to see whether any strong proof that Agent Orange causes cancer had developed since the last time I checked in on the subject many years before. The search engine led me to numerous sites that would make a person think that there was clear proof with respect to a fairly long list of cancers. They talked about dioxin, a chemical found in Agent Orange, as "super toxic." Even the Veterans

Administration site would lead you to think that the science clearly established the cancer risk of dioxin exposure. Only Wikipedia noted, after
spreading the alarm, that "the effect of long-term low-level exposure has
not been established."[37]

Finally, after much effort, I found my way to a report from the National
Academy of Sciences—which was not displayed on the first page under
Agent Orange or dioxin—indicating that the cancer risk of dioxin exposure
had been greatly exaggerated. It was there on the Web, but it was not, in the
rule of thumb sense, available.

When people are drawn to information because of fear—or anger, or
lust, or through any systematic bias—the automatic vote counting of search
engines move that information toward the top of the list. At that point the
mind's availability shortcut will lead people to believe the things at the top
of the list are more probable or more significant than they really are. This
can happen with health risks or rumors, terrorist threats or tax debates. The
algorithms magnify the inherent biases in human thinking and spread the
error instantly around the world. In this respect, at least, the information
revolution has not produced a utopian improvement of human nature; it
has done the opposite.

CHAPTER TEN

THE SECRETS OF STORY

Humans have an innate ability to get inside other people's heads. With it they can imagine the world as it appears and feels from perspectives other than their own. This capacity develops at around three years old, about the same time that a child develops a narrative sense of herself,[1] which is probably no coincidence. Our mind-reading ability is far from perfect, but like our mental rules of thumb, it survives in us because it works well enough most of the time.

In one of the classic tests for whether a child has developed the ability to imagine another's perspective, researchers tell the child a story, dramatizing it with two puppets. At first the puppets are playing with a marble and two open-ended boxes. They hide the marble under one box then leave the room. A little while later, one of the puppets returns, plays with the marble some more, puts it under the other box, and leaves. The first puppet then returns to the room, and the child is asked where this puppet will look for the marble. Children who have begun to develop the capacity to see the world through another's eyes will point to the first box, even though they know the marble is under the second.[2]

This ability may seem almost mechanical, unconnected with the emotions. But as children grow, they develop an array of mind-reading skills that bring their emotional systems fully into play—using empathy, recognition of minute differences in facial expressions (making it possible to distinguish most of the time between a genuine and a put-on smile), sensitivity to body language and to the prosody (melody) of a speaking voice.

These skills are important to social animals, especially those capable of deceit. If an individual depends on other members of her social group for protection against predators, her ability to know when somebody is going to cheat and put her at risk will confer a big advantage in the process of natural selection. So, by the way, will the ability to cheat and get away with it. The two abilities are in continuous competition.

Language advances both the bright and dark side of our mind-reading ability. The supple complexity of human language separates us from all other species. Its use is as central to our life as eating, seeing, or moving around. Words are not entirely necessary for the telling of stories—think of pantomime or silent films—but the telling of stories is as deeply rooted in humans as language. Neuroscientist Antonio Damasio called it "a brain obsession."[3] I'm pretty sure he meant that as a compliment.

Storytelling is so fundamental to human life that Carl Jung built a whole psychology around the idea that certain archetypal stories exist independent of cultures. At least one prominent neuroscientist has made a connection between archetypes and the basic mechanisms of the brain. Certain deep emotional structures (the inborn fear of snakes, for example) manifest themselves in myths and legends passed down through the oral tradition from generation to generation (the temptation of Eve, for example).[4] E. O. Wilson also linked the archetypes with inherited behavioral patterns, such as revulsion at incest. These patterns, he argued, "bias cultural evolution" toward certain core narratives, such as the oedipal story.[5]

Jung's theories have been a matter of intense debate for a century, but nobody debates that language and story give people a special way of thinking. Without words, the development of the clumps of information that conserve working memory would be limited. Without stories, children would lack what has been called the "vocabulary of emotion," through which they come to recognize both the things that cause a feeling and the normal response to it.[6] Without metaphor, our capacity for conceptualization would be frozen in literalness.[7]

In many instances—including most ordinary conversation—speech precedes conscious thought. "What good could talking to yourself do," asked one philosopher, "if you already know what you intended to say?"[8] Using language as a way of discovering something, not just of expressing it, is not the mark of imperfect mental skills, it is the skill. Pulitzer Prize–winning novelist Robert Olen Butler actually distinguished between artists' and nonartists' writing on the basis of how little the writer knows before starting: "Before they write a single word, the nonartists know exactly the effect they wish to have on readers, whether emotional or intellectual. . . . But the artist *does not know.* She doesn't know about the world until she creates the object. For the artist, the writing of a work is as much an act of exploration as it is expression, an exploration of images, of moment-to-moment sensual experience."[9]

THE WAY THE HEART TALKS TO ITSELF

Story speaks of and to the emotions. In a sense, a story is the name of an emotion that previously had no name.[10] In fact, one way of looking at emotions is that they themselves have a narrative structure: they begin with a sense of reality and a personal interpretation of it then proceed to an action or plan of action to respond to it.[11]

Story works by engaging in an audience the very mechanisms that we all use to get inside other people's minds. Narratives also evoke mental imagery. We don't see the plight of miners; we see one miner trapped in the cold darkness deep under the earth. Such images can outcompete sense perceptions in the struggle for attention.[12] This is what gives them the power to enlighten us. But it also makes us ripe for manipulation.

Stories work because as we experience a story, it becomes a part of the narrative of our own lives.[13] Reading a story is an act both of empathy and self-exploration. Like love.[14]

Philosophers and psychologists have looked upon story as a powerful force in establishing personal identity.[15] Our ongoing, internal autobiography is always subject to revision by the author, of course, but the autobiography itself can affect reality. A person chooses to include, in the narrative of herself, certain elements that seem to fit the story she is living. Eventually the story starts telling her how to behave.[16]

The work of psychiatrist Roy Schafer has complicated the picture with the question who is narrating what to whom. We won't be able to get very far in puzzling out the journalistic issues in narrative without dealing with such matters. As we do, it will be good to recall that the complexities don't originate in the conventions of journalism or even of literary narrative. They originate in the human condition.

When we tell the story of ourselves to ourselves, Schafer wrote, we are implicitly saying that there is both a self telling the story and a self to whom the story is being told. It just happens that both selves bear our own name. When we tell other people stories of our self, we also break into multiple voices. For example, who exactly is telling the tale when we say, "I'm not myself today?" And who is the tale about? These issues do not stop with the riddles of the first person. As Schafer noted, "We narrate others just as we narrate selves."[17]

As complicated and ambiguous as all this is, novelist and literary critic David Lodge saw in story a way out of the skepticism of the times: "In a world where nothing is certain, in which transcendental belief has been undermined by scientific materialism, and even the objectivity of science is qualified by relativity and uncertainty, the single human voice, telling its own story, can seem the only authentic way of rendering consciousness."[18] Could this be the extraordinary appeal of the memoir and the personal blog? Unfortunately for journalists, story is also rigged with traps.

THE TRUTH ABOUT TALES

Much of what follows will relate most directly to written or spoken narrative, both of which will persist in the digital, interactive environment. In fact, the information revolution, despite predictions that it would bring the death of print culture, actually ignited an explosion of written communications. Even letter writing, which the telephone had rendered almost extinct, became ubiquitous. Though visual presentation of story—on film and in graphic novels, for example—has special strengths and challenges, the secrets of written and oral storytelling provide a foundation for analyzing narrative in any form.

A few words about the word "narrative." It has come to have a number of related meanings. The first and most important is the presentation of information as action in time. This is the sense of the word in which narrative stands in contradistinction to exposition. Another meaning is narrative as a particular perspective. In politics, for example, people talk about establishing their candidate's narrative regarding a situation. In this sense of the word, narrative can actually refer to exposition or polemical expression. Finally, there is narrative as a conversation with oneself, especially about oneself. I will for the most part be using narrative in the first sense.

The very things that make narrative attract attention put it into a state of tension with the Standard Model of Professional Journalism. Story arises, wrote one historian, precisely from the "desire to have real events display the coherence, integrity, fullness, and closure of an image of life that is and can only be imaginary."[19] The more journalistic narrative draws from the proven techniques of literature, the more it departs from the strictest definitions of truth telling.

Many students of story—whether literary, journalistic, or historical—have concluded that story engages people best when it reveals the world through the consciousness of an individual or a number of individuals rather than omnisciently.[20] This creates a problem for truth telling, which starts with a problem of truth knowing. "In life we never know anyone but ourselves by thoroughly reliable internal signs," wrote literary theorist Wayne Booth, "and most of us achieve an all too partial view even of ourselves."[21] Then, too, nonfiction narrative plays a kind of trick on the audience, which is useful but somewhat uncomfortable for journalists who believe in disinterestedness. In the presence of story, the audience lowers its guard, suspends its disbelief,[22] and accepts statements about things it should know are unknowable.

Fiction itself has wrestled with this epistemological problem. At one point, it became fascinated with objectivity, an aesthetic that held the imagined story to disciplines very similar to those in the Standard Model. Booth described these disciplines as neutrality, impartiality toward the characters, and *impassibilité* (an unimpassioned approach). Art was ahead of journalism here in reflecting the intellectual current of the time. As early as the middle of the nineteenth century, for example, Flaubert said fiction needed to be rigorously disciplined in its methodology in order to achieve the precision of the physical sciences.[23] Such authors as Henry James and Joseph Conrad experimented with recounting the story entirely through what James called "centers of consciousness"—that is to say, refracting reality through the limited perspectives of specific individuals.

For a while, objectivity fell out of fashion. Not long after Lippmann sketched the outlines of a professional methodology for journalism, novelists such as James Joyce were flagrantly violating every rule the Flauberts of the world had tried to impose. In the middle of the twentieth century the idea of literary objectivity appeared again in the work of authors such as Alain Robbe-Grillet, who tried to limit themselves to flat statements of the surface of things in order to purge their fiction of any effort to impart a moral lesson, or even to mean. But this movement did not last very long, the works that it produced being mind-numbingly dull. Moreover, *le tout monde* of literary theory was also discovering the sublimity of the notion that everything one says is conditioned by power relationships established by the culture. In other words, what one says always teaches something, no matter how dull one is prepared to be in order to avoid it.

The argument that expression always carries at least implicit value judgments has particular force with respect to narrative. This goes beyond the exercise of tricking out the choices a writer has made even in the most seemingly flat and neutral account of an event. It bursts through the distinction journalists have tried to make between explanation and editorializing. The "deep grammar of narrative history," said historian Robert J. Richards, makes moral judgment inevitable.[24] The "invisible air of the narrative," he said, "will carry the sweet smell of virtue, the acrid stench of turpitude, or simply the bittersweet of irony."[25]

Moral judgment. That is about as far from the Standard Model as one can get short of outright lying, which as we have seen, a purist could say is also inherent in the deep grammar of narrative. The writer renders a verdict, no matter what rhetorical devices she may use to hide it.

Because of the way it connects with emotion, story can be particularly morally persuasive. This is why politicians like to drape their proposals in ministories of real individuals whose hardships the proposals will alleviate. A story told from the internal point of view has even more force, working on and through the mind-reading, empathic capacity of the brain. The most powerful effect occurs when the audience takes a story deeply as its own. "The vulgar lover's argument," wrote philosopher Ronald DeSousa, "is 'Come into my play: let me audition you for this part.' But the real seducer says, 'I come to you from your own play. Look: here is your part.'"[26]

MATTERS OF PERSPECTIVE

The usual way to think about point of view is to start with James's centers of consciousness. Through whom is the reader observing the action? First person. Third person. Plus variations: First person unreliable (I observe the action, but I'm wrong about the facts, their context, or their meaning). Third person intimate (in which the writer narrates what someone else sees, thinks, and feels). Third person objective (in which the writer stays outside someone else's head but follows her around). Third person omniscient (in which the writer knows when so much as a sparrow falls or a character's expectation of joy rises). And so on.

Before considering point of view at this level, though, we need to start deeper down—with the author herself. Booth's book *The Rhetoric of Fiction* examined the relationship between a story's actual author, implied author, and narrator. "We must never forget," wrote Booth, "that though the author can to some extent choose his disguises, he can never choose to disappear."[27] Some modern fiction plays with the assumptions readers make about the real author, the author as she wants readers to think of her, and narrators who go by the author's name. But even without the narrative games that bring these figures explicitly into the text, they are always there.

The real author is the journalist sitting at her terminal. A couple of kids and a spouse at home. Mortgage payments to make. Mixed feelings about her aging parents. A brainful of childhood experiences that keep attaching like Velcro to events that occur in the here-and-now. And so on. This author does not ordinarily want to reveal herself in her work, and not only for professional reasons.

The implied author is the person the real author wants the reader to think about if she thinks about the author at all. Follower of the disciplines of the Standard Model. Able to keep personal opinions and problems from influencing the work. Thoughtful, perhaps, though not elitist, God forbid. Very worldly. Skeptical, maybe even just a shade cynical.

Finally there is the written narrator. In first person journalism this is a character going by the name of "I" and bearing an intimate relationship with the implied author. In journalism borrowing from the techniques of fiction, the narrator can be one of the people the story is about.

Writers invent implied authors to help shape the reader's attitude toward the work as a whole, that is, to create a perfect reader. The ultimate aim, Booth wrote, is to "eliminate all distance between the essential norms" of the implied author and the reader.[28]

The Standard Model prescribes certain characteristics of the implied journalist author. In so doing it attempts to create readers who believe that they are reading an accurate, unbiased report of observable fact. Some of the techniques used to establish the character of the Standard Model's implied author are flat and impersonal recitation; the presentation of material in rough order of its significance (what used to be called the inverted pyramid style); heavy use of quotation rather than direct assertion. All these attempt to draw the reader into believing that the journalistic work is authoritative.[29]

What the Standard Model's implied author decidedly is not, of course, is a real person. No real person is ever as detached as the Standard Model's implied author, except perhaps a monster. So there is artifice at the center of even the Standard Model, despite its insistence on strict standards of truth telling.

The voice of the detached, unfeeling professional journalist has the side effect of distancing the reader both from the implied author and from the work itself. The detached author envisioned by the Standard Model can seem disturbing to nonjournalists. This is because readers relate to implied authors the way they do to other characters—and other human beings. They use their mind-reading skills and their empathy. They use emotion in making judgments. Philosopher Susanne Langer saw the conventions of journalism as odd in this respect: "If you can get people to take your fiction as fact, it seems that 'the air of reality' must have been achieved. Yet oddly enough, newspaper reports, which usually (according to their editors) have 'foundation in fact,' quite commonly lack just that air of immediate and important reality."[30]

One way to achieve what she calls "the sense of life" is for the implied author to reveal more human characteristics than the Standard Model permits. This is what commentators do. They hold themselves out as passionate, engaged human beings. They show sadness. They flash with anger. They may even self-deprecatingly recognize their own foibles, although being a stuffed-shirt can work, too. Witness William F. Buckley, Jr., George Will, and at a different extreme of intellectual sophistication, Lou Dobbs. Again, the implied author is not the real person. When I was writing editorials, I noticed that I was actually more opinionated in public than around the dinner table.

The reason you are seeing more and more attitude in the presentation of news is that an emotional voice cuts through the competitive clutter and seizes people's attention. Attitude works so well, in fact, that Anthony Lewis—whose column in the *New York Times* had plenty of it—said in 2008, "We're suffocating in opinion in this country. I believe in freedom of opinion, but we need facts."[31]

Narrative throbs with the sense of life. When done well, it works better than attitude—though attitude is a much easier skill to master. Human interest has always been a journalistic category, but this approach to news is sharply on the rise.[32] The reason seems clear: sensing the increasing difficulty of attracting attention in a radically more competitive environment, journalists have reached out more and more to make a human connection.

Some of the mannerisms of journalists in pursuit of human interest can be silly. A very thoughtful and generally reserved friend of mine becomes quite agitated when he talks about the way that every story in the paper seems to start with a paragraph or two of narrative before the story launches into an exposition of the issue in the detached manner prescribed by the Standard Model. If I understand the source of his irritation, it is the obviousness, sentimentality, and ultimate futility of the initial effort to create human interest. Or maybe he just thinks it wastes a couple of paragraphs of his time.

When a long article about health policy begins with a short anecdote about somebody who has cancer then forgets about her, the emotional effect is not powerful. On close examination it might even seem morally repulsive. Was the writer simply using the poor cancer victim? I'm not sure the anecdotal approach is even marginally effective. Nonetheless, everybody—not just newspaper reporters—seems to be using it. Just think of a typical NPR report from the field. It starts with the sounds of somebody doing something (hammering, splashing in a pool), followed quickly by the narrator explaining that Aamir Ajamabad (or Tim O'Shaunessy or Nguyen Van Thi) spends his days building coffins (or cutting bog or harvesting rice) and worrying about his family's future.

Longer form narratives also seem much more common than a couple of decades ago, along with the prodigal son of the group, the fictionalized docudrama about actual events. With respect to them, the ethical question isn't about the artifice involved in creating implied authors or about how one person knows the internal state of another. The issue is their lack of concern for any of this, starting with simple fact accuracy.[33]

Dramatization in visual news media can be done responsibly, but it requires discipline and critical intelligence. The first requirement is that dramatizations present themselves clearly as such. Every effort must be made to keep the audience from confusing the actors with the real people they portray. Beyond this, nothing should be dramatized that has not been thoroughly verified as fact. Dramatizing events in which different sources have different versions should be avoided, unless in a kind of *Rashomon* approach, with each version getting its moment on stage. This is especially important when the event depicts someone in an unfavorable light.

As media continue to merge, dramatization and narrative journalism will continue to draw closer to one another; so must the news disciplines that govern them.

: : :

Paul Ricoeur made an observation concerning the implied author and implied reader of narrative that illuminates journalism's current situation. The real author disguises her true self. But she cannot force the real reader to become the ideal reader. The tools she has for bringing a reader around are limited. For the most part she must take the reader she gets, and that reader is, well, real.[34]

One way of understanding the situation journalism faces in the midst of the information revolution is that the audience member implied in the Standard Model has not changed. But the real audience member has. Journalists sense the change and grasp for methods like narration to attract attention in our message-inundated environment.

THE PROBLEM OF THE PERSONS

The fundamental problem with journalism in the third person intimate point of view is epistemological.[35] How can a journalist know what someone else is thinking? One way is to hear it from that very person, though this does not by any means guarantee accuracy. The person who tells the journalist may have forgotten. Her mind may have reassembled a memory in light of what she knows now rather than being perfectly true to what she was thinking then. Or she may even be consciously or unconsciously suppressing the truth. In fact, it is hard to imagine many people being absolutely truthful about what goes through their minds. A lot of it would mortify them to say aloud. James Joyce's extraordinary expression of this unfiltered internal buzz, especially in *Ulysses,* shocked the world. It is hard to shock anybody with novels anymore, but it does seem to work with respect to real people, witness the brisk trade in memoirs of degradation and depravity.

In attempting to write from the third person intimate point of view, attribution pierces the illusion. Journalism professor Walt Harrington offered this advice to narrative writers of news: "*When possible write from inside the heads of your characters. . . .* Remember to try to keep your subjects talking to each other or seeming to think their quotes, rather than having them make their remarks to you."[36] Often the journalist simply does not attribute at all, but this leaves the reader in the dark about where the information came from.

Of course, there are degrees of distance from verifiable fact. It is one thing for a journalist to report that "John felt faint as he gazed down at the bloody, lifeless body of his son," after having been told this by John himself. It is another if a friend of John tells the journalist that John told her this. Still another if the journalist simply imagines what the father must have felt and reports it as fact.

Much of the problem of attribution can be solved by the addition of an afterword describing the sources of the third person internal perspectives offered in a journalistic narrative. Julia Keller's powerful Pulitzer Prize–winning 2004 account in the *Chicago Tribune* of a tornado smashing through a small Illinois town used this approach effectively.[37]

The Standard Model used to resist, though it never utterly rejected, the use of first person reporting in newspapers. Occasionally a reporter was permitted to share her personal experiences, but usually the technique was reserved for telling colorful but unimportant bits of exotica or at the end of a correspondent's tour of duty in a difficult place or when the reporter has become an impossible-to-deny part of the story—for example, by suffering injury or kidnapping or imprisonment.

Television, of course, was different because the reporter ordinarily presented herself on camera in the report. This convention originated with radio. Edward R. Murrow during the Battle of Britain told what it was like to be right there; listeners sometimes actually heard the bombs going off. Magazine journalism has had a more personal perspective than late twentieth-century newspapers generally permitted; this used to be the distinguishing characteristic of the medium. Magazines have also regularly engaged in extended first person reports. *Harper's* under the legendary editorship of Willie Morris in the 1960s specialized in them, leading the movement then known as the New Journalism. But in newspapers, first person conflicted with the conventions of impersonal authoritativeness.

In earlier eras, however, before the Standard Model really took hold, first person narration was much more common. Here is an example:

> Capt. Charles A. Lindbergh alighted at the Paris flying field at 10:21 o'clock tonight, having flown alone from New York in 33 hours and 29 minutes. It was a record for all time.

"Am I in Paris?" were the pilot's first words as the French aviators and mechanics dragged him from the cockpit of "The Spirit of St. Louis," in which he had crossed the Atlantic—the first man ever to encompass the feat, single handed.

"You're here," I told him, as the mob jabbered in French, which was not the least understood by the bewildered American.[38]

That story led the *Chicago Tribune* on May 22, 1927, under an eight-column all-caps banner headline that said, LINDBERG LANDS IN PARIS. Nothing prepared you for the line, "'You're here,' I told him . . . ," which strikes today's newspaper reader as jarring simply because we're so used to reporters pretending that they have not played any part in the story.

I have long thought the avoidance of first person is a mistake. First person makes human contact with readers. Done well, it can generate empathy and induce readers to reenact the story in their own minds. Moreover, many of the epistemological problems of third person intimate point of view go away. The writer has privileged and authoritative access to her own thoughts. Who is to deny them?

The *Chicago Tribune*'s Paul Salopek filed a dispatch after leaving Afghanistan, where he had found a way to cross the Hindu Kush to join the Northern Alliance for its final assault on the Taliban and capture of Kabul. In the dispatch he not only used first person to powerful effect. He also used second person, addressing directly the dead and displaced of the town of Rabat. Here it is in its entirety:

> What happened to you, people of Rabat?
>
> You who baked wheaty nan in kitchens where iron stoves rust, punctured by shrapnel?
>
> You who dug fine irrigation canals, mending leaks with fistfuls of mud and carefully placed stones? American B-52s have turned the canals into graves for the Taliban.
>
> On the morning of the final attack, the harsh ordinariness of your lives lay exposed to the sun: old buckets, a woman's white-heeled shoe, a rotting sweater, a turban unraveled like a fleeing snake. In one mud-walled alley a plastic whistle lay—once blown by a favorite daughter or son?
>
> The advancing Northern Alliance rebels ignored your ghosts.
>
> Tough Solangis, they slogged under the weight of their ammunition past your ruined homes, joking and singing on the footpaths your men had trod to barley fields: just another day's work to be done.

One platoon of rebels took cover in the courtyard of a rich man's house, shitting in full view of each other beneath dead plum trees. Like the rag ends of village life scattered in the dust, there were no secrets to hide.

These hard men cared nothing for you, people of Rabat.

The sunny yards where your sticky harvests of raisins dried, or the flat mud roofs where you kept noisy pigeons in cages of wire, these were just more places to die on the road to Kabul.

But I remember. I know which block on your main street dips across a broad, sandy gulch that floods during the rains, but is good for a soccer match after school. I know where your oldest vineyard grows, behind a wall with a blue door that now hangs crazily on its hinges.

Who lived in the mud fortress where commander Bashir directed machine-gun fire at the Taliban front line? He must have been a tall man. The steps up to his shattered watchtower are steep.

And your poorest must have huddled in the maze of small, unkempt houses across the field from the mosque—where a Solangi's feet were blown off by a booby trap that exploded with a dirty brown pop.

The Solangis walked out of your village in the tracks left by their tank, headed south. That was Nov. 12, the day before Kabul fell. Advancing on the Taliban trenches, some held hands firmly, as people falling from buildings do.

Where are you, people of Rabat? Wheezing in some camp in Pakistan? Selling sweets on a Tehran street corner? Or are you dead beneath your fields?

Leaving Afghanistan the other day, I pressed my face against the window of a United Nations mercy flight, searching for your emptied homes. I distinguished nothing. The dusty Shomali Plain stretched below like the page of a crumbling manuscript that has been written on and erased, too many times.[39]

Salopek is a remarkable writer. Few can manage first and second person point of view the way he can. But his piece shows that, used well, they can deeply engage a reader's empathy—for the people of Rabat, for the Northern Alliance soldiers, for the writer himself—and express things that would otherwise simply be inexpressible.

Of course, a first person journalist needs to understand, as Salopek clearly did, that she is creating herself as a character, with all the complicated questions of authenticity and artifice that this entails. And if she is reporting small events of which she is the only available witness, she will always be subject to the accusation that she simply made the story up. The work of Polish newspaper journalist Ryszard Kapuściński faced a barrage of this as his fame grew after his death.[40] (If you've read none of Kapuściński's work, start with his reporting from Africa.[41] It provides extraordinary examples of the power of first person journalism.) Even when the event is enormous and witnessed by many people, the use of first person seems to attract questions of veracity. Generations after the event, Henry Wales, the author of the *Tribune*'s Lindbergh story, stood accused by a colleague of lying about his presence at the scene.[42]

First person does seem to offer special temptations to fabricate. When I was a young reporter at the *Chicago Daily News* a prominent columnist for another newspaper stood accused of fabricating a number of details an exclusive interview he had with a leading political figure of the day. They stood at odds with some well-established facts about the politician. The wry night city editor said there was a lesson there.

Not to lie, I said.

No, he said. When the wind blows, make the curtain move.

I think he was being ironic. He went on to become a distinguished journalism professor.

: : :

It takes a lot of skill to do extended first person storytelling well, and unfortunately journalists generally receive no formal training in it. First person narration requires much more writerly technique than a flat, detached presentation. It takes something close to a fiction writer's artistry to create and sustain the character of "I." It also takes a particular kind of self-awareness. In the first person, a philosopher observed, "it is human—all too human— to take one's own side.[43]

Done poorly, first person narration deteriorates into narcissism. Instead of seducing the reader by introducing the "I" into her story, a first person writer can easily put the reader off by trying to force the reader into the writer's story. Norman Mailer's first person accounts are a dangerous model for journalists for this reason. Even a writer of Mailer's gifts can fall into Narcissus's pool.

One more risk of first person narration: When the narrator displays no emotion, it can produce what Lodge described as "a peculiarly disturbing effect of alienation . . . , especially when violent death is involved."[44] He used the example of Camus' *The Stranger*. When the "I" sees the usual objects of human passion in a perfectly detached way, she can seem a sociopath. So marrying the detachment of the Standard Model with the first person would be a very dangerous approach for a journalist.

JOURNALISM AS AN ART

Journalism is no more an art than it has been a science. It stands somewhere between, too practical to be an art, too messy, immediate, and perishable to aspire to science. But the more it recognizes its need to connect with the emotions of its audience, the more it will borrow from the ways of art.

Structure is a generally hidden but fundamental question that all art confronts. For the written arts, the most basic challenge is how to deal with what William James called the blooming, buzzing confusion of reality. "Does the world really present itself," asked one historian, ". . . in the form of well-made stories, with central subjects, proper beginnings, middles, and ends, and a coherence that permits us to see 'the end' in every beginning?"[45] Of course not. Artists shape the confusion into form. Even truth-disciplined historians arrange events to create in readers expectations that, when realized, make events seem inevitable.[46]

The interplay between the expected and the unexpected has a great a role in narrative art. Very early, philosophers linked this to something deep in the nature of the human mind. Aristotle observed that incidents "have the very greatest effect on the mind when they occur unexpectedly and at the same time in consequence of one another."[47] This seems related to the pattern-seeking drive of the human brain. Musical compositions, for example, often establish a harmonic or rhythmic pattern and then frustrate it; when the pattern finally completes itself, we feel emotional release.[48] Psychologist Gerald Clore proposed that the intensity of experience may be a function of the amount of cognitive restructuring it provokes: "What makes suspense an intense experience may be the fact that one alternately entertains first one outcome and then another, each with opposite implications. As one's cognitive mold of the situation flip flops in this way, a lot of cognitive restructuring is experienced and the overall experience of intensity increases correspondingly."[49] This makes sense, given what we know about the way that cognitive challenge produces emotional arousal.

I have come to believe that deep in the structure of all art lies the creation and meaningful violation of expectations. When Mozart produced a figure and repeated it, his genius drove him to vary the pattern at some critical point. That is why we listen to his music to this day. Information theory tells us that only the improbable communicates. The perfectly probable is white noise, the dull repetition of a pile driver. The brain quickly establishes the pattern and tires of it because it tells the brain nothing new. But make the pile driver skip a beat, and the brain comes alive to the change. In the jazz standard "How High the Moon," the melody states itself then repeats, but with two bars missing. The brain doesn't get what it expects. Still, what it does get makes perfect sense. That's why jazz musicians whose parents were not born when Morgan Lewis wrote the tune are still improvising variations on it.

In literary art—as in most others—ambiguity plays a role similar to that of the creation and violation of expectation. "What is . . . ambiguous and irreducible to the theme in all the great works of art," Merleau-Ponty wrote, "is not a provisional weakness which we might hope to overcome. It is the price we must pay to have literature."[50] In literature, observed a great philosopher of story, "several things are meant at the same time, without the reader being required to choose between them."[51] In other words, the work of literary art gives pleasure by allowing a reader to suspend herself among the possible interpretations. We savor the ambiguity of artistic expression because we recognize something in it that is deeply of ourselves. Opposite emotions often come so close to one another that they seem to touch—love and hate, desire and fear. We appreciate the richly multiple meanings of literature because we ourselves have multiple meanings.[52]

Anyone who has been in a good discussion of a great novel or story has to recognize this aspect of a literary text. Did Marcel Proust's Swann really fall in love with Odette because she reminded him of a Botticelli painting? Did Stephen Crane's soldiers have to behave the way they did, just like the ants running across the faces of the dead? Discussions of journalistic texts do not proceed this way. Or if they do, it is only to note a weakness in the execution.

When I worked at the *Chicago Daily News,* I once wrote a lead paragraph in the form of a question. My editor threw the story back at me.

People don't put a coin in the box so that we can ask them questions, he said. They expect us to tell them the answers.

This time he wasn't being ironic.

THE ROUND AND THE FLAT

Even though people don't come to journalism to find a state of uncertainty, journalists can use the insight about the emotional force of ambiguity to strengthen their narratives—at least around the edges. Melodrama and caricature do satisfy a lot of people in the news audience, just as they do on soap operas, but a little complexity of character works in even the most popular forms of storytelling. I am not suggesting that a character as elusive as Bartleby the Scrivener will keep a general audience's attention. But such wildly successful TV shows as *The Sopranos* demonstrate that emotional and moral complexity, done well, do not drive people away. The question is whether there is any compelling practical or ethical reason for journalism to present its subjects that way.

E. M. Forster's distinction between flat and round characters may help here. It suggests that more sophisticated plotting and characterization is, in fact, more truthful. Flat characters, Forster wrote in *Aspects of the Novel*, "are constructed round a single idea or quality: when there is more than one factor in them, we get the beginning of the curve toward the round."[53] Round characters, on the other hand, are those that can surprise us convincingly. They have "the incalculability of life" about them.[54]

This incalculability not only offers the emotional satisfaction of surprise but also reflects the true complexity of actual human beings as we experience them. People do not come with labels marked good and evil, satisfying as it may be in the throes of love or hatred to think that they do. Journalistic narrative inhabited only by flat characters—people who are perfectly sympathetic, perfectly awful, perfectly right, or perfectly wrong—can often get away with it. The audience may not demand much more. Or it may not know what it is missing. But this is not only a lazy way of telling a story; it is fundamentally not truthful.

This provides some help in understanding how serious journalism should think of celebrity. In the first instance, it should not flatten these people, even though everything, starting with their own PR people, seems to conspire to produce that result. The proper approach to celebrities begins with curbing initial enthusiasm for the new movie star, the power hitter, the political savior. The time to begin building round characters is immediately. This does not mean tearing someone down as soon as she raises her head; it does mean recognizing that the remarkable person who is suddenly attract-ing a lot of attention is just that—a person.

Then we come to the dark side of the cycle of celebrity, the ritual killing of a star. We need to remember that gossip is all about reputation, starting with the reputation of the gossiper. One obvious way that an individual can try to enhance her reputation is by running down someone else's. Eventu-ally, however, the dirt rubs off on the one doing the dirtying. If a journalist or news organization wants a decent reputation, being a moral scourge may be a dangerous way to get it. Pretty soon the scourge will start sounding like one of those preachers who hurls hellfire Sunday morning at those whose concourse he enjoyed Saturday night. And should the scourge be caught in one sin, it can be the end.

Of course, there is a powerful ethical reason to treat celebrities as suf-fering human beings worthy of journalist's respectful care. This is a human duty we owe to every other person. But the point is that there is a good, selfish reason as well.

The metaphor of flat and round can also help us think about other aspects of narrative. Predictable plot structures create little surprise. Nar-rative techniques too obviously designed to tug at our hearts can backfire. Journalists tempted to use them should bring to mind the remark, attrib-uted to Oscar Wilde, about one of Dickens's caricatures of innocence: "One would have to have a heart of stone to read the death of little Nell without dissolving into tears . . . of laughter." Sentimentality not only can make the audience feel manipulated; it also almost always is too simplistic to be true.

Events that capture enormous public attention because of their human dimension should invite serious journalists to try to understand what it is about them that most deeply engages people. Sometimes the answer will be apparent: Sympathy for someone whose love was stolen. Anger at someone who has hurt others. But sometimes the answer can light up something central about the way we live.

The controversy around the appointment of Clarence Thomas to the U.S. Supreme Court provides an example. I was editor then, and when a former employee of Thomas accused him of sexual harassment, my spirits sagged. I knew it was a big story, but it saddened me to see the Supreme Court damaged once again by a confirmation spectacle. Our coverage probably reflected my grimness—until Ann Marie Lipinski returned to town. She was then metropolitan editor and went on to be editor. She saw the story as a way to write about relations between black men and women, about the way whites and blacks saw each other's reactions to the controversy; in short, she saw a way to tell the story that not only satisfied people's fascination with the details but also explained to them their fascination.

Conceptualizing a story in a round way marks the work of the very best reporters and editors. Jim Squires, my predecessor as editor of the *Tribune*, was brilliant at this. I'll never forget one conversation he had with Lipinski. Then a reporter, she had covered the enormous funeral for Harold Washington, Chicago's first black mayor, who had died suddenly at his desk in City Hall.

Tell us what happened, the editor told her, but in telling it I want you also to tell the story of the deep, abiding relationship between black politics and the black church. You saw it right there in the sanctuary.

She had. And her story was wonderful.

: : :

The intensity of competition for people's attention in our message-immersed environment can lead to a race to the lowest common denominator of emotional presentation: If it bleeds, it leads. Make 'em laugh or make 'em cry.

The fact is that hack journalists have always fallen back on these shortcuts. In this time of enormous change perhaps the hacks have a temporary advantage. But great journalists today get through to people without surrendering their values. Whenever Salopek wrote, people went to his work—in print and on the Web. This was because he wrote so beautifully. A number of CNN reporters and commentators somehow have managed to transcend the demands of the form and present sophisticated work. Garrison Keillor, the popular host on radio of *A Prairie Home Companion* who came late to journalism, produces one of the freshest, most engaging newspaper columns in the business.

We need to hold creativity at a very high premium. Journalists who want to keep to their core social mission and central values while still attracting a broad audience have to imagine new forms of presentation. Then, as technology changes, they need to imagine new ones. It is not just a matter of using multiple media—though that is part of it. It requires abandoning the time-tested and embracing experiment, which means a willingness to try and fail. One of the many things I admired about Michael Kinsley's work as editor of the editorial page of the *Los Angeles Times* was the wiki editorial feature he attempted to establish. It didn't work, because people sunk it with trash. He paid a price in ridicule. The profession should have showered him with praise.

CHAPTER ELEVEN

A KIND OF TRUTH

The Standard Model of Professional Journalism has been under attack on multiple fronts. A climate of skepticism is undermining audience belief in news media's ability to present an accurate depiction of reality. A democratic resurgence facilitated by the Internet is turning people away from expert authority. The science of the mind has refuted the idea that emotion and reason can be separated or that one is invariably better than the other for guiding human conduct. And the need to connect emotionally with the audience to get its attention in a highly competitive, message-immersed environment is making detachment, neutrality, and the neat separation of fact and opinion self-defeating.

Early in the information revolution, communications professor Daniel Hallin saw where things were heading. "Today," he wrote in 1998, "the professional model of journalism has substantially broken down"[1] because "the social conditions for [it] no longer exist."[2] This leaves us in the throes of a moral crisis that goes beyond the embarrassment of a few journalists from prominent organizations publishing lies. It is deeper than the opportunism of charlatans pretending they care about fairness or balance while doing whatever it takes to attract attention to themselves. Charlatans have always been with us. The economic collapse of newspapers has exacerbated the problem, but the problem would be there even if advertising revenues had not crashed.

The twenty-first-century moral crisis strikes deeply because some ethical principles that we used to think were enduring turn out to have been quite perishable. This leaves us like the pilgrim stripped of religious faith by science in poet Matthew Arnold's "Stanzas from the Grande Chartreuse," written as the Industrial Revolution took hold. Journalists find themselves "Wandering between two worlds, one dead, / The other powerless to be born."[3]

The challenge now is to begin building a new professional model on a firmer foundation, one that permits journalists to do what they must in order to get through to people but to do it in a morally defensible way. The new elements of news discipline must handle more than the traditional questions of accuracy and independence. Since journalists need to use emotion to succeed in the new information environment, their ethical disciplines have to deal with the issue of audience manipulation. I will begin with the issue of truth telling and discuss manipulation in the next chapter.

THE HUMAN CONDITION

Let's take it as established that we can't escape the prison of subjectivity. We see things from our own point of view. We are able to imagine others' perspectives, and this may help us understand the world. But we are stuck with living in our own. Let's also take it as established, however, that subjectivity does not doom us to an inability to find a kind of truth.

Let's acknowledge that much that we thought we knew about how the brain makes its way to understanding has been wrong, that the cognitive systems in the brain can mislead as much as the emotional, and that the emotions provide a kind of knowledge without which it is difficult to live and make judgments in the world. But let's also recognize that by studying the neural shortcuts—emotional and otherwise—that lead to error, we can learn to recognize and compensate for them.

Let's take it as established that Absolute Truth eludes us, as skeptics since the ancient Greeks have periodically enjoyed demonstrating. But let's also understand that we can determine that some statements of the case are closer to being right than others. The earth revolves around the sun and the moon around the earth. That beats the idea that the sun revolves around the earth, otherwise humans would never have been able to set foot on the moon.

Finally, let's agree that self-interest can color what we see. But let's take it as the proper moral aspiration of all humans to learn to get beyond ourselves.

For all the flaws in its understanding of the way the human mind actually works, the Standard Model arose to provide journalism a discipline at a time when journalists' confidence was shaken.[4] Now that confidence is again at low ebb, here are some thoughts about news disciplines fit for our times.

THE TRUTH DISCIPLINE

Only the most radical and unpersuasive skeptics would assert that journalists shouldn't even try to tell the truth, however loosely that may be defined. So let's start there.

The challenge of describing what kind of truth journalism might aspire to has been around for quite a while. Lippmann dealt with it in *Public Opinion.* "The hypothesis, which seems to me the most fertile," he wrote, "is that news and truth are not the same thing, and must be clearly distinguished."[5] Since he wrote those words, capital *T* Truth has come even more into doubt. It is not what journalists can hope to express. They need to pursue something more modest, and yet at the same time more than simple fact accuracy.

Not that simple fact accuracy is simple to accomplish. My successor as editor of the *Tribune,* Howard Tyner, pioneered a system for measuring how well the paper was doing in this regard—day by day in getting names, ages, addresses, and such details right. His system, which became a model for the *New York Times* and other newspapers, allowed editors and reporters to locate the repeating sources of error and correct them. Wherever possible it used the computer to help solve these problems. Without these creative methods, improving even basic fact accuracy too often eluded our grasp.

The larger discipline of truth has to begin with a refusal to express anything you know to be false. This actually says more than might be apparent on the face of it. It includes an element of independence. As the Hutchins Commission asserted, "When the man who claims the moral right of free expression is a liar, a prostitute whose political judgments can be bought, a dishonest inflamer of hatred and suspicion, his claim is unwarranted and groundless. From the moral point of view, at least, freedom of expression does not include the right to lie as a deliberate instrument of policy."[6] The legal right is another matter, of course. But what is most interesting here is the connection made between lying and the selling of "political opinion." It suggests that the lack of independent judgment is a form of deception when it is hidden from the audience, especially when it involves money. There is nothing wrong with advertising. Somebody pays to put out his message, and everyone knows whose message it is. But when somebody accepts money to communicate something without identifying it as a paid message, he deceives the audience. Sadly, you can smell this sort of thing on local TV news all the time, beginning with interviews of the stars of programs featured on the channel. I cannot be sure, but I have also sensed that financial weakness has led advertisers to demand and get coverage that economically stronger news operations would not have given.

Independence and the refusal to lie go at the top of the list of our new disciplines for news, just as they were at the top of the list of the traditional disciplines. The increasing use of narrative and first person forms adds some complexity. A journalist needs to be thoughtful about the artifice of the implied author he projects. It would violate the truth discipline, for example, for a journalist to present himself as someone who is impartial when he makes no effort to be. Likewise, in first person work, the "I" created by a journalist needs to express the honest responses of the actual author. Insincerity violates the truth discipline. Journalists writing in the first person are not required to reveal all the intimate contradictions inherent in the fact that they are real people. No reasonable person in the news audience expects that; most would be bored by it. But presenting oneself with reasonable candor, predispositions and all, is required.

The next level of the discipline of truth involves what has traditionally been called "objectivity," though most thoughtful journalists have recognized for a long while the philosophical emptiness of "objectivity" in the sense of a perfectly selfless representation of reality. When journalists use the word today, they mean something much looser, a set of techniques aimed at the fulfillment of the Standard Model of Professional Journalism. As we attempt to refine that model, it is worth dusting off the idea of objectivity and seeing if anything is left of it.

Philosopher Ronald DeSousa made a set of intriguing distinctions that help calibrate just how much our inevitable emotionality and subjectivity limit our ability to describe reality with some rigor. Subjectivity can mean one of four things, he wrote: "Phenomenology ('what it's like' to have my experiences); projection (the illusion that the shadows of my own attitude are real properties of the world); relativity (the fact that some properties come into being only as a result of an interaction between a subject and the world); and perspective (the 'I-ness of I'; the elusive fact that every experience and every choice is necessarily made from a certain point of view, or point of agency)."[7] To simplify his argument a bit, our ways of knowing the world—other than projection but including emotion—are about as reliable as sense perceptions and should not lead us to give up on the aspiration to something like disciplined objectivity. Or another way of putting it, in most cases we need only be as wary of our overall subjectivity as we are of what we see, hear, smell, and feel to the touch. We know these can deceive us, but they are usually reasonably reliable.

The critique of journalistic objectivity does not end with epistemology. Communications professor Ted Glasser has mounted a frontal assault on it based on its practical consequences. He listed three things that made him conclude that serious journalists should be working "to liberate journalism from the burden of objectivity":

First, objectivity conflicts with the "watchdog" role of the press by calling into question the idea that the press should be an adversary of government.

Second, it "emasculates the intellect by treating it as a disinterested spectator."

And third, it is "biased against the very idea of responsibility." By this he meant that an objective reporter feels he has done his job when he reports accurately what a certain kind of person (for example, a public official) tells him, whether or not he has any reason to believe that it is true. "Objectivity," Glasser wrote, "requires only that reporters be accountable for HOW they report, not what they report." Only by transcending objectivity, he argued, can a journalist make himself responsible for telling the truth.[8]

This builds on the critique that followed the Red Scare of the 1950s in which journalists reported uncritically the attacks people like Senator Joseph McCarthy made on people they claimed had been members of the Communist Party. The news reports of McCarthy's assertions were accurate in the sense that they accurately repeated the accusations. But this meant only that their stories transmitted the fabrications precisely.

Notice that Glasser's first two objections to objectivity really concern neutrality, which we will deal with a bit later. Only the third point questions what Bill Kovach and Tom Rosenstiel call the "journalism of verification."[9]

THE DISCIPLINE OF VERIFICATION

"Truth for us," wrote William James, "is simply a collective name for verification-processes, just as health, wealth, strength, etc., are names for other processes connected with life, and also pursued because it pays to pursue them."[10] Philosopher A. J. Ayer defined a strong and weak sense of verification. In the strong sense a proposition is verifiable if "its truth could be conclusively established in experience." But Ayer asserted that verification in this sense is impossible. He contended that "no proposition, other than a tautology [in effect, a definition, like 2 + 2 = 4], can possibly be anything more than a probable hypothesis."[11] Note how well this resonates with the way the brain functions at its most fundamental level.

To be verifiable, a proposition also has to be falsifiable. This insight came from philosopher of science Karl Popper.[12] Evidence that seems to support a hypothesis does not mean much if you have set it up so that refutation is impossible. When that happens, you have simply defined away the problem of proof, not solved it. It is, in effect, confirmation bias in the extreme.

Historical hypotheses, such as many of the statements made by journalists, tend not to be falsifiable in the strictest sense.[13] You cannot, for example, run history over again a different way and see whether things come out differently. But Popper's notion is still a helpful guide. When asserting a fact, a journalist can usefully ask himself, What would it take to make me disbelieve it? Could anything make me disbelieve it? If the answer is no, it's trouble.

What Kovach and Rosenstiel mean by verification is less rigorous than what James or Ayer or Popper meant. For Kovach and Rosenstiel the standards are quite individual to each journalist or organization, but there is a loose set of methodologies generally accepted by the profession.[14] "Practices such as seeking multiple witnesses to an event, disclosing as much as possible about sources, and asking many sides for comment are, in effect, the discipline of verification," they wrote.[15] If your mother says she loves you, check it out.

Without trying to write a code of conduct, they did come up with five rules they called "the intellectual principles of a science of reporting":

1. Never add anything that was not there.
2. Never deceive the audience.
3. Be transparent as possible about your methods and motives.
4. Rely on your own original reporting.
5. Exercise humility.[16]

Notice that they did not include neutrality or detachment.

But what of Glasser's argument that verification conflicts with journalistic responsibility? Imagine, for example, a circumstance in which a public official states something as a fact. As a journalist you verify that he said it. Is this enough to permit you to report it publicly?

Glasser said no, that would be irresponsible, if what he said was wrong.

But the mere statement may itself be important for people to know. For example, imagine that a president denied public accusations by an international human rights organization that the United States was engaged in torture. The journalist may have doubts about the denial but not be able to back them up with evidence. Say that all he has is the queasy feeling provoked by his emotional systems. Is the intuition that the president is lying enough to justify a journalist withholding the president's statement? Should he publish the statement but say that he doesn't believe it?

The journalist should pay attention to his gut feeling. It should summon him to investigate further. But until he comes up with evidence refuting the president's assertion, he should report it, along with the fact that the journalist had found no independent evidence either supporting or casting doubt on the statement.

Every circumstance will be slightly different, depending on how important it is to public knowledge that somebody has asserted something, how verifiable the statement is, how strong the public interest in knowing the fact that the statement has been made. But given the importance of the issue and the dispute as to the basic facts, after his initial report the journalist needs to investigate further.[17]

So Glasser's point was overstated, though he was right that in practice journalists often hide behind their methodology. Nothing about the discipline of verification in principle keeps journalists from taking responsibility for the underlying accuracy of what they report someone has told them.

In the end, it is just this simple: When verification is done well, it produces journalism incomparably more accurate than would have been produced without it.

VARIATIONS OF VERIFICATION

There are times when journalists are justified in going ahead without straightforward verification, when indirect methods are enough. Tom Goldstein pointed to one useful approach in his book *Journalism and Truth*. It is the notion of "consilience," a word that means coming together. "Consilience occurs," Goldstein wrote, "when one class of facts supports the conclusion induced from a second class of facts."[18] Philosopher Paul Ricoeur described something like this in historical works. A kind of verification—he calls it "objectivity"—occurs when various historical accounts "interlock with one another in the manner of geographical maps," or "like different facets of the same precious stone."[19]

Some rough intuition about consilience formed the basis for the "two source rule" made famous by Bob Woodward and Carl Bernstein during the Watergate scandal. If two people, both in a position to know, independently of one another assert the same thing, this can provide some comfort about its veracity. Of course, both sources may have heard it from the same liar. Or they may be secretly in cahoots. Even short of conspiracy, in the midst of a big story like the Watergate, one way or another everybody has links to everyone else. And everyone has ulterior motives.

Sometimes it is impossible to find a second source. Consilience can help. I used something like it in a 1972 story in the *Washington Post* reporting that Chief Justice Warren Burger had misused the prerogatives of his position to postpone a decision in *Roe v. Wade* until the next term of the Court.[20] Justice William O. Douglas had written a scathing dissent to the order putting the case over and then left town for the summer, telling clerks to file the dissent if the decision of the case actually was delayed. His colleagues eventually managed to persuade him not to file the dissent, so the public knew nothing of the controversy until the *Post* published the story.

I had an excellent source—who made me promise not only to keep his identity in confidence but also to keep my byline off the story for fear that it would point in his direction. I could not find anyone else to verify his account, but he gave me many details that I was able to compare with the public records of the Court. Every detail that I could verify in the public record checked out perfectly. Moreover, his account as a whole proved exquisitely consistent with the direction the Court was heading in published opinions until the very end of the term, when the record suggested that something had happened beneath the surface. It all fit. Of course, my source could have concocted an elaborate lie that squared perfectly with everything in the public record. He was certainly smart and skilled enough to do so. But I had a longstanding relationship with him that led me to trust him, and after I laid out the complex consistency between his story and the records of the Court, my editors at the *Post* gave the go-ahead. The article ran without a byline on page one on July 4, 1972. (I am not sure that as editor I would have trusted a twenty-something reporter in these circumstances. Today I would also have a brisk debate with the reporter about whether we could put so much reliance on an anonymous source when the story amounts to an attack on a named individual.)

When the story ran, the chief justice immediately denied it. Eventually Bob Woodward and Scott Armstrong got the internal documents and included a complete narrative of the matter in their book *The Brethren*.[21] The documents showed that my story was accurate. Burger's denial was not.

Consilience is not the only technique that can help journalists with verification short of what they would ordinarily require. It is not necessary, nor possible, to specify them all in advance. But journalists ought to be able to articulate what methods they are using, and their editors and colleagues ought to challenge them and make them defend their approach. This process of discussion is not proof against error, but it goes a long way in that direction.

Imprecise as the methodology of verification may be, in the end journalists need to be driven by what Ricoeur called the need "to do justice to the past." It is, he wrote of historians, like being "someone with an unpaid debt."[22] A journalist pays the debt by verifying by one method or another every statement he makes. And if something still doesn't seem right, the debt is still outstanding. The journalist can only pay it by going back again and again.

GUARDING AGAINST SYSTEMATIC ERROR

Every journalist should receive training in the brain's rules of thumb. Understanding how these cognitive and emotional shortcuts can trick us into error will help them pay the debt to reality fully and on time. Let's begin with mind reading and its limitations.

We have encountered many reasons why we should not simply distrust intuitions about what is going on in other people's heads. But intuition needs to interact with discipline, especially since natural selection seems to have favored erring on the side of detecting deception. Add to this the fact that journalists operate in an environment full of people trying to deceive them in large ways and small. The lie detection mechanisms of the journalist's mind learn to expect the worst. People may call this cynicism, but in fact it is nothing more than the brain's associative learning. The trouble for journalists is that it can lead to quite disproportionate false positives for deception. Experience teaches journalists to be wary of false negatives; they need to worry about false positives, too.

Related to this is the fundamental attribution error, the tendency to attribute behavior to a person's motives and free choices rather than to causes beyond his control. My experience in government made me recognize how often the margin of responsible choice is narrow, a lot narrower than I'd ever imagined from the outside looking in. Understanding and correcting for the fundamental attribution error would improve journalism more than almost anything I can think of.

Not only do we regularly misattribute behavior to choice and disposition, we also intuitively ascribe motive. This is a useful skill, honed by natural selection from prehistoric times. But the skill is highly error prone. Nevertheless, even journalists who otherwise dutifully adhere to the Standard Model and its strict truth discipline seem prepared to abandon them anytime they have an opportunity to imagine what lies deep in the mysteries of the human heart. Motives ascribed by journalists are often extremely reductive—greed, ambition, lust.[23] Usually the journalist makes no effort at verification. Nor, given the complex and occult nature of human motives, would it even be possible in most cases to verify them. The best a journalist can hope for are verifiable pieces of evidence that suggest what a person's motives might be—things he says to others, for example. Reported as such—as pieces of evidence—this is fine. It is the leap beyond the evidence—or worse, without evidence—that violates the truth discipline.

: : :

The brain's novelty and negativity biases drive human curiosity, which invites journalism to satisfy it. But this should not end the discussion. Journalists need to recognize these biases and not simply surrender to them. Novelty and negativity can put certain things at the top of the mind and, through the operation of the availability rule of thumb, mislead a journalist into believing they are more probable than more positive things. A journalist who recognizes this can correct for it by looking for external, verifiable indicia of probability. Beyond that, just because the audience is curious about the new and the negative does not mean journalists should slavishly follow, especially when they know it can lead the audience into error. The capacity to make a judgment about significance is, after all, what distinguishes a journalist from an algorithm.

The legal rules of evidence that govern what juries may be exposed to by the lawyers trying the case require judges to strike a balance concerning

evidence that carries a special emotional charge. The balance is between
the prejudicial effect of the evidence (the likelihood that it will be over-
weighted by a jury) and the probative value of the evidence (how valuable
it is in determining who should prevail in the case). Journalists should
strike something like this balance when dealing with novelties and nega-
tivities that they know run the risk of misleading the audience. How big is
the risk? How important is the information? The judgment will be imprecise, but the chance of making it wisely increases if a journalist realizes that
he needs to try.

: : :

The availability rule of thumb underlies the persuasive power of narrative.
By stimulating human empathy in the audience, it turns the abstract into the
emotionally important, thus putting it top of mind. This can lead the audience into important material that it otherwise might disregard. But journalists should exercise particular care that the human story they choose to tell is
representative of the phenomenon they are trying to light up with it.

Journalists themselves can fall prey to availability errors, especially when
they actually witness something highly emotional. This can be so difficult
to compensate for that editors must intervene, not to deny the emotional
importance of the event, only to make sure that the reporter has not lost
perspective.

On the other hand, emotionally charged events can also lead reporters
and editors to a deeper and broader understanding. In 1992 fifteen-year-old
Laquanda Edwards was shot down at the notorious Cabrini-Green public
housing project. David Silverman, the *Tribune* reporter who covered the
story, wrote a poignant lead paragraph: "You will forget her name. You will
forget her face. And the last mark she left—a blood stain on the pavement
in front of her apartment building at Cabrini-Green—was washed away
Friday."[24] It was a deeply moving article. It haunted me. Then a few months
later a bullet struck seven-year-old Dantrell Davis in the head as he walked
from Cabrini-Green to school with his mother. He died ten feet from the
school door.

I talked with other editors at the *Tribune* about how we should respond
to these awful events. There had been a lot of stories in the paper about
the murder of innocent children, but nothing connected them with one
another. We decided that the *Tribune* would report in detail the life and

death of every youngster murdered in Cook County over the course of the following calendar year.

The series, called "Killing Our Children," included a lot of emotionally powerful individual narratives. Put together, they revealed some patterns that we did not anticipate. Child abuse killed more children than anything else. And the shaking of infants was particularly lethal. Silverman's article and the availability rule of thumb had put the matter of homicide of children to the front of our minds. But only a lot of detailed reporting revealed the context in which to understand it.

: : :

One psychologist has identified an example of the probability tricks the brain plays that relates specifically to narrative journalism. Think of the kind of story in which one event leads to another, which leads to another, and so on, to the conclusion. The more links in such a story—that is, the more elaborate the narrative detail—the more credible it will probably seem to the reader. The detail, in effect, draws the reader into the action. But statistically, the more links necessary to lead to the conclusion, the less likely the story as a whole will be correct. This is simply because each introduces a certain chance of error, and the chances multiply to establish the overall probability of error.[25]

The lesson in this is not that journalists should minimize detail. It is that they need to recognize the problem and not let themselves be mesmerized by the power of detail. In fact, they need to be stricter about verification the greater the number of links that have to be right for the essence of the narrative to be right.

The formal education of journalists should include, as a required course, the study of probability and statistics, because our mental shortcuts don't work well at all in this area. Journalists don't need to be able to do multiple regression analysis or design a proper null hypothesis. But they do need to be able to analyze statistical research in order to translate it into plain English for their audience. And they need to have an internal set of alarms that go off when they are about to fall into a trap laid by the brain's probability rules of thumb.[26]

The very process of examining such matters can lead to important journalism. At one point the investigative reporter John Crewdson was concentrating his work on the subject of risk: how our society perceives it, how we measure it for purposes of making public policy, how we communicate it in the news, and so on. This led to a remarkable series of articles on the risk of dying of cardiac arrest on airliners (which was vastly greater than the risk of dying in a crash) and the relatively low cost of avoiding the risk.[27] This led to the airlines putting defibrillators on every aircraft.

: : :

The strong tendency of the human mind to divide people into "us" and "them" and the way that even perfectly equal treatment in reporting negative behavior can still teach children prejudice create a huge challenge for journalists. That the problem is well known does not diminish its difficulty.

Journalists need to take steps to minimize the risk that they make decisions based on prejudices they themselves have learned. One of the best ways of doing this is to have news decisions made by groups of people who have learned different things growing up in very different environments. We call this diversity. We might just as well call it avoiding group confirmation bias.

Journalists may have to disregard the audience's natural curiosity about novelty and negativity in the interest of avoiding sending inaccurate messages about probability when the messages slot into our brains' "us" and "them" grooves. With respect to the groups most often hurt by prejudice, editors may also need to go out of their way to include positive depictions in order to counterbalance the effect on children who have little routine exposure to people from these groups. This is slippery business, of course, as it can depart from the strict goal of coverage that simply reflects reality. But if the group hurt by prejudice is significantly underrepresented in newsroom decision making, this might actually be thought of as nothing more than a compensatory strategy to counteract group confirmation bias and make news coverage's fit with reality more precise. Still, even doing all of this, we have to recognize the modest extent to which journalists can rectify the tendency to racial bias. All institutions in society need to help do that, even search algorithms.

: : :

Psychiatrist Hans Kohut saw enormous opportunity to improve the work of historians through education that would help them to understand better the deep sources of their own responses to the events they write about.

The "ever deepening awareness of the tendency to make the history we write serve certain psychological ends . . . ," he wrote, "should allow us to move toward greater objectivity." He even suggested that the historian (or by extension the journalist) explicitly discuss the subjective element in his work, that is, "the way the historian's specific emotional involvement influences his perceptions."[28]

First person journalism can certainly do this, though amateurs should always be duly humble about how much they understand their own motives. Whether or not they find a way to be explicit about it in their reports, an awareness of the subjective element can sharpen the verification techniques journalists use.

ABANDONING NEUTRALITY?

The pressure of today's information environment has already led to a widespread retreat from the Standard Model of Professional Journalism's insistence on neutrality and disinterestedness. These values have always been fragile, if only because in the final analysis no human being can fully live up to them. More particularly, in the last half of the twentieth century serious journalists placed increasing emphasis on what has been called interpretative reporting or explanatory journalism as ways of helping the public understand some of the complexities of modern public policy. Interpretation and explanation by their nature are not neutral. Ideally they offer a perspective that is informed by genuine and deep understanding of the subject, though we have seen that this kind of expertise has fallen into democratic disrepute.

More recently, journalists in all media have inclined more and more toward more direct and unfettered commentary. This permits a more emotionally charged presentation of information, which is more effective at getting an audience than the traditional flat, detached mode of presentation. This tendency is only likely to increase over time as competition for attention and the emotional arousal caused by message inundation increases. The shift toward opinion is not temporary or faddish; it is durable.

Kovach and Rosenstiel have argued that objectivity never really meant that journalists had to be utterly disinterested. "The method is objective," they wrote, "not the journalist." In fact, they warned that detached presentation can be deceptive. The "neutral voice, without a discipline of verification," they wrote, "creates a veneer covering something hollow."[29]

So how much is lost in the abandonment of disinterestedness and neutrality? One comment by William James gives me some consolation. "The most useful investigator, because the most sensitive observer," he wrote, "is always he whose eager interest in one side of the question is balanced by an equally keen nervousness lest he become deceived."[30] The more that journalists let themselves engage in direct commentary, the more they need to be nervous about being wrong and to look with an open mind for evidence tending to refute their assertions. This is a particularly demanding discipline.

I myself vastly prefer news reports disciplined by the Standard Model. They allow me to draw my own conclusions based on evidence presented in one place from a variety of sources and policy perspectives. In *News Values* I argued that journalists should be intellectually honest in presenting their reports.[31] Under this approach, there is nothing wrong with a journalist openly favoring a particular disputed policy or version of reality so long as he reports facts and arguments that tend to refute his position as forcefully as he would like his facts and arguments to be presented in the work of those taking the other side of the argument. I still think any policy debate is enriched when all its participants discipline themselves this way, but it does not lend itself to passionate presentation of the sort that cuts through the overload and grabs an audience.

E. M. Forster's metaphor of round and flat characters in narrative may offer journalists a useful way to think about how to discipline direct commentary in their work. "The test of a round character," Forster wrote, "is whether it is capable of surprising in a convincing way. If it never surprises, it is flat. If it does not convince, it is flat pretending to be round."[32]

Arguments, too, are flat or round. The flat ones grind on in a totally predictable way. The flat liberal or conservative, the flat fundamentalist or atheist not only sees everything through an ideological lens; all he sees *is* the lens. No stray light comes through. No challenge to the orthodoxy. Round arguments, on the other hand, respond to the complexity of events. They recognize the limitations of their own assumptions. They may veer in unexpected directions, not in pursuit of novelty, but in response to data that challenges the well-trod path of their general approach.

Unfortunately confirmation bias is the enemy of intellectual honesty and roundness of argument. Once a journalist comes to a conclusion and goes public with it, the tendency to overstate the significance of everything that supports it is great. The tendency to disregard everything that conflicts is even greater. In this respect, abandonment of neutrality requires even greater discipline than adherence to the Standard Model did.

Let me give some examples that may make the flat-round distinction clearer. Peggy Noonan, the *Wall Street Journal* political columnist, specializes in round argument. So do Michael Kinsley and George Will. Charles Krauthamer rarely curves, nor does Paul Krugman, though he is certainly one of the most intellectually accomplished writers who has ever regularly adorned the pages of a newspaper. On television CNN's John King is round; MSNBC's Keith Olbermann and Fox's Bill O'Reilly are flat. On the Web Andrew Sullivan is round on most subjects; William Kristol is flat on everything.

As a reader, I will try to find news sources that want to serve people like me. That means intellectual honesty in reporting, or at least roundness of argument. In their absence, I will just have to spend more time sorting through a variety of news sources in order to decide for myself what is right. Pity to have to go to extra effort, but it is what I do when deciding whether to read a particular book, watch a particular movie, or buy a particular piece of music, areas of discourse in which opinionated critics have traditionally done most of the talking.

CHAPTER TWELVE

A MATTER OF RESPECT

One thing the idea of disinterestedness and distrust of emotional presentation did for twentieth-century journalists was to absolve them from having to worry much about defining and disciplining themselves against manipulation. Twenty-first-century journalists do not have that luxury. The question is everywhere.

An analysis of news stories randomly selected from the Lexis/Nexis database of television, newsmagazines, and large and small city daily newspapers for the years 1980–99 showed that even back then—as cable television surged and the Internet was taking hold—sensationalism was on the rise, as was the incidence of human interest stories, crime and disaster stories, and the use of first person.[1] Another analysis, this one of front pages of twenty American newspapers on four arbitrary dates in 2001 and again in 2004, showed that even in that short time the number of stories with what journalists call feature leads (narrative or descriptive rather than expository, usually with a human interest approach) increased by 36 percent. Stories taking a hard news approach—the sort that most often meet the strictest application of the Standard Model—declined accordingly.[2]

Struggling to avoid financial collapse, the *Chicago Tribune* went as far as any major newspaper to remake itself for the new information environment. After a radical redesign in 2008, usually only one or two stories appeared on its standard-size front page along with enormous photos and lots of headlines. Many of the stories that did get front-page treatment were very distant from news of public affairs. Big graphics often dominated interior pages, along with lists of "Five Things You Should Know About" this or that. Tribune's chief innovation officer Lee Abrams, who reinvented rock-and-roll radio in the 1970s, drove much of this transformation. Historian of post–World War II radio Marc Fisher described Abrams's approach this way: "He wants newspapers to be something people love. He's all about the emotion, which is the part that newspapers have traditionally been scared to death of."[3] (Nothing wrong with that thought, but journalism first has to be all about informing the public. Moreover, what works in one medium doesn't necessarily work in another. The audience expects something very different from reporters than from rock DJs. At the Tribune papers where Abrams drove the most change, circulation declined. The *Chicago Tribune* has since moderated its approach.)

Meanwhile, at New York Reality TV School, potential contestants were taught to act out in what the *Wall Street Journal* called "gold-standard" spontaneous outbursts;[4] many of those delivering the TV news, especially on cable, seemed to have taken the same course. Cartoonist Garry Trudeau showed them no mercy in a 2005 *Doonesbury* strip featuring TV correspondent Roland Hedley reporting from New Orleans after Hurricane Katrina. Says Hedley: "Are there any new developments? Yes. And I'll be reacting to them viscerally throughout this report. I'll be outraged over the lack of progress, confrontational with those responsible, and visibly moved by the continuing saga of those victimized. It's possible that I'll weep. Why? Because it isn't just about the story. It's about my *relationship* to the story! Join me as I join the story. Carol?"[5]

Responding to the challenge of the information revolution, journalism is more than dipping its toe into emotion. It has dived in headlong. The water is deep and dark, and there are no real standards to buoy it up.

The first place to look for ethical guidance turns out to be in the emotions themselves. Many philosophers and scientists now see the brain's emotional systems as central to our moral life.[6] But we can't expect them to give us simple, easy-to-apply rules. As far back as Aristotle, ethical thinkers have realized that tough moral questions defy such rules. The situations in which issues present themselves are infinitely varied, which makes all ethics at some level situation ethics.[7] Nor can we simply follow our gut impulses; we have to think with our whole brains if we want to behave morally. Nonetheless, a good way to start thinking about how to avoid manipulation is through that very basic human feeling—empathy. This does not mean opening oneself fully to the feelings and sufferings of the people a journalist is reporting on. In many instances, a reporter needs to keep a certain emotional distance to be able to do her work—just as a surgeon does. It does mean having an abiding respect both for the people in news stories and the audience.

Before dealing with the complexities of this, there is another problem with serious journalism we should confront up front—the problem of dullness and its opposite.

THE CHALLENGE OF PALLID AND VIVID INFORMATION

Even though the classical idea of the human mind got a lot wrong, it was right about the way demagogues work on the emotions of the crowd. The brain assigns weight to a piece of information by its emotional vividness (the miners trapped underground). Demagogues use this to focus people where they want them focused and distract them from what they don't want them to notice. Unfortunately, some highly significant information has little effect on our thinking simply because it is so pallid that we are easily distracted away from it.[8]

One election year I made myself very unpopular with the League of Women Voters and other decent, like-minded folks dedicated to the rational education of the electorate when I declined to follow the long *Tribune* tradition of publishing a special section of the newspaper devoted to basic information about each candidate—age, biography, and so on—plus the candidates' answers to a list of questions about public policy presented to them by the League. Talk about pallid. When I worked on the editorial page, I used to have to read this kind of material as part of the process of evaluating candidates for *Tribune* endorsement. Even having a high sense of responsibility for making the right decision was not enough to make such dry, unrevealing recitations an important factor in my judgment. So when I had the chance, I declined to publish the special section because I knew it would make absolutely no difference to our readers. Almost nobody would actually read it. A single wave of negative advertising on television, on the other hand, could win or lose the election. I was sorry that this was so. But it was.

Luckily, the bland personal data and guarded, unrevealing written statements of the candidates were not terribly significant. But even some terribly important information can be numbingly dull, and serious journalists need to figure out how to inform people about it. Unfortunately, the only antidote to the dullness of data is cleverness in presentation. Really excellent graphic displays can help—making the visual impression forceful even when the detail is bland. Very good writing also works, but it requires talent, practice, and hard work. The one thing that will not do is for the journalist to rest on the significance of the information and put the onus on the audience. Yes, journalists are teachers, but they do not have the power to give grades. In fact, the class is in charge; the teacher is the one who has to pass the test.

: : :

Early in my career I found myself working on a story at the other end of the emotional spectrum. As soon as I wrote it, I knew it would scare every parent who read it. The story provides a case study in the kind of ethical issues emotionally charged information raises.

It was February of 1974 at the height of flu and cold season. Somebody had tipped the *Tribune* that doctors had seen a rise in the incidence of a rare condition called Reye's syndrome, which affects children who have been fighting viral infections and causes potentially grave liver and brain damage. Another reporter and I were able to verify that four children in the Chicago area had already died of Reye's that season and three others had been hospitalized. We also learned that nineteen more cases had presented themselves in Wisconsin, resulting in five deaths. Our article cited a study from four years earlier reporting only 120 cases anywhere in the world that year. We could not say what caused the disease, though we indicated that the Chicago Board of Health said it was not communicable. We did report that that one theory was that aspirin used during a viral infection could be the culprit.[9]

As a very junior reporter, I did not have much say in whether to publish this story, though I believed strongly that it should run. The argument against publishing would have been that the story would alarm, perhaps unnecessarily, thousands and thousands of parents with children suffering from influenza and colds. Today, using what we know about the mind's rules of thumb, we might say this was a case in which the vivid availability of the image of a dying child would cause a vast overestimation of the probability of the real risk of the disease. On the other hand, this was not a matter, like the CTA crime wave stories I confessed to earlier, in which publishing the story would scare people into overestimating the risk of something that we knew was utterly normal. Clearly something was going on that had doctors baffled. We didn't know very much about the odds, but we did know it wasn't a normal February flu season.

The discussion before publishing the story, such as I can remember it, was not particularly intense. The principal question was whether we were sure of our facts. To the extent that we talked about unduly frightening people, we fairly quickly dismissed the concern based on the fact that a number of children had already died. In other words, we may not have ᵗʰᵉ ⁿrobabilities, but we were quite sure that the stakes were mor-

ˢᵗᵒʳʸ ran there was some criticism

ence of Reye's continued to

balance between probative

ter, I think it was reasonable

ath whose parents simply did

ptoms were just from severe

syndrome, but most doctors

ognize it. They did not know

hough we had pointed out the

disease. Today the medical pro-

for fever to anyone under eigh-

ief that the probability of Reye's

reality) was very high. But the

that direction—though uncom-

bably their family doctors—were

of the information was extremely

ce of their parents not knowing

lren were hospitalized with Reye's syndrome in the Chicago area that that eason, and fourteen of them died. I have no idea, of course, whether what we published saved anyone's life, let alone how much unnecessary anguish we caused. What I do know is that, because of the rarity of the disease and the unfamiliarity of most doctors with it, we did not have the luxury of making anything more than a very rough judgment.

This is often the kind of decision journalists must make, but today they at least have better analytic tools available to them as they make it. In this case I believe we would have ended up in the same place had we used those tools. But if the facts were just a little different, an understanding of the systematic biases in the brain might lead in the opposite direction.

PERSUASION OR MANIPULATION?

The issue of manipulation has not passed the notice of journalists. An article in the *American Journalism Review* about a seeming increase in feature stories about death and dying asked, "When does a story become less about providing information and more about manipulating emotions? When does it become more voyeuristic than revealing? At what point does an effort to elucidate slide into pathos?"[10]

The nature of those questions shows how thin the line between persuasion and manipulation really is. In his book on writing Joseph M. Williams demonstrated this using an example that at first glance nobody would think of as manipulative, the Declaration of Independence.[11] And yet, as Williams showed, Thomas Jefferson chose whether to use the active voice (Joe did something) or passive voice (something was done by Joe) in a way that had a powerful subliminal effect.

In Jefferson's bill of particulars King George always acts. *He refuses* assent to wholesome laws. *He forbids* his governors to pass important laws. And so on. Moreover, when describing how the colonists behaved, Jefferson also used the active voice. *We warned* our British brethren. *We appealed* to their sense of justice. And so on. But when Jefferson discussed the fundamental assumptions upon which he based the assertion of a right of revolution, he wrote almost entirely in the passive voice. All men *are created* equal. They *are endowed* by their Creator with rights. It *becomes necessary* for one people to break away from another. Jefferson, Williams noted, used that passive voice style relentlessly "to strip the colonists of any free will of their own and to invest agency in higher forces that coerce the colonists to act."[12] Jefferson, Williams wrote, "manipulated, managed, massaged—call it what you will—his language to support his logic in ways not apparent to casual reading."[13]

Williams concluded that you must go beyond the rhetorical devices in themselves to decide whether their use is acceptable or unacceptable: "It is finally an ethical issue. Do we trust a writer who seeks to manage our responses not just explicitly with a logical argument but implicitly through his prose style? . . . We are . . . likely to say *Yes* about Jefferson, but only if we agree that his intended ends justified his means, a principle that we ordinarily reject on ethical grounds."[14] As we will see, the Declaration of Independence is not an unusual case. We will often have to look beyond the rhetorical technique itself to make an ethical decision about using it.

For some students of democratic processes, quibbling with niceties of active and passive voice simply misreads the way politics should work. In their book *Affective Intelligence and Political Judgment,* for example, a trio of scholars ridiculed the notion that politics requires "strenuous civic virtue" characterized by civility, thoughtfulness, and high-minded political engagement. "Despite its nutritive benefits," they wrote, "political spinach is not always, well, appetizing."[15] I suppose that when I declined to publish the League of Women Voters' section, I was pushing away a plate of spinach.

However, the trouble with dismissing the ethical question about means is that people usually find it even harder to be morally clear-headed about ends. So in the absence of ethical examination, there is a great danger that better knowledge of the flaws in the human mind will simply provide the unscrupulous a practical guide for how to take advantage of them.[16]

Under the prevailing conditions of intense competition for attention it does not take much to persuade a journalist that she has to unfetter herself from ethical quibbles or else be at a decisive disadvantage against those who feel no compunction. You cannot dismiss this point lightly. One way to put the question to ourselves most starkly is to ask how journalists can hope to reach entertainment fans—those who have tuned out of news entirely, now that they have lots of alternative ways to spend their time. In particular, how can anyone expect to reach them with important but pallid public policy information?

Political scientist Markus Prior offered a grim assessment.[17] He imagined three possible approaches. The first was to use the law to reduce public choices so that people would be forced back to the news. He recognized this is a very bad idea. The second approach he called "mobilization," which targets entertainment fans in such a way as to break through to them. Though Prior in 2007 didn't see this as particularly promising, the Obama campaign showed that in a very special situation and with the sophisticated use of a whole spectrum of new methods—from e-mail to blogging "truth squads"—political engagement by young people could be increased. How this could meet the ordinary, day-to-day challenge of presenting the news is not clear, except by the very kind of heightened emotional presentation of information that raises the question of manipulation. Finally, Prior proposed what he called "socialization," largely through education of the young in civics and the importance of being a well-informed participant in the political system. Nothing wrong with trying harder with this, and perhaps educators can use some of the products of the information revolution that young people seem to respond to. But Prior is right when he called this the most difficult approach.[18]

A better pedagogy may be to teach young people how they can be tricked by skillful manipulators. Demonstrate to them the way a vivid, human image can mislead their brains about probabilities. Show them the way unmediated democratic mechanisms such as Internet search algorithms can lead them into erroneous conclusions—not only because people lie on the Web but because even true statements can mislead. (A stomach ache actually might be caused by a fatal tumor, after all. It's just that this is extremely rare.) English classes could even make a point of demonstrating the difference between round characters and flat caricatures and the way melodrama can play us for fools.

Even if such efforts were wildly successful (itself an unrealistic assumption given how much trouble we have educating children on the basics), communicators in our message-immersed environment would still need to increase the emotional volume in order to be heard. And this brings us back to the question of how to do it in a socially responsible way.

One answer lies in a fresh application of a very old moral concept—the Golden Rule. Do unto others as you would have them do unto you. Seen through a neuroscientific lens, the Golden Rule is a profound invitation to empathize. It summons the brain's mind-reading ability to feel within ourselves the desires of others. But at the same time it recognizes the power of self-interest. Its genius is in using what we would want from others as the measure of our own conduct.

"We write ethically," proposed Williams, "when as a matter of principle, we would trade places with our intended readers and experience the consequences they do after they read our writing. Unfortunately, it's not quite that simple."[19] The whole history of the human race suggests that living up to the Golden Rule never is.

Nonetheless, as a guide for thinking about—and more importantly discussing—the issue of manipulation, Williams's proposal is probably as good as we can hope for. It comes down, in the end, to respect for the audience. Wayne Booth put it this way: "The hack is . . . the man who asks for responses he himself cannot respect."[20] George W. S. Trow made the point the other way around. When journalists dumb it down, he wrote, "they feel a little contempt for themselves—which they transform, by a magic process known only to themselves, into contempt for you."[21]

Williams proposed a corollary to his version of the Golden Rule: Writers should never knowingly use language in their own interest rather than the audience's.[22] This provides a particularly useful guide for journalists, whose social mission it is to serve the audience's interest. In this sense the use of emotion or rhetorical tricks solely to get attention is not journalism. Former *Los Angeles Times* editor John Carroll called it "pseudo-journalism."[23] The difference is not in the means but in the ends.

Unfortunately, having sound ends, let alone adherence to the Golden Rule, does not necessarily reveal itself in the very expression of the work the way neutrality and detachment did in the Standard Model's flat, unemotional style. One way serious and responsible news organizations could indicate to the audience that they respect it would be to call themselves and other organizations to account when they misuse emotion. This practice is not unprecedented. Already journalists do something like it with respect to the rhetoric and advertising during major political campaigns. With a clearer understanding of the way the brain works they would be able to do a more sophisticated job of this.

Finding the ways of telling true stories, of writing expository pieces from a clear—even intense—point of view while making the audience see that it is being treated with respect is one of the greatest challenges for young journalists today. They will not meet it by falling back on the old journalistic categories of feature story, magazine article, anecdotal lead, human interest, and so forth. Proof that it is possible can be found on the National Public Radio program *This American Life,* where the voice of the presenter or interviewer is never harsh, never authoritative in the manner of traditional broadcast news. Some of the best presenters speak in contemporary vernacular that makes them seem more like ordinary folks than oracles, even when their reports are highly sophisticated.[24]

: : :

Now let's see how Williams's ethical principles might apply to an actual journalistic situation. I will use an article that happened to run in the *Chicago Tribune* the day before I wrote this section of the book. It was not an especially stark example of the ethical issues raised by emotional presentation. In fact, it is a fairly typical treatment, and this makes it useful for our purposes.

The *Tribune* piece[25] began with an anecdote about the efforts of the mother of a seven-year-old girl with brain cancer to get from state government information about radioactive spills at a nuclear plant near their home. After four years of frustration, the article reported, the mother finally pried from the state information on huge and repeated radioactive spills at two plants.

The article as a whole was not about nuclear safety. It was about what the reporters clearly saw as flaws in the state's open records laws. It can hardly be surprising that a newspaper that regularly uses open records laws in doing its work believed in the political ends this kind of story served. Even journalists who believe that they and their peers should avoid advocacy on most matters defend being strong advocates of freedom of information acts and other mechanisms of government transparency.[26] When the question of ends gets little debate, questioning the means is even more important.

The article opened with child cancer and radioactivity, which today are as good as snakes and spiders at provoking fear. Was the paper justified in using that fear to attach to the more pallid issue of state information policy?

The mother never did find an environmental cause for her daughter's cancer, the story acknowledged, though this admission was hardly enough to dispel the aura of fear. Those radioactive spills lay there like emotional quicksand for the unwary.

The journalists used the availability rule of thumb as surely as when an auto manufacturer depicts a beautiful woman, her lovely hair blowing wildly in the breeze, next to the driver of one of its convertibles. The sexual imagery of the former wildly distorts a potential male buyer's assessment of the probability of future happiness if he buys the convertible. The frightening image of the nuclear spill anecdote puts it top of mind, distorting the probability assessment of the danger of not having a more liberal open records law.

Are there circumstances in which using this particular anecdote would have been legitimate? It would have been more justified if the story had centered on health risks and the anecdote dealt with a person actually harmed because of the time it took to get information about the risk. Even then the article should have reflected, even if only in general, upon how often withholding state information leads to bad health consequences. And it should have given reasons why, if this risk is not great, it needs to be addressed (perhaps because the cost of doing so is so small that even a slight health risk overpowers it).

Not long after the open records article ran, the *Tribune* published an article disclosing that for two decades the residents of a Chicago suburb drank chemically contaminated water without knowing it. The article linked the situation to the weakness of disclosure provisions of environmental laws. The fear in this case was well earned and related directly to the inadequacy of legal requirements.[27]

What kind of anecdote would have been appropriate for the *Tribune's* earlier open records article? Probably a narrative of pure frustration, without the fear. Well written, such a story can engage readers' empathy. We have all had the experience of trying to get a government bureaucracy to do what it is paid by taxpayers to do. We tell them to one another all the time. The *Tribune* has a repeating feature called "What's Your Problem?" that recounts such stories. It seems to be popular with readers. Stories of frustration with bureaucracy have risen to the level of art that has endured because of its emotional power, works such as Franz Kafka's *The Trial* or Dickens's *Little Dorrit* with its depiction of the infuriating Circumlocution Office. Nothing either required or justified the use of the nuclear fear anecdote.

Finally, there are those large and repeated radioactive spills. Eventually the article returned to them, noting that through the mother's efforts officials finally disclosed that one nuclear power plant had spilled millions of gallons of tritium, a radioactive form of hydrogen. The spill wasn't liquid hydrogen, the millions of gallons was mostly water. What was the concentration of tritium? What concentration is dangerous to humans? If you are going to talk about millions of gallons of radioactive material going to the public, you have a responsibility to educate yourself—and then the public—about how great the danger really is. In this particular instance federal, state, and local regulatory agencies had asserted that the spills created no health risk. A journalist who doubted this assessment should have mounted evidence contradicting it, evidence from somewhere other than the audience's amygdalas.

The open records article did not pass the test posed by the Golden Rule; the contaminated drinking water article did. The open records article treated the audience in a way that the journalists themselves would not have wanted to be treated. Imagine their response if state officials warned them that releasing the information about the spills would set off panic, leading to dangerous crowds trampling anyone in their path as they fled the area. The reporters would have seen right through this. They would have found the warning contemptuous of them. They should have treated their audience with the same respect with which they would want to be treated.

: : :

Visual images carry special emotional force. A photo of a starving child, a dead American soldier being dragged through the streets, a prisoner being humiliated, the bloody bodies of women and children lying dead in a ditch. We may not even be able to look. More often, we cannot take our eyes away.

The *Tribune* opened its series on the murder of young people, "Killing Our Children," with a photo of a dead young man on a very bloody gurney at Cook County Hospital. I made the decision. The young man had been murdered on the streets. No one else appeared in the photo, which was much more graphic than we would normally have thought of publishing. And yet it did represent the very thing that had motivated us to enter upon a year-long crusade. We chose to run the picture, to the chagrin of many readers who called and wrote to object to being subjected to such a gruesome sight. This is one decision that I continue to debate with myself to this day.

It is difficult to strike an ethical balance between the value of such an image in communicating an important truth and the degree to which its very power will be misleading. Did the fact that a dead American soldier's body could be dragged through the street mean that the U.S. military had no business being in Somalia? Did the photos from Abu Ghraib speak to something fundamentally wrong in the way the United States was pursuing the war in Iraq? Were the bodies in the ditch in My Lai an image of systematic U.S. atrocity in Vietnam?

There is still debate about each of those questions, this many years afterward, so we can't expect decision makers in a news organization will be able to give a perfect answer on deadline. But they do need to ask themselves the right questions and discuss them seriously.

Knowing what I now know about the way the brain works, I think I would have pulled back from running the photo of the dead youngster on the bloody gurney. Our ends were good ones. The subject we were dealing with was vital. But for many readers the image overpowered any light our reporting shed that day.

In making ethical decisions about emotional presentations of news, decision makers will usually face great uncertainty about consequences. They will be using standards like the Golden Rule, whose application will be subject to many possible interpretations. And they will know that their audience will have no idea how concerned they were about treating it with respect.

The best they can do is to raise the issues as clearly as possible for discussion by people who take them seriously and come at them from varied backgrounds and experiences. Imprecise as this may be, if everyone producing journalism followed such a process, I promise you that society would be better off for it, even if it didn't recognize why.

CHAPTER THIRTEEN

A NEW RHETORIC
FOR NEWS

A newspaperman of a certain age, born of an upright Underwood typewriter, should be wary about making suggestions to younger generations of journalists about how to present the news. The only thing I am sure about is that they will have to create a new rhetoric and that understanding our brain and our history can help them. Nonetheless, in the course of years of research for this book, I have had some thoughts about where the rhetoric of news needs to go. Having walked through a sizable graveyard of disproven predictions about the future of news and buried a few ideas of my own there, I present those that follow with richly earned humility.

Despite the fragmentation of the audience brought about by the information revolution, for our purposes it makes sense to divide potential news consumers into two categories. The first consists of very well-educated, public policy–oriented, generally well-to-do people. They may hold good jobs in business. They may work in universities or other parts of the knowledge industry. Probably most of the people you know are in this group. They continue to want their news to display many of the characteristics promoted by the Standard Model of Professional Journalism—scrupulous verification, comprehensiveness, intellectual honesty, and sophistication. This group forms the core of the audience today for the *New York Times, Wall Street Journal,* and *Washington Post,* in print and on the Web, as well as the *Jim Lehrer News Hour* and radio programs like National Public Radio's *All Things Considered.*

Nonetheless, what we have seen about the effect of message immersion and distrust of expert authority suggests that this audience is shrinking and will continue to shrink. (The retreat of metropolitan newspapers from comprehensive, sophisticated coverage of national and international affairs as well as of science and the arts has allowed for audience growth among the national competitors. This is not because the size of the overall audience for such an approach is increasing; it is because competition for it is decreasing. The aging of the population may also mute the change for a time, but this will not outlive the Baby Boom generation.)

So even the competitors for the audience of news sophisticates will have to alter their rhetoric. Although the news sophisticates want many of the old virtues, they are affected by the same message-immersed stresses as everyone else. So tighter editing of stories will be required. (The front page of the *Financial Times* is an excellent example of how much can be told in a few well-chosen paragraphs.) Use of emotionally engaging approaches will also need to be part of the rhetoric for news sophisticates. An example of creativity in this regard has been NPR's *This American Life*. One of the rhetorical devices it uses to great effect is having the subjects of stories tell the story themselves with minimal intrusion or prompting from the journalistic interlocutor.

Though they need to refine their rhetoric, competitors for the news sophisticates must not stop distinguishing between what is important and what is not, what art is excellent and what is trivial, which ideas are profound and which superficial. No matter what the Web enthusiasts tell them, they should never try to channel the wisdom of the hive, because the news sophisticates define themselves as not being part of any swarm.

It is tempting for traditional journalists like me to concentrate on serving news sophisticates because they care more than anyone else about the same things we journalists care about. But the most difficult challenge the information revolution poses to journalists seeking to fulfill their social mission is how to reach the growing category of people who are not attracted to journalism that adheres to the Standard Model. Unless we are ready to relegate this large and growing group of people to getting their news from largely trivial local television reports and the scattergun, unmediated front-screen services like Google News, we have to figure out how to get their attention and hold it long enough to inform them about things of importance.

Time and again people arguing about the future of news have made the distinction between what people want to know and what they need to know. This is a useful distinction, but only as a step toward getting beyond it. If concentrating on what people want to know means succumbing to direct democratic rule of the sort you can find on the Internet, it is a retreat too far. It abandons the social mission in order to serve it. We have seen how search engine algorithms can magnify the systematic biases in human thought. We have seen how the marketplace of ideas, even in conditions of market perfection, does not produce truth or even accuracy the way that a perfect economic marketplace produces efficient satisfaction of people's wants. Fulfilling the social purpose of journalism requires us to give people what they need to know.

At the same time, failing to attend to what people want is also a recipe for journalistic failure. We have to take the audience as it is, not as we would wish it to be. As we have seen, it has changed significantly in the past couple of decades, and it is going to change lots more. The rhetoric of news is going to have to change radically to reach it.

As journalists think this through, the place to begin must always be the social mission of journalism and the disciplines of independence, verification, and respect. Holding solidly to these, they must let loose of such other elements of the Standard Model as neutrality, disinterestedness, and distrust of emotion. These should be adhered to only when they help get important information through to people in service of the social mission.

The next step is to look at approaches that have been very successful in attracting public attention. Let's start far afield from the news.

Cinema's use of jump-cut kinetic imagery touches the brain's instinct to orient to movement. Movies have also learned to tell a story from multiple perspectives, breaking with the suspect mode of omniscience while retaining in the hands of the director the ability to pull the mosaic of perspectives together into a meaningful whole. Think of the 2004 movie *Crash*.

Memoir invites empathy and belief by offering itself as nothing more than one person's perspective. It has captured public attention from fiction by purporting to be true and deeply felt (as novels used to pretend when the form was young), which makes them seem relevant in just the way news wants to be.

Let's not neglect the ear. The human voice, especially when it is speaking intimately, beckons attention. Nonspeech also causes our ears to cock, especially when it is unexpected: the roar of a lion in our living room, the clatter of factory machinery, the sound of a knock on a door. Music has a special relationship to human emotion. In some ways it embodies pure emotion, feeling before words, celestial wonder in the Bach B-Minor Mass, John Coltrane's rapture, rage in Metallica, torment in Mahler.

Let's move on to a place where most serious journalists would prefer never to tread—the tabloids. I don't mean the kind of supermarket tabloids that make up stories about Martians and people giving birth to cats. I'm referring to blaring, street-sale papers ranging from the London tabs to the *National Enquirer.* There are a lot of ways in which these are not good models, of course. They often decline to let truth get in the way of a great story. They are tasteless. Most important for our purposes, they are often utterly trivial. That is, they give away everything at the start. Instead of beginning with a decision about what people need to know and then using emotional rhetoric to get it through to them, they begin with what it will take to sell the paper. Then they stop.

But they do know how to get attention. Strong, short, irreverent tabloid-type headlines, for example, can attract attention to matters of importance. Think of the marvelous, often sarcastic or even off-color heads and captions in the *Economist.* One front cover example: a headline that read "Paleolithic Pornography."[1] The story was about dusty, old archaeology. Change Paleolithic to prehistoric and pornography to porn and you would have a tabloid headline. The tabloids also know how to use visual images for their emotional impact. Too often Standard Model newspapers have simply used big pictures in the belief that this will grab attention—big, dull pictures. Reaching lots of people will require a rethinking of still photography by media that can't display kinetic images.

It is also worth studying tabloid television for things that can be put in service of serious journalism. Again what is most problematic about this kind of TV is that it gives away too much by deciding what to tell based only on what people want to be told. Still, deployed in service of journalism's social mission, its emphasis on extended narrative marked whenever possible by suspense, its understanding of celebrity (which can draw attention to problems of genuine importance), and its deployment of the personality of the presenter to create interest all can be of use to serious journalists.

Here is one example of a journalistic challenge and an approach worth experimenting with: how to get attention for investigative reporting of the sort in which a reporter follows a string day by day until a knot of official deception unravels. The trouble with this kind of story is that often in the early stages it is hard for the audience to appreciate the importance of each day's revelation. And yet it is important to keep the pressure on through day-by-day publicity in order to scare or embolden people to reveal hidden information. The popular police procedural genre may suggest an approach. A first person reporter, abandoning the pretense of invisibility, could use the suspense created by his very pursuit of the story to keep people's interest. Doing this while upholding the principles of verification would require artistry, but the techniques of investigation required artistry, too, before they became widely practiced and tested through experience.

There are risks in departing from time-worn journalistic presentation models. Not the least of them is that paying great attention to getting people's attention can quickly lead to cynicism and manipulation. In this regard the new information environment requires even more discipline than the old one. Journalists need to have their values extremely well established as they venture into the unknown or else they might go native, adopting not only the techniques of tabloids but also their utter lack of concern for the social mission.

In experimenting with new ways of presenting the news, it will also be vital to remember that experiments may fail. They may not attract and hold attention after all. They may not be able to advance the social purpose they were intended to serve. They may make it difficult to hold to the verification or respect disciplines.

There have been all sorts of experiments that haven't worked. *USA Today* in its time was a brilliant experiment, though it needed to be and was refined after it initially exploded on the scene. But multiple efforts to copy it—forgetting that it was designed specifically for an audience of business travelers away from home—failed miserably. Likewise the use of news briefs to solve the problem of time pressure on readers. This experiment has been replicated countless times, always with the same result. The *Wall Street Journal* is the only paper I know that has made it work. The ubiquitous human anecdote lead is an experiment that has become a cliché. All this simply goes to show that it is very easy for an experiment to fail, but it is very hard to admit that it has failed.

I find myself leaning toward print examples because it is what I have known best and longest. But, though print will probably still have a place in it, the future belongs to digital, interactive presentation of news. This is especially so for news that has a chance of getting important things through to the large majority of people.

There are three enormous challenges in interactive presentation. The first is to invent devices that mediate the ill effects of the radical democratization of judgment, especially about significance and accuracy, without alienating the audience. Wikipedia's journey from anarchy to mechanisms to avoid efforts to alter content to serve a political or other agenda will be worth following closely in this regard.[2] There have also been a number of experiments with interactive ways to develop well-grounded credibility ratings.[3] Journalists need to be thinking deeply about similar approaches to rating the significance of news reports.

The second big challenge is getting interactivity to serve the social mission powerfully. Often traditional journalists have approached this question defensively. As recently as 2009 I heard a debate at the highest level of a great newspaper company about whether to allow anonymous or pseudonymous comments from readers on a newspaper's Web site. Because of the social mores of discussion on the Web, the question before the newspaper was really whether its Web site would have any chance at all of being a center of discussion in the interactive environment. On the other hand, while there have been many interesting experiments with citizen journalism—letting nonprofessional journalists do basic reporting—and many examples of cell phone videos breaking through repression to get the truth out, much more needs to be done in this regard. The opportunity for improving serious journalism is great, but mediating mechanisms must be found against the risks of wild inaccuracy and propaganda.

The third big challenge is that the interactive medium minimizes the possibility of by-product learning. Because it is a seek-and-find medium, serendipity does not throw people in the path of news that might interest them without their having known that it would. Every story needs to compete for attention on its own. Joseph Pulitzer used to argue that he used sensationalism on his front pages to lure people into the heart of the paper—especially the editorial page—where they would be educated. I'm not sure this ever worked. But today it is not a strategy that makes any sense. Every story needs to fight for attention on its own, and the more important the story, the harder it should fight.

The greatest opportunity in the interactive medium is the profound integration of material appealing to the eye and ear. Used well, this can make it possible to get attention for even very important but difficult material. Think of Al Gore's brilliant polemic about global warming, *An Inconvenient Truth*. This points the way to the still imperfectly realized promise of multimedia. As the cost of bandwidth continues to decline, success will go to those who figure out how to put images, video, words, and sound together in compelling new ways.

To appreciate the potential, think back to the days before PowerPoint presentation software. Trying to get information through to an audience in person in those days meant giving a speech without boring people into slumber. Perhaps you could put up an acetate overhead or two, but they were lifeless. Or you could use a slide projector, which immediately suggested to everyone that they were in for something like a walk through your vacation photographs. PowerPoint made it possible for the best presenters to integrate the words they spoke with brief pieces of projected written text that underscored important points. Vivid imagery could be integrated with written words. Eventually video and sound were added. Creative presenters were able to push their messages through multiple senses and multiple networks in the brain. Gore's global warming film has been called the world's greatest PowerPoint presentation.

The interactive medium will integrate the attention-holding, jump-cut kineticism of video, the repeated perspective changes of cinema, the invitation to empathy of the human voice, the capacity of written words both to create emphasis and provide fine detail, even the emotional underscoring of music to attract and hold attention.

If I were contemplating a journalistic career today, knowing what I have learned over the past decade or so, I would concentrate on two things. First, I would do whatever I could to prepare myself to have something to communicate. For this reason I would still want to go to law school to prepare for journalism. But instead of a single-minded concentration on learning how to write, I would be looking to range broadly to determine what skills I might use to reach people in new ways. In fact, I would try to get myself in the mindset to learn a technique and then move on in search of ways to replace it with a better one. The rapid change in technology requires this. I would recognize that the personal challenge was greater than it had been for my predecessors, but I hope I would find this exhilarating.

: : :

I began thinking about the issues in this book the way that a reporter starts an investigation. A big thing was happening, but something seemed wrong in the way we were understanding it. I began to pull the string. The trail led me to conclusions I would never have expected that I would come to. I found no villains. Just human beings trying to cope with an environment that was changing more rapidly than they knew how to handle. Now that I've unraveled one garment, I recognize that beneath it are layers and layers more. Enough to keep fine, young, dedicated, public service journalists busy perfecting their craft—and the new professional disciplines that guide it—for a long, long time.

In the preface I listed a number of questions that journalism professor Tom Goldstein and former *New York Times* executive editor Max Frankel used to ask their students at Columbia University Journalism School.[1] I promised that neuroscience would offer answers to them. Let's end where we began.

"Why does bad news crowd out the good?" We now know that the brain has a strong bias toward negative information and that this bias can be explained by the pressures of natural selection.

"Why does news of conflict crowd out news of cooperation?" The answer is similar, with an overlay of the binary bias that directs us to see the world in terms of "us" versus "them."

"Why do we care where the famous eat and sleep? And why are they newsworthy in the first place?" Because we establish a strong, surrogate emotional bond with celebrities in an increasingly transient, disembodied, and lonely society. Celebrities help hold very large and disparate social groups hold together.

"Should recent news trump previous news? Must news focus on 'today' and 'yesterday'? Should nearer news trump the distant?" The brain's rules of thumb (such as availability) make the recent and the near seem more important than the more distant in time and space. This works reasonably well most of the time today and was vitally important on the African savannah when our ancestors were struggling to become our ancestors. But it can also obscure important matters that occur far away or have their impact over long periods of time rather than in the moment.

Of course, just giving the neuroscience explanations does not answer Goldstein and Frankel's larger question, which was normative: Just because curiosity *is* attracted to these matters, *should* journalists slavishly follow? The pressure to say yes has more intensity today than any time in the past hundred years. But our need to understand the complex world around us has also become more intense. So the normative question remains valid. Understanding the ways of the brain does not give a complete answer, but it is a strong start.

NOTES

PREFACE

1. Postman, *Amusing Ourselves to Death.*
2. Gardner, Csikszentmihalyi, and Damon, *Good Work.*
3. Kovach and Rosenstiel, *Warp Speed,* 6–7.
4. Jackson, *Distracted,* 14.
5. Lippmann, *A Preface to Morals,* 157.
6. Goldstein, *Journalism and Truth,* 20.

CHAPTER ONE

1. Lippmann, *Public Opinion,* 229.
2. Merleau-Ponty, *Phenomenology of Perception,* 26.
3. For example, Schudson, *Why Democracies Need an Unlovable Press* and *Discovering the News;* Glasser, "Objectivity Precludes Responsibility."
4. Janeway, *Republic of Denial;* Posner, "Bad News."
5. Moore, "Cramming More Components onto Integrated Circuits".
6. McLuhan, *Understanding Media,* 207.
7. Ricoeur, *Time and Narrative,* 3:235.
8. See Fuller, *News Values,* for a more complete discussion of these matters.

CHAPTER TWO

1. *The Education of Henry Adams,* 1130.
2. Menand, *The Metaphysical Club,* 59.
3. James, *Pragmatism,* 510.
4. Steel, *Walter Lippmann and the American Century,* 77.
5. Wiebe, *The Search for Order,* 161.
6. Lippmann, *Liberty and the News,* 5–6.
7. Ibid., 7.
8. Ibid., 48.
9. Ibid., 49.
10. Wiebe, *The Search for Order,* 112–23.
11. Lippmann, *Liberty and the News,* 9.
12. Goldstein, *Journalism and Truth,* 37–38.
13. Lippmann, *A Preface to Morals,* 19.
14. Carey, *Communication as Culture,* 57.
15. Lippmann, *Public Opinion,* 227.
16. Ibid., 19.
17. Lippmann, *The Phantom Public,* 4.
18. Pound, "The Cult of the Irrational," quoted in Schudson, *Discovering the News,* 126–27.
19. Schudson, *Discovering the News,* 122.
20. Steel, *Walter Lippmann and the American Century,* 280.
21. Ibid., 200–201.
22. Lippmann, *A Preface to Morals,* 220–21.
23. Lippmann, *Public Opinion,* 223–24.
24. Ibid., 36.
25. Ibid., 47.
26. Schudson, *Why Democracies Need an Unlovable Press,* 76.
27. Ibid., 4.
28. Neuman, Just, and Crigler, *Common Knowledge,* 20.
29. Gitlin, *Media Unlimited,* 168.
30. Boorstin, *The Image,* 57.
31. Braudy, *The Frenzy of Renown,* 545.
32. Marshall, *Celebrity and Power,* 225.
33. Braudy, *The Frenzy of Renown,* 282.
34. Ibid., 615.

35. De Zengotita, "Attack of the Super-zeroes" 41.
36. Ibid., 42.
37. Dunbar, *Grooming, Gossip and the Evolution of Language.*
38. Ibid., 123.
39. Cacioppo and Patrick, *Loneliness,* 247.
40. Ibid., 259; see also Dunbar, *Grooming, Gossip and the Evolution of Language,* 205.
41. Trow, *Within the Context of No Context,* 73.
42. Ibid., 118.

CHAPTER THREE
1. Jacob von Uexküll, quoted in Merleau-Ponty, *The Structure of Behavior,* 159.
2. Plato, *Phaedo,* 52.
3. Aristotle, *Nicomachaen Ethics,* 1809.
4. Ibid., 1776; Aristotle, *Rhetoric,* 2195–98.
5. Nussbaum, *Upheavals of Thought,* 22.
6. Epictetus, *Discourses,* 347.
7. Lippmann, A *Preface to Morals,* 329–30.
8. Dawes, "Shallow Psychology," 3.
9. Pascal, *Pensées,* No. 277, 78
10. Jefferson, "Dialogue between My Head & My Heart."
11. Scottish Enlightenment philosopher David Hume is one example. Hume, *A Treatise of Human Nature,* 266. Another is Jürgen Habermas. Though he is a leading contemporary spokesman for reason, he included emotion in his idea of rational discussion. Even expressing a feeling or mood can be rational, he argued, so long as the person doing so can persuade others that he is sincere in what he says about it. Habermas, *The Theory of Communicative Action,* 1:15.

12. Cacioppo and Patrick, *Loneliness,* 22.
13. Panksepp, *Affective Neuroscience,* 81–82; see also Edelman, *Bright Air,* 218–27. This is an area where thoughtful experts differ. Scholars such as Steven Pinker minimize the differences between the human brain and human-made information processors. See Pinker, *How the Mind Works.*
14. Merleau-Ponty, *Phenomenology of Perception,* 169.
15. Phenomenologist philosophers such as Merleau-Ponty remind us that science's belief in its exclusive focus on what is available to third-person observers is naive, because all the scientist's own behavior, including what he does in the lab, arises from his first-person, subjective self. Ibid., ix; see also Gallagher and Zhavi, *The Phenomenological Mind,* 18.
16. Niebuhr, *The Nature and Destiny of Man,* 1:1.
17. Wilson, *Consilience,* 54.
18. Barrett, *The Illusion of Technique,* 149.
19. Harth, *Windows on the Mind,* 65.
20. Panskepp, *Affective Neuroscience,* 74.
21. Ratey, *A User's Guide to the Brain,* 11.
22. Hebb, *The Organization of Behavior,* 70.
23. LeDoux, *Synaptic Self,* 136.
24. Centuries before Hebb formulated his rule, David Hume got to the same insight by asking himself this simple question: How can I know that one thing causes another? He began from the premise that a person can only know for sure the impressions he receives through the senses and the ideas that he derives from them. Then what of cause and effect? All a mind actually perceives is the contiguity

in time and place of the two sense-impressions—a bat hitting a ball and the ball sailing over the outfield fence, for example—and the fact that one sense-impression precedes the other. When the same two sense-impressions occur together, one following the other, again and again, the brain makes the association that it thinks of as cause and effect. "All knowledge resolves itself into probability," he wrote. (Hume, *A Treatise of Human Nature*, 122). Neurons that fire together wire together.

CHAPTER FOUR

1. Shubin, *Your Inner Fish*, 185.
2. Dennett, *Darwin's Dangerous Idea*, 52–60.
3. Wilson, *On Human Nature*, 34. There has been debate about the extent of human evolution over recent millennia. Evolution of *Homo sapiens* has occurred, of course. We know that because some humans have white skin, some brown. Some people have Tay-Sachs, some sickle cell anemia. The dispute concerns whether large changes have occurred in the brain. Jaynes, *The Origin of Consciousness*; Cochran and Harpending, *The 10,000 Year Explosion*. But no one suggests that the fundamental structures of the brain have changed or could change in a matter of a few centuries.
4. Gould, "Evolution: The Pleasures of Pluralism."
5. Pinker, *How the Mind Works*, 305.
6. Sacks, *Musicophilia*, 94.
7. LeDoux, *The Emotional Brain*, 157–69.
8. Pinker, *How the Mind Works*, 287.

9. Harth, *Windows on the Mind*, 118–33.
10. Dennett, *Consciousness Explained*, 135.
11. Ratey, *A User's Guide to the Brain*, 131.
12. Damasio, *The Feeling of What Happens*, 301–2.
13. Kohut, *The Analysis of the Self*, 302.
14. Gerald Edelman has theorized that a Darwinian process operates within the living brain. "The genetic code," he wrote, "does not provide a specific wiring diagram. . . . Rather, it imposes a set of constraints on the selectional process." Edelman, *Bright Air*, 83. His theory holds that closely connected collections of neurons are strengthened as they are used and weakened with disuse. At certain points, those that aren't used simply disappear.

CHAPTER FIVE

1. Hume, *A Treatise of Human Nature*, 266.
2. LeDoux, *Synaptic Self*, 323.
3. Some do try. Steven Pinker, for example, defined intelligence as overcoming obstacles "by means of decisions based on rational (truth-obeying) rules." Pinker, *How the Mind Works*, 62. Others are not so sure the grinding away of such algorithms captures how the brain really works. Daniel Dennett has argued that just because our actions usually accomplish what we intend and thus seem to be reasonable "does not mean they are rational in the narrower sense: the product of serial reasoning." Dennett, *Consciousness Explained*, 252.
4. Nussbaum, *Upheavals of Thought*, 109.
5. Damasio, *Descartes' Error*, 43.
6. Ibid., 52–53; emphasis in original.

7. Excessive rationality can itself be problematic. It is often found in sociopaths. In extreme cases it can be considered psychopathic. Panksepp, *Affective Neuroscience*, 42.

8. Damasio, *Descartes' Error*, 192–93.

9. LeDoux, *Synaptic Self*, 320–22.

10. See Cosmides and Tooby, "Evolutionary Psychology and Emotions," 92, for a list of the conditions most relevant to the evolution of emotions.

11. LeDoux, *Synaptic Self*, 206.

12. LeDoux, *The Emotional Brain*, 112–14. There have been objections to this whole exercise, including an argument that a few basic emotions could not possibly give rise to the rich variety of human feelings. Jaak Panksepp had a neat answer: "Had molecular biologists been fooled by comparable assertions, they may never have attempted to seek an explanation for the vast diversity of life in the permutations of the four nucleotides in DNA." Panksepp, "Basic Emotions Ramify Widely in the Brain," 86.

13. Keltner and others, "Facial Expression of Emotion," 426.

14. Ratey, *A User's Guide to the Brain*, 267.

15. LeDoux, *The Emotional Brain*, 157–69.

16. Ibid., 59.

17. In 1960 philosopher Magda Arnold called this function of our emotions "appraisal." She used this word because emotions seem able to categorize things as helpful or hurtful, drawing us toward things that enhance our well-being and pushing us away from things that threaten it. Appraisal theory remains a lively subject of philosophical and neuroscientific debate. LeDoux, *The Emotional Brain*, 49–53, 64–67. As a descriptive word, "appraisal" is probably as good as any, though it does imply a kind of logical process that does not capture the way emotions actually work.

18. Loewenstein and Lerner, "The Role of Affect in Decision Making," 627.

19. Ricoeur, *Freedom and Nature*, 189.

20. Pinker, *How the Mind Works*, 185.

21. Dennett, "Cognitive Wheels: The Frame Problem in AI," well summarized in DeSousa, *The Rationality of Emotion*, 193–94.

22. Damasio, *Descartes' Error*, 173.

23. LeDoux, *The Emotional Brain*, 68.

24. DeSousa, "Emotions: What I Know, What I'd Like to Think I Know, and What I'd Like to Think," 68.

25. Damasio, *Descartes' Error*, 173.

26. LeDoux, *The Emotional Brain*, 18.

27. Averill, "Emotion and Anxiety," 37.

28. See Pinker, *The Blank Slate*, for a book-length broadside attack on social constructionism. See also Wilson, *Consilience*, 40.

29. Berntson, Cacioppo, and Sarter, "Bottom-Up: Implications for Neurobehavioral Modes of Anxiety and Autonomic Regulation," 1105–8.

30. Scherer, "Emotion Serves to Decouple Stimulus and Response," 127.

CHAPTER SIX

1. Wilson, cartoon in the *New Yorker*.

2. Lippmann, *Public Opinion*, 46.

3. Linda Stone, quoted in "A Survey of New Media," 24.

4. Birkerts, *The Gutenberg Elegies*, 206.

5. Klingberg, *The Overflowing Brain*, 20–22.

6. Ratey, A *User's Guide to the Brain*, 121;
   see also Davidson and others, "Parsing the Subcomponents of Emotion and Disorders of Emotion," 15.
7. Dennett, *Consciousness Explained*, 144; emphasis in original.
8. Bower and Forgas, "Affect, Memory, and Social Cognition," 138–39.
9. Schwarz, "Feeling as Information," 539.
10. Mandler, *Mind and Body*, 171.
11. Edland and Svenson, "Judgment and Decision Making under Time Pressure," 28; Maule and Hockey, "State, Stress, and Time Pressure," 86.
12. LeDoux, *Synaptic Self*, 178–79.
13. Bower and Forgas, "Affect, Memory, and Social Cognition," 141.
14. Zetter and others, "Physiological and Pharmacological Function of Affect," 939; Stemmler, "Methodological Considerations in the Psychophysiological Study of Emotion," 226–27.
15. Ellsworth and Scherer, "Appraisal Process in Emotion," 580; Ellsworth, "Some Reasons to Expect Universal Antecedents of Emotion," 191.
16. Kaiser and Wehrle, "Situated Emotional Problem Solving in Interactive Computer Games," 276–80.

   When researchers induce emotions in experimental subjects, it turns out to be hard to produce only one emotion at a time. The emotions produced just aren't specific, but they do tend to be either only negative or only positive. Polivy, "On the Induction of Emotion in the Laboratory." It appears that anything that emotionally arouses a person—at least at moderate levels—makes her to pay more

attention to information with the same positive or negative valence as the emotion induced in her. There are conflicting views of this. See Stemmler, "Methodological Considerations in the Psychophysiology of Emotion," 228–33.

17. You can take one version of this test on the Web by going to http://www.snre.umich.edu/eplab/demos/sto/stroopdesc.html.
18. Hugdahl and Stormark, "Emotional Modulation of Selective Attention," 276, 80.
19. Klingberg, *The Overflowing Brain*, 73.
20. Ibid., 165.
21. Öhman, Flykt, and Lundqvist, "Unconscious Emotion," 322.
22. Ackerman and Ayers, "A National Endowment for Journalism."
23. Lippmann, *Public Opinion*, 223–24.
24. Newspaper Association of America, "Total Paid Circulation, 1940–2007."
25. Prior, *Post-Broadcast Democracy*, 134.
26. Neuman, Just, and Crigler, *Common Knowledge*, 113–14.
27. Prior, *Post-Broadcast Democracy*, 284.
28. Ibid., 19.
29. Commission on Freedom of the Press, *A Free and Responsible Press*, 1.
30. Mullainathan and Shleifer, "The Market for News."
31. Posner, "Bad News," 9.
32. Ibid., 11; emphasis in original.
33. Shriver, "By the Numbers," 34.
34. Lippmann, *Public Opinion*, 46.
35. Wakeman, *The Hucksters*, 21–22.
36. Taber, Redden, and Hurley, "Functional Anatomy of Humor," 349; Mobbs and others, "Humor Modulates the Mesolimbic Reward Centers," 1041.

37. Johnson, *The Meaning of the Body,* 34–35.
38. Ratey, *A User's Guide to the Brain,* 73.
39. Jackson, *Distracted,* 72
40. See Lanham, *The Economics of Attention,* 53–54.
41. Schudson, *Discovering the News,* 89.
42. Ibid., 90.

CHAPTER SEVEN

1. Pinker, *The Blank Slate,* 157.
2. Tooby and Cosmides "The Past Explains the Present," 418–19.
3. Goldie, "Emotion, Feeling, and Knowledge of the World," 99–100.
4. Linderman, *Plenty-coups, Chief of the Crows,* 169; emphasis added.
5. Nabokov, *Two Leggings: The Making of a Crow Warrior,* 197.
6. Clore, "Why Emotions Are Felt," 105–7; Goldie, "Emotion, Feeling, and Knowledge of the World," 100.
7. Nisbett and Ross, *Human Inference,* 31.
8. Lippmann, *Public Opinion,* 7.
9. Ellsworth, "Some Reasons to Expect Universal Antecedents of Emotion," 151.
10. Öhman and Wiens, "On the Automaticity of Autonomic Responses in Emotion," 261.
11. Ellsworth and Scherer, "Appraisal Process in Emotion," 576–77.
12. Rozin, "Introduction: Evolutionary and Cultural Perspectives on Affect," 844; Cacioppo and Gardner, "Emotion," 206.
13. Dunn, "Emotional Development in Early Childhood," 339.
14. Smith and others, "Being Bad Isn't Always Good," 210.
15. Loewenstein and Lerner, "The Role of Affect in Decision Making," 629. The negativity bias can even be found in the body outside the brain. Muscular withdrawal reflexes are stronger and relax more slowly than approach reflexes, especially where the stimulus is intense. Berntson and Cacioppo, "The Neuroevolution of Emotion," 191.
16. Bless, "The Interplay of Affect and Cognition," 202–3. There is evidence that negative events grow to seem more negative than positive events grow to seem more positive as they become closer in space and time. Rozin, "Introduction: Evolutionary and Cultural Perspectives on Affect," 844.
17. Dennett, *Consciousness Explained,* 179.
18. Tversky and Kahneman, "Extensional versus Intuitive Reasoning," 47–48.
19. These categories are not mutually exclusive. The availability rule of thumb, for example, may lead to errors in assessing probability or in forecasting future emotions. The representativeness rule of thumb can produce a starting point for thinking that creates a framing bias. The Nobel Prize–winning pioneer of the field, Daniel Kahneman, argues that an "affect" rule of thumb should join the list in a prominent position. Kahneman and Frederick, "Representativeness Revisited," 56. I have treated the emotional effects in my discussion of the other rules of thumb.
20. Sunstein, *Laws of Fear,* 77–79.
21. McClure and others, "Conflict Monitoring in Cognition-Emotion

Competition," 208–10. Note that the second case also presents the individual with another even more highly emotional choice: whether to throw the worker off the bridge or to jump off the bridge into the path of the trolley himself.

22. A study of medalists in the 1992 Olympics provides a wonderful example of framing. Bronze medalists on average were happier with the outcome than silver medalists. That seems odd until you realize that a lot of the bronze medalists probably framed their situation this way: almost got no medal. But silver medalists probably saw their situation this way: could have gotten gold. Medvec, Madey, and Gilovich, "When Less Is More," 625–35.

23. This question is a variation on one from Nisbett and Ross, *Human Inference*, 25.

24. Loewenstein and Lerner, "The Role of Affect in Decision Making," 622.

25. Ibid., 624.

26. Jennings, Amabile, and Ross, "Informal Covariant Assessment," 225.

27. Nisbett and Ross, *Human Inference*, 163.

28. Pinker, *How the Mind Works*, 143.

29. Ibid., 344.

30. Nisbett and others, "The Use of Statistical Heuristics in Everyday Inductive Reasoning," 528–30.

31. Loewenstein and Lerner, "The Role of Affect in Decision Making," 620–21.

32. Ibid., 625–26.

33. Ibid., 625.

34. Cacioppo and Berntson, "The Affect System and Racial Prejudice," 106–7.

CHAPTER EIGHT

1. National Opinion Research Center, General Social Surveys, 1972–2006, "Confidence in Press."

2. Sundar and others, "Blogging for Better Health," 84.

3. Janeway, *Republic of Denial*, 29–41.

4. Lippmann, *A Preface to Morals*, 19–20.

5. Janeway, *Republic of Denial*, 110.

6. Krauss, "Ethanol, Just Recently a Savior, Is Struggling."

7. Saul, "In Vitro Clinics Face Questions on Risks over Multiple Births."

8. Bruner, *Acts of Meaning*, 60–61.

9. Stephens, "We're All Postmodern Now," 3.

10. Keynes, *The General Theory*, 383.

11. Niebuhr, *The Nature and Destiny of Man*, 1:258.

12. German social theorist Jürgen Habermas has been one of the most influential academic voices on behalf of the possibility of rational discourse. At the heart of his argument is the idea that rational deliberation can occur so long as everyone in the conversation is trying to find the truth, expresses herself in a straightforward and nonmanipulative manner, and accepts the principle of equality. Habermas, *Communication and the Evolution of Society*, 2–4, 32; usefully synthesized by Sunstein, *Republic.com 2.0*, 144–45.

13. Turkle, *Life on the Screen*, 18.

14. Bruner, *Actual Minds, Possible Worlds*, 95.

15. Bruner, *Acts of Meaning*, 34.

16. See Cobley, *Narrative*, 3; McNair, *News and Journalism in the UK*, 24–25.

17. McNair, *News and Journalism in the UK*, 24.

18. Ibid., 26–27.

19. Scholes, "Afterthoughts on Narrative," 207–8.

20. McNair, *News and Journalism in the UK,* 39.

21. "To those who suppose that emotion is nothing but innate reactions we say this: Consider the cultural variety in the causes of emotions and the variety of complex emotions from one society to another. And to those who suppose that emotion is nothing but social construction, we say this: Consider the existence of emotions in social mammals, the universality of certain modes of emotional response, and the known neurophysiology of emotional responses." Johnson-Laird and Oatley, "Cognitive and Social Construction in Emotions," 472.

22. Haidt, *The Happiness Hypothesis,* 123.

23. Schudson, *Why Democracies Need an Unlovable Press,* 88.

24. See Pinker, *The Language Instinct,* 149.

25. Dewey, *Logic: The Theory of Inquiry,* 108.

26. Popper, *The Open Society and Its Enemies,* 2:382–83; emphasis in original.

27. Wiebe, *Self-Rule,* 17–40.

28. Ibid., 22.

29. Wiebe, *The Segmented Society,* 24–25.

30. Wiebe, *Self-Rule,* 157.

31. Trow, *My Pilgrim's Progress,* 155.

32. Putnam, "The Strange Disappearance of Civic America," 47.

33. See Prior, *Post-Broadcast Democracy,* 20–21.

34. Wiebe, *Self-Rule,* 259.

35. Ibid., 257.

36. Hardin, *Trust and Trustworthiness,* 1.

37. Ibid., 152.

38. Zak, Kurzban, and Matzner, "Oxytocin Is Associated with Human Trustworthiness."

CHAPTER NINE

1. Turner, *From Counterculture to Cyberculture,* 71.

2. Barlow, "Declaration," quoted in ibid., 13.

3. Kelly, "The Computational Metaphor."

4. Wolfe, "Digibabble, Fairy Dust, and the Human Anthill," 218.

5. Carey, *Communication as Culture,* 152.

6. Ibid., 160.

7. Turner, *From Counterculture to Cyberculture,* 202.

8. Miller, "Swarm Theory."

9. Ibid., 146.

10. Lanier, "Digital Maoism."

11. See Brown and Duguid, *The Social Life of Information,* 18, n. 11.

12. Brand, quoted in a transcription of the discussion in "'Keep Designing,'" 49.

13. There were some ways that news providers may have been able legally to take action in common to get paid for their work, at least paid by search engines and other aggregators. One early effort was the creation of an organization called the New Century Network, but it did not survive. The industry was not ready to pursue such ideas seriously until the crisis hit.

14. Scott, "Pundits in Muckrakers' Clothing," 50.

15. See Isaacson, "How to Save Your Newspaper."

16. Milton, *Areopagitica,* 961.

17. *Abrams v. U.S.,* 250 U.S. 616 (1919).

18. De Tocqueville, *Democracy in America,* 409.

19. www.google.com/technology/ (as of January 17, 2008). The description has since changed to eliminate the word "democratic," but the sense of it remains the same.
20. Lanier, "Digital Maoism."
21. Aristotle, *Politics*, 2094.
22. Wood, *The Creation of the American Republic*, 404.
23. McLuhan, *Understanding Media*, 7.
24. Ibid., 15.
25. Sunstein, *Infotopia*, 104.
26. Ibid., 130.
27. Bickel, *The Morality of Consent*, 100.
28. Sunstein, *Infotopia*, 28.
29. Ibid., 27.
30. Sunstein, *Laws of Fear*, 98.
31. D'Andrade, *Cognitive Anthropology*, 208–9.
32. Brooks, "Greed and Stupidity."
33. Stross, *Planet Google*, 28.
34. Ibid., 79–80.
35. Keen, *The Cult of the Amateur*, 93.
36. White and Horvitz, "Cyberchondria: Studies of Escalation of Medical Concerns in Web Search."
37. "Agent Orange," *Wikipedia*, consulted February 17, 2009.

CHAPTER TEN

1. Basch, *Practicing Psychotherapy*, 38.
2. See Wimmer and Perner, "Beliefs about Beliefs."
3. Damasio, *The Feeling of What Happens*, 189.
4. Panksepp, "Subjectivity May Have Evolved in the Brain as a Simple Value-Coding Process," 314.
5. Wilson, *Consilience*, 217–18.
6. DeSousa, *The Rationality of Emotion*, 182.
7. Johnson, *The Meaning of the Body*, 195.
8. Dennett, *Consciousness Explained*, 301.
9. Butler, *From Where You Dream*, 47.
10. Oatley, "Creative Expression and Communication of Emotions," 485.
11. Shweder "'You're Not Sick, You're Just in Love,'" 37.
12. Deacon, *Symbolic Species*, 430.
13. Nussbaum, *Upheavals of Thought*, 236.
14. See Oatley, "Creative Expression and Communication of Emotions," 487, 499.
15. Arendt, *Human Condition*, 97.
16. Jaynes, *Origin of Consciousness*, 64.
17. Schafer, "Narration in Psychoanalytic Dialogue," 31.
18. Lodge, *Consciousness and the Novel*, 87.
19. White, "The Value of Narrativity," 23.
20. Bruner, *Actual Minds, Possible Worlds*, 25–26; Ricoeur, *Time and Narrative*, 3:144–45; Harrington, *Intimate Journalism*, xx.
21. Booth, *The Rhetoric of Fiction*, 3.
22. Ricoeur, *Time and Narrative*, 3:186.
23. Booth, *The Rhetoric of Fiction*, 67–68.
24. Richards, "The Moral Grammar of Narratives," 3.
25. Ibid., 12.
26. DeSousa, *The Rationality of Emotion*, 258.
27. Booth, *The Rhetoric of Fiction*, 20.
28. Ibid., 157.
29. Journalism's implied authors vary according to the writer's intention in a particular article. Michael Schudson observed, "The classic 'hard news' story operates more to convey useful information efficiently than to build

a shared world with readers emotionally. At this end of journalistic writing, the reporter mimics a piece of machinery. . . . At the other end, the reporter resembles a literary or photographic artist, connecting worlds more than conveying data." Schudson, *The Sociology of News,* 192.

30. Langer, *Feelings and Form,* 291.
31. Lewis, quoted in "Law & Media Program Hosts Greenhouse, Lewis," 8.
32. Weldon, *Everyman News,* 30–44, 165–241.
33. Goldstein, *Journalism and Truth,* 9–13.
34. Ricoeur, *Time and Narrative,* 3:170.
35. See Fuller, *News Values,* chap. 5.
36. Harrington, *Intimate Journalism,* xliv; emphasis in original.
37. Keller, "After the Storm's Fury."
38. Wales, "Lindberg Lands in Paris."
39. Salopek, "Hints of Lives Are All That Remain."
40. Shafer, "The Lies of Ryszard Kapuściński."
41. Kapuściński, *The Shadow of the Sun.*
42. Root, *The Paris Edition,* 34.
43. Goldie, "Narrative and Perspective," 205.
44. Lodge, *Consciousness and the Novel,* 83.
45. White, "The Value of Narrativity," 23.
46. Richards, "The Moral Grammar of Narratives," 7.
47. Aristotle, *Poetics,* 2323.
48. Johnson, *The Meaning of the Body,* 144.
49. Clore, "Why Emotions Vary in Intensity," 392.
50. Merleau-Ponty, *Signs,* 77.
51. Ricoeur, *The Rule of Metaphor,* 91.
52. Langer, *Feelings and Form,* 242.
53. Forster, *Aspects of the Novel,* 67.
54. Ibid., 78.

CHAPTER ELEVEN

1. Hallin, "A Fall from Grace?" 43.
2. Ibid., 47.
3. Arnold, "Stanzas from the Grande Chartreuse," 272.
4. Schudson, *Discovering the News,* 121–59.
5. Lippmann, *Public Opinion,* 226.
6. Commission on Freedom of the Press, *A Free and Responsible Press,* 10.
7. DeSousa, *The Rationality of Emotion,* 141.
8. Glasser, "Objectivity Precludes Responsibility."
9. Kovach and Rosenstiel, *The Elements of Journalism,* 70.
10. James, *Pragmatism,* 581.
11. Ayer, *Language, Truth and Logic,* 37–38.
12. See "Karl Popper," *Stanford Encyclopedia of Philosophy.*
13. Ricoeur, *Time and Narrative,* 1:156.
14. Michael Schudson has pointed out that the original understanding of objectivity was only "that a person's statements about the world can be trusted if they are submitted to established rules deemed legitimate by a professional community." Schudson, *Discovering the News,* 7.
15. Kovach and Rosenstiel, *The Elements of Journalism,* 71.
16. Ibid., 78.
17. See Fuller, *News Values,* 22–26, for another treatment of this issue.
18. Goldstein, *Journalism and Truth,* 39.
19. Ricoeur, *Time and Narrative,* 1:176.
20. Fuller, "Move by Burger May Shift Court's Stand on Abortion."
21. Woodward and Armstrong, *The Brethren,* 165–89.

22. Ricoeur, *Time and Narrative*, 3:152.
23. Carey, "Why and How: The Dark Continent of American Journalism," 180–81.
24. Silverman, "Sniper Ends Girl's Dream to Flee Cabrini."
25. Fischhoff, "For Those Condemned To Study the Past," 348.
26. There is evidence that education in statistics can have a "profound effect" on people's everyday reasoning, but it is by no means proof against error. Nisbett and others, "The Use of Statistical Heuristics in Everyday Inductive Reasoning," 528–30. Our mental rules of thumb are so powerful that they lead even scientists who use statistical methods in their work to make predictable errors. Kahneman and Tversky, "Subjective Probability," 46.
27. Crewdson, "Code Blue: Survival in the Sky."
28. Kohut, *How Does Analysis Cure?* 38–39.
29. Kovach and Rosenstiel, *The Elements of Journalism*, 74.
30. James, *The Will to Believe*, 471.
31. Fuller, *News Values*, 28–33.
32. Forster, *Aspects of the Novel*, 78.

CHAPTER TWELVE

1. Patterson, "Doing Well and Doing Good," 2–5.
2. Weldon, *Everyman News*, 37.
3. Love, "The Lee Abrams Experience: How To Hear the Man Who Would Transform Tribune."
4. Kaylan, "Reality TV: In Fame's Antechamber."
5. Trudeau, *Doonesbury*, December 25, 2005.

6. Ricoeur, *Freedom and Nature*, 122; Nussbaum, *Upheavals of Thought*, 1.
7. Nussbaum, *Love's Knowledge*, 73.
8. Nisbett and Ross, *Human Inference*, 55–56. The idea of "pallid" information is theirs.
9. Fuller and Satter, "Rare Disease."
10. Shapiro, "Return of the Sob Sisters," 52.
11. Williams, *Style*, 223–30.
12. Ibid., 228.
13. Ibid., 229.
14. Ibid., 230; emphasis in original.
15. Marcus, Neuman, and MacKuen, *Affective Intelligence and Political Judgment*, 134.
16. One example of this kind of thinking can be found in psychologist Drew Westen's *The Political Brain*, which argued that after the electoral victories of George W. Bush Democrats needed to start manipulating the public's emotions as well as the Republicans did. Westen began with the premise that Democrats needed to win for the good of the country. Thus he saw the problem not as manipulation but rather the reluctance to manipulate.
17. Prior, *Post-Broadcast Democracy*, 281–88.
18. Ibid., 286.
19. Williams, *Style*, 215.
20. Booth, *The Rhetoric of Fiction*, 396.
21. Trow, *My Pilgrim's Progress*, 50.
22. Williams, *Style*, 216.
23. Carroll, "The Wolf in Reporter's Clothing."
24. A good example can be found in the episode entitled, "The Watchmen."
25. Lightly and Hawthorne, "Illinois Open Records Law Often a Closed Door."

26. See Shister, "A Matter of Degree: The Role of Journalists as Activists in Journalism Business and Policy."

27. Hawthorne, "Poison in the Well."

CHAPTER THIRTEEN

1. *Economist,* May 14, 2009.

2. Crovits, "Wikipedia's Old-Fashioned Revolution: The Online Encyclopedia Is Fast Becoming the Best."

3. See Newstrust, http://newstrust.net/; Transparency Initiative of Media Standards Trust (UK), http://www .mediastandardstrust.org/projects/ transparency.aspx.

AFTERWORD

1. Goldstein, *Journalism and Truth,* 20.

SUGGESTED READING

THE SCIENCES OF THE BRAIN

The ante to be paid in order to start understanding brain science can seem forbidding, but a number of books and DVDs offer a sophisticated yet accessible way in. Citations for these works are in the bibliography.

John J. Ratey's *A User's Guide to the Brain: Perception, Attention, and the Four Theaters of the Brain* is an excellent place to start. Ratey's speciality has been attention deficit disorder, which gives *A User's Guide* particular relevance in understanding the aspects of our brain that the information revolution has challenged. The book is especially good in describing the symphonic complexity and coordination of mental activity, though it leans toward the clinical and at times can be repetitive.

Two video courses by the Teaching Company are excellent in easing a novice into brain science. The first is given by Jeanette Norden, a professor of cell and developmental biology specializing in the brain at the School of Medicine at Vanderbilt University. Norden's course, *Understanding the Brain*, makes the daunting topic of brain anatomy accessible, though occasionally the sheer complexity of the subject defeats her. The other course is given by Robert Sapolsky, professor of biology and neurology at Stanford University and winner of a MacArthur Foundation Fellowship. In *Biology and Human Behavior: The Neurological Origins of Individuality,* Sapolsky puts together the biological pieces that influence the way we think and act. He is an engaging and accessible lecturer, which allows him to integrate a variety of subjects—from genetics to neurochemistry— each of which is quite difficult in itself.

We are lucky that a number of first-rate neuroscientists are good writers as well. Joseph LeDoux, professor of neuroscience and psychology at New York University, has done pioneering research in the field. His excellent book *Synaptic Self: How Our Brains Become Who We Are* begins at the level of the individual neuron, describing how nerve cells communicate and connect with one another and how this shapes our mental life. In *The Emotional Brain: The Mysterious Underpinnings of Emotional Life,* LeDoux introduces the larger emotional systems and the way they interact.

The influential work of Antonio Damasio, professor of psychology and neurology at the University of Southern California, has helped reshape the way we understand the role of reason and emotion in the workings of the brain. This fundamental revision of the classical model of the mind has had enormous implications in many fields. Damasio's books deal with both neuroscience and philosophy in a sophisticated, engaging, understandable way. The place to start is *Descartes' Error: Emotion, Reason, and the Human*

Brain. It lays out the evidence that, contrary to the classical ideas handed down from Plato through Freud and beyond, emotion is not neatly separated from cognition and reason nor inferior to them in understanding the world. Damasio extends this insight in *The Feeling of What Happens: Body and Motion in the Making of Consciousness,* which explores how both brain and body are implicated in knowing. In *Looking for Spinoza: Joy, Sorrow, and the Feeling Brain,* Damasio uses the work of the seventeenth-century philosopher to deepen our understanding of how the body—including the brain—both takes in the world and defends itself against threatening changes.

The Nature of Emotion, edited by leading psychologists Paul Ekman and Richard J. Davidson, includes articles that will enrich the understanding of a nonspecialist who has already gone some distance in learning about the brain. The anthology treats questions such as "What Is the Function of Emotions?" and "Can We Control Our Emotions?" which have particular relevance to understanding the way our brains might be dealing with the information revolution. One warning: Several articles are more suited to clinical or academic audiences.

Swedish neuroscientist Torkel Klingberg's research on attention and working memory relates directly to the challenge journalists face in reaching audiences. *The Overflowing Brain: Information Overload and the Limits of Working Memory* is a very accessible introduction to the field. Evolutionary biologist Neil Shubin's *Your Inner Fish: A Journey into the 3.5-Billion-Year History of the Human Body* offers a delightfully engaging introduction to the way our evolutionary past shapes our present bodies. Leda Cosmides and John Tooby bring the same evolutionary approach to bear on human behavior in the Internet-available "Evolutionary Psychology: A Primer."

Richard Nisbett and Lee Ross's *Human Inference: Strategies and Shortcomings of Social Judgment* provides a solid introduction to the brain's shortcuts that usually help but sometimes frustrate our ability to understand the world around and inside of us. Law professor Cass Sunstein has brought insights about these shortcuts to bear both on public policy issues and, importantly for journalists, the ways of the information revolution in three excellent and well-written books, *Infotopia: How Many Minds Produce Knowledge, Laws of Fear: Beyond the Precautionary Principle,* and *Republic.com 2.0.*

PHILOSOPHY

Philosophers have historically led the way in clarifying how the human mind functions, and this continues. Unfortunately, finding philosophy books that do not repel the general reader is difficult, but a few works repay a nonexpert reader's effort.

Martha C. Nussbaum's *Upheavals of Thought: The Intelligence of Emotions* uses everything from classic philosophical texts to modern literature to examine the importance of emotion as a way people have of getting what she calls "news of the world." Ronald DeSousa deals with the same theme in *The Rationality of Emotion,* though in a less accessible way. DeSousa's book is particularly useful, though, in disentangling our ideas about objective and subjective knowledge, which have tripped up journalistic thinkers for more than a century. Susanne Langer's *Philosophy in a New Key* led the way in understanding that the mind has more than one useful mode of knowing and describing the world—roughly speaking, the scientific and the artistic. Though not for the fainthearted, a book by Shaun Gallagher and Dan Zahavi—*The Phenomenological Mind: An Introduction to Philosophy of Mind and Cognitive Science*—provides a way into a vein of philosophy that provides profound insights about the mind that the basic ideology of science excludes.

Finally, Louis Menand's *The Metaphysical Club: A Story of Ideas in America* provides a fascinating intellectual portrait of the era that shaped how journalists began to professionalize and define their disciplines.

OTHER IMPORTANT THEMES

Celebrity provides a window into the effects of the information revolution. History helps open the curtains. Leo Braudy's remarkable *The Frenzy of Renown: Fame and Its History* gives a detailed and nuanced view of both the changing and the durable aspects from the earliest period of recorded history to the present. Robin Dunbar's *Grooming, Gossip, and the Evolution of Language* goes even further back, offering an intriguing theory about the origins of gossip in primate behavior. It implies that that the practice deserves more respect than it usually gets, since it is an important way of holding social groups together.

Though the title of Wayne C. Booth's *The Rhetoric of Fiction* makes clear that it does not deal with journalism, his book provides extraordinary insights about the way narrative works, especially about the various levels of the relationship between the writer and the audience. More than any other book of literary theory, this one has connected for me the actual experience of writing and the actual experience of reading.

Fred Turner's *From Counterculture to Cyberculture: Stewart Brand, the Whole Earth Network, and the Rise of Digital Utopianism* is a fascinating and very round history of the ideological origins of the Internet.

Finally, in our skeptical and uncertain times, the first addendum to volume 2 of Karl Popper's examination of freedom of thought, *The Open Society and Its Enemies,* delivers a tonic to the spirit. Don't let the title, "Facts, Standards, and Truth: A Further Criticism of Relativism," put you off. Popper's insights into the philosophy of knowing culminate in an eloquent description of how a humble understanding of the limits of knowledge make the life of the mind soar.

A note on Web addresses: I have made every effort to make sure these were up to date when this book went into production, but of course they do sometimes change.

Ackerman, Bruce, and Ian Ayers. "A National Endowment for Journalism." *Guardian* (U.K.), February 13, 2009. Available at http://www.guardian.co.uk/commentisfree/cifamerica/2009/feb/12/newspapers-investigative-journalism-endowments.

Adams, Henry. *The Education of Henry Adams.* In *Novels, Mont Saint Michel, and The Education,* edited by Ernest Samuels and Jayne Samuels, 715–1181. New York: Library of America, 1983.

"Agent Orange." Wikipedia. Available at http://en.wikipedia.org. Consulted February 17, 2009.

Arendt, Hannah. *The Human Condition.* Chicago: University of Chicago Press, 1958.

Aristotle. *Nicomachean Ethics.* In Barnes, *The Complete Works of Aristotle,* 2:1729–1867.

———. *Poetics.* In Barnes, *The Complete Works of Aristotle,* 2:2316–40.

———. *Politics.* In Barnes, *The Complete Works of Aristotle,* 2:1986–2129.

———. *Rhetoric.* In Barnes, *The Complete Works of Aristotle,* 2:2152–2269.

Arnold, Matthew. "Stanzas from the Grande Chartreuse." In *The Poems of Matthew Arnold, 1840–1867,* 270–75. London: Oxford University Press, 1926.

Averill, James R. "Emotion and Anxiety: Sociocultural, Biological, and Psychological Determinants." In *Explaining Emotions,* edited by Amélie Oksenberg Rorty, 37–72. Berkeley: University of California Press, 1980.

Ayer, Alfred Jules. *Language, Truth and Logic.* New York: Dover Publications, 1952.

Barlow, John Perry. "Declaration of the Independence of Cyberspace." Quoted in Turner, *From Counterculture to Cyberculture,* 13.

Barnes, Jonathan, ed. *The Complete Works of Aristotle: The Revised Oxford Translation.* Vol. 2. Princeton, NJ: Princeton University Press, 1984.

Barrett, William. *The Illusion of Technique.* Garden City, NY: Anchor Press/Doubleday, 1978.

Basch, Michael Franz. *Practicing Psychotherapy: A Casebook.* New York: Basic Books, 1992.

Berntson, Gary G., and John T. Cacioppo. "The Neuroevolution of Motivation." In *Handbook of Motivation Science,* edited by James Y. Shah and Wendy L. Gardner, 188–200. New York: Guilford Press, 2007.

Berntson, Gary G., John T. Cacioppo, and Martin Sarter. "Bottom-Up: Implications for Neurobehavioral Models of Anxiety and Autonomic Regulation." In Davidson, Scherer, and Goldsmith, *Handbook of Affective Sciences*, 1105–16.

Bickel, Alexander. *The Morality of Consent.* New Haven, CT: Yale University Press, 1975.

Birkerts, Sven. *The Gutenberg Elegies: The Fate of Reading in an Electronic Age.* New York: Fawcett Columbine, 1994.

Bless, Herbert. "The Interplay of Affect and Cognition: The Mediating Roles of General Knowledge Structures." In Forgas, *Feeling and Thinking,* 201–22.

Boorstin, Daniel J. *The Image: A Guide to Pseudo-Events in America.* New York: Harper Colophon, 1961.

Booth, Wayne C. *The Rhetoric of Fiction.* 2nd ed. Chicago: University of Chicago Press, 1983.

Bower, Gordon H., and Joseph P. Forgas. "Affect, Memory, and Social Cognition." In *Cognition and Emotion,* edited by Eric Eich, John F. Kihlstrom, Gordon H. Bower, Joseph P. Forgas, and Paula M. Niedenthal, 87–168. Oxford: Oxford University Press, 2000.

Brand, Stewart. Quoted in a transcription of a panel discussion in "'Keep Designing': How the Information Economy Is Being Created and Shaped by the Hacker Ethic." *Whole Earth Review,* May 1985, 44–55. Available at http://www.wholeearth.com/issue-electronic-edition.php?iss=2046.

Braudy, Leo. *The Frenzy of Renown: Fame and Its History.* New York: Vintage Books, 1997.

Brooks, David. "Greed and Stupidity." *New York Times,* April 2, 2009, op-ed page.

Brown, John Seeley, and Paul Duguid. *The Social Life of Information.* Boston: Harvard Business School Press, 2002.

Bruner, Jerome. *Acts of Meaning.* Cambridge, MA: Harvard University Press, 1990.

———. *Actual Minds, Possible Worlds.* Cambridge, MA: Harvard University Press, 1986.

Butler, Robert Olen. *From Where You Dream: The Process of Writing Fiction.* New York: Grove Press, 2005.

Cacioppo, John T., and Gary G. Berntson. "The Affect System and Racial Prejudice." In *Unraveling the Complexities of Social Life: A Festschrift in Honor of Robert B. Zajonc,* edited by John A. Bargh and Deborah K. Apsley, 95–110. Washington, DC: American Psychological Association, 2001.

Cacioppo, John T., and Wendi L. Gardner. "Emotion." *Annual Review of Psychology* 50 (1999): 191–214.

Cacioppo, John T., and William Patrick. *Loneliness: Human Nature and the Need for Social Connection.* New York: W. W. Norton & Co., 2008.

Carey, James W. *Communication as Culture.* Rev. ed. New York: Routledge, 2009.

———. "Why and How: The Dark Continent of American Journalism." In *Reading the News,* edited by Robert Karl Manoff and Michael Schudson, 146–96. New York: Pantheon, 1986.

Carroll, John. "The Wolf in Reporter's Clothing: The Rise in Pseudo-Journalism in America." Available at http://jcomm.uoregon.edu/lectures-awards/ruhl-lecture-2004.

Clore, Gerald L. "Why Emotions Are Felt." In Ekman and Davidson, *The Nature of Emotion,* 103–11.

———. "Why Emotions Vary in Intensity." In Ekman and Davidson, *The Nature of Emotion,* 386–93.

Cobley, Paul. *Narrative.* London: Routledge, 2001.

Cochran, Gregory, and Henry Harpending. *The 10,000 Year Explosion: How Civilization Accelerated Human Evolution.* New York: Basic Books, 2009.

Commission on Freedom of the Press (Hutchins Commission). *A Free and Responsible Press: A General Report on Mass Communication: Newspapers, Radio, Motion Pictures, Magazines, and Books.* Chicago: University of Chicago Press, 1947.

Cosmides, Leda, and John Tooby. "Evolutionary Psychology and Emotions." In Lewis and Haviland-Jones, *Handbook of Emotions,* 91–115.

———. "Evolutionary Psychology: A Primer." Available at http://www.psych.ucsb.edu/research/cep/primer.html.

Crewdson, John. "Code Blue: Survival in the Sky." *Chicago Tribune,* June 30, 1996, special section.

Crovits, L. Gordon. "Wikipedia's Old-Fashioned Revolution: The Online Encyclopedia Is Fast Becoming the Best." *Wall Street Journal,* April 6, 2009, columns page.

Damasio, Antonio R. *Descartes' Error: Emotion, Reason, and the Human Brain.* New York: Avon Books, 1998.

———. *The Feeling of What Happens: Body and Emotion in the Making of Consciousness.* San Diego: Harcourt, 1999.

———. *Looking for Spinoza: Joy, Sorrow, and the Feeling Brain.* Orlando, FL: Harcourt, 2003.

D'Andrade, Roy. *The Development of Cognitive Anthropology.* Cambridge: Cambridge University Press, 1995.

Davidson, Richard J., Diego Pizzagalli, Jack B. Nitschke, and Ned H. Kalin. "Parsing the Subcomponents of Emotion and Disorders of Emotion: Perspectives from Affective Neuroscience." In Davidson, Scherer, and Goldsmith, *Handbook of Affective Sciences,* 8–24.

Davidson, Richard J., Klaus R. Scherer, and H. Hill Goldsmith, eds. *Handbook of Affective Sciences.* Oxford: Oxford University Press, 2003.

Dawes, Robyn M. "Shallow Psychology." In *Cognition and Behavior,* edited by John S. Carroll and John W. Payne, 3–11. Hillsdale, NJ: Lawrence Erlbaum Associates, 1976.

Deacon, Terrence W. *The Symbolic Species: The Co-evolution of Language and the Brain.* New York: W. W. Norton & Co., 1997.

Dennett, Daniel C. "Cognitive Wheels: The Frame Problem in AI." In *Minds, Machines, and Evolution: Philosophical Studies,* edited by Christopher Hookway, 129–52. Cambridge: Cambridge University Press, 1984.

———. *Consciousness Explained.* Boston: Little, Brown & Co., 1991.

———. *Darwin's Dangerous Idea: Evolution and the Meanings of Life.* New York: Simon & Schuster, 1995.

de Sousa, Ronald. "Emotions: What I Know, What I'd Like to Think I Know, and What I'd Like to Think." In Solomon, *Thinking about Feeling,* 61–75.

———. *The Rationality of Emotion.* Cambridge, MA: MIT Press, 1987.

de Tocqueville, Alexis. *Democracy in America.* Translated by Harvey C. Mansfield and Delba Winthrop. Chicago: University of Chicago Press, 2000.

Dewey, John. *Logic: The Theory of Inquiry.* In *John Dewey, the Later Works.* Vol. 12, *1938,* edited by Jo Ann Boydston. Carbondale: Southern Illinois University Press, 1986.

De Zengotita, Thomas. "Attack of the Superzeroes: Why Washington, Einstein, and Madonna Can't Compete with You." *Harper's Magazine,* December 2004.

Dunbar, Robin. *Grooming, Gossip and the Evolution of Language.* London: Faber & Faber, 2004.

Dunn, Judy. "Emotional Development in Early Childhood: A Social Relationship Perspective." In Davidson, Scherer, and Goldsmith, *Handbook of Affective Sciences,* 332–46.

Edelman, Gerald M. *Bright Air, Brilliant Fire: On the Matter of the Mind.* New York: Basic Books, 1992.

Edland, Anne, and Ola Svenson. "Judgment and Decision Making under Time Pressure: Studies and Findings." In Svenson and Maule, *Time Pressure and Stress in Human Judgment and Decision Making,* 27–40.

Ekman, Paul, and Richard J. Davidson, eds. *The Nature of Emotion: Fundamental Questions.* New York: Oxford University Press, 1994.

Ellsworth, Phoebe. "Some Reasons to Expect Universal Antecedents of Emotion." In Ekman and Davidson, *The Nature of Emotion,* 150–54.

Ellsworth, Phoebe C., and Klaus R. Scherer. "Appraisal Processes in Emotion." In Davidson, Scherer, and Goldsmith, *Handbook of Affective Sciences,* 572–95.

Epictetus. *Arrian's Discourses of Epictetus.* In *The Stoic and Epicurean Philosophers: The Complete Extant Writings of Epicurus, Epictetus, Lucretius, Marcus Aurelius,* edited by Whitney J. Oates, 223–457. New York: Random House, 1940.

Fischhoff, Baruch. "For Those Condemned to Study the Past: Heuristics and Biases in Hindsight." In Kahneman, Slovic, and Tversky, *Judgment under Uncertainty,* 335–51.

Forgas, Joseph P., ed. *Feeling and Thinking: The Role of Affect in Social Cognition.* Cambridge: Cambridge University Press, 2001.

Forster, E. M. *Aspects of the Novel.* New York: Harcourt Brace Jovanovich (A Harvest/ HBJ Book), 1956.

Fuller, Jack. "Move by Burger May Shift Court's Stand on Abortion." *Washington Post,* July 4, 1972.

———. *News Values: Ideas for an Information Age.* Chicago: University of Chicago Press, 1996.

Fuller, Jack, and David Satter. "Rare Disease Blamed Here in Deaths of 4." *Chicago Tribune,* February 18, 1974.

Gallagher, Shaun, and Dan Zahavi. *The Phenomenological Mind: An Introduction to Philosophy of Mind and Cognitive Science.* London: Routledge, 2008.

Gardner, Howard, Mihaly Csikszentmihalyi, and William Damon. *Good Work: When Excellence and Ethics Meet.* New York: Basic Books, 2001.

Gilovich, Thomas, Dale Griffin, and Daniel Kahneman, eds. *Heuristics and Biases: The Psychology of Intuitive Judgment.* Cambridge: Cambridge University Press: 2002.

Gitlin, Todd. *Media Unlimited: How the Torrent of Images and Sounds Overwhelms Our Lives.* New York: Henry Holt & Co. (Metropolitan Books), 2001.

Glasser, Theodore J. "Objectivity Precludes Responsibility." *Quill,* February 1984. Available at http://www.columbia.edu/itc/journalism/j6075/edit/readings/glasser.html.

Goldie, Peter. "Emotion, Feeling, and Knowledge of the World." In Solomon, *Thinking about Feeling,* 91–106.

———. "Narrative and Perspective: Values and Appropriate Emotions." In *Philosophy and the Emotions,* edited by Anthony Hatzimoysis, 201–20. Cambridge: Cambridge University Press, 2003.

Goldstein, Tom. *Journalism and Truth: Strange Bedfellows.* Evanston, IL: Northwestern University Press, 2007.

Gould, Stephen Jay. "Evolution: The Pleasures of Pluralism." *New York Review of Books,* June 26, 1997. Available at http://www.stephenjaygould.org/reviews/gould_pluralism.html.

Habermas, Jürgen. *Communication and the Evolution of Society.* Translated by Thomas McCarthy. Boston: Beacon Press, 1979.

———. *The Theory of Communicative Action.* Vol. 1, *Reason and the Rationalization of Society.* Translated by Thomas McCarthy. Boston: Beacon Press, 1984.

Haidt, Jonathan. *The Happiness Hypothesis: Finding Modern Truth in Ancient Wisdom.* New York: Basic Books, 2006.

Hallin, Daniel. "A Fall from Grace?" *Media Studies Journal,* Spring/Summer 1998, 42–47.

Hardin, Russell. *Trust and Trustworthiness.* New York: Russell Sage Foundation, 2002.

Harrington, Walt. *Intimate Journalism: The Art and Craft of Reporting Everyday Life.* Thousand Oaks, CA: Sage Publications, 1997.

Harth, Eric. *Windows on the Mind: Reflections on the Physical Basis of Consciousness.* New York: William Morrow & Co., 1982.

Hawthorne, Michael. "Poison in the Well: Crestwood Officials Cut Corners and Supplied Residents with Tainted Water for 2 Decades." *Chicago Tribune,* April 22, 2009.

Hebb, Daniel. *The Organization of Behavior: A Neuropsychological Theory.* Mahwah, NJ: Lawrence Erlbaum Associates, 2002.

Holmes, Oliver Wendell, Jr. Dissenting opinion in *Abrams v. U.S.,* 250 U.S. 616 (1919).

Hugdahl, Kenneth, and Kjell Morten Stormark. "Emotional Modulation of Selective Attention: Behavioral and Psychophysiological Measures." In Davidson, Scherer, and Goldsmith, *Handbook of Affective Sciences*, 276–91.

Hume, David. *A Treatise of Human Nature*, edited by David Fate Morton and Mary J. Norton. Oxford: Oxford University Press, 2000.

Isaacson, Walter. "How to Save Your Newspaper." *Time Magazine*, February 5, 2009. Available at http://www.time.com/time/business/article/0,8599,1877191,00.html.

Jackson, Maggie. *Distracted: The Erosion of Attention and the Coming Dark Age.* Amherst, NY: Prometheus Books, 2008.

James, William. *Pragmatism.* In *Writings, 1902–1910*, edited by Bruce Kuklick, 479–624. New York: Library of America, 1987.

———. *The Will to Believe and Other Essays in Popular Philosophy.* In *Writings, 1878–1899*, edited by Gerald E. Meyers, 445–704. New York: Library of America, 1992.

Janeway, Michael. *Republic of Denial: Press, Politics, and Public Life.* New Haven, CT: Yale University Press, 1999.

Jaynes, Julian. *The Origin of Consciousness in the Breakdown of the Bicameral Mind.* Boston: Houghton Mifflin Co., 1976.

Jefferson, Thomas. "Dialogue between My Head & My Heart." In *Writings*, edited by Merrill D. Peterson, 866–77. New York: Library of America, 1984.

Jennings, Dennis L., Teresa M. Amabile, and Lee Ross. "Informal Covariant Assessment: Data-Based versus Theory-Based Judgments." In Kahneman, Slovic, and Tversky, *Judgment under Uncertainty*, 211–30.

Johnson, Mark. *The Meaning of the Body: Aesthetics of Human Understanding.* Chicago: University of Chicago Press, 2007.

Johnson-Laird, P. N., and Keith Oatley. "Cognitive and Social Construction in Emotions." In Lewis and Haviland-Jones, *Handbook of Emotions*, 458–75.

Kaiser, Susanne, and Thomas Wehrle. "Situated Emotional Problem Solving in Interactive Computer Games." In *Proceedings of the 9th Conference of the International Society for Research on Emotions*, edited by N. H. Frijda, 276–80. Storrs, CT: ISRE Publications, 1996.

Kahneman, Daniel, and Shane Frederick. "Representativeness Revisited: Attribute Substitution in Intuitive Judgments." In Gilovich, Griffin, and Kahneman, *Heuristics and Biases*, 49–81.

Kahneman, Daniel, Paul Slovic, and Amos Tversky, eds. *Judgment under Uncertainty: Heuristics and Biases.* Cambridge: Cambridge University Press, 1982.

Kahneman, Daniel, and Amos Tversky. "Subjective Probability: A Judgment of Representativeness." In Kahneman, Slovic, and Tversky, *Judgment under Uncertainty*, 32–47.

Kapuściński, Ryszard. *The Shadow of the Sun.* Translated by Klara Glowczewska. New York: Vintage International, 2002.

"Karl Popper." *Stanford Encyclopedia of Philosophy*. Available at http://plato.stanford .edu/entries/popper/.

Kaylan, Melik. "Reality TV: In Fame's Antechamber." *Wall Street Journal*, July 19–20, 2008.

Keen, Andrew. *The Cult of the Amateur: How Today's Internet Is Killing Our Culture*. New York: Doubleday/Currency, 2007.

Keller, Julia. "After the Storm's Fury." *Chicago Tribune*, December 7, 2004. Available at http://www.pulitzer.org/works/2005-Feature-Writing.

Kelly, Kevin. "The Computational Metaphor." *Whole Earth* 95 (Winter 1998): 72. Available at http://www.wholeearth.com/issue/article/63/the.computational.metaphor.

Keltner, Dacher, Paul Ekman, Gian C. Gonzaga, and Jennifer Beer. "Facial Expressions of Emotion." In Davidson, Scherer, and Goldsmith, *Handbook of Affective Sciences*, 415–32.

Ketter, Terence A., Po W. Wang, Anna Lembke, and Nadia Sachs. "Physiological and Pharmacological Induction of Affect." In Davidson, Scherer, and Goldsmith, *Handbook of Affective Sciences*, 930–62.

Keynes, John Maynard. *The General Theory of Employment, Interest, and Money*. San Diego: Harcourt (A Harvest Book), 1964.

Klingberg, Torkel. *The Overflowing Brain: Information Overload and the Limits of Working Memory*. Translated by Neil Betteridge. Oxford: Oxford University Press, 2009.

Kohut, Heinz. *The Analysis of Self: A Systematic Approach to the Psychoanalytic Treatment of Narcissistic Personality Disorders*. Madison, CT: International Universities Press, 2001.

———. *How Does Analysis Cure?* Edited by Arnold Goldberg, with the collaboration of Paul Stepansky. Chicago: University of Chicago Press, 1984.

Kovach, Bill, and Tom Rosenstiel. *The Elements of Journalism: What Newspeople Should Know and the Public Should Expect*. New York: Three Rivers Press, 2001.

———. *Warp Speed: America in the Age of Mixed Media*. New York: Century Foundation Press, 1999.

Krause, Clifford. "Ethanol, Just Recently a Savior, Is Struggling." *New York Times*, February 12, 2009.

Langer, Susanne K. *Feelings and Form*. New York: Charles Scribner's Sons, 1953.

———. *Philosophy in a New Key*. New York: New American Library (A Mentor Book), 1948.

Lanham, Richard A. *The Economics of Attention: Style and Substance in the Age of Information*. Chicago: University of Chicago Press, 2006.

Lanier, Jaron. "Digital Maoism: The Hazards of the New Online Collectivism." Available at http://www.edge.org.

LeDoux, Joseph. *The Emotional Brain: The Mysterious Underpinnings of Emotional Life*. New York: Simon & Schuster, 1996.

——. *Synaptic Self: How Our Brains Become Who We Are.* New York: Penguin Books, 2003.

Lewis, Anthony. Quoted in "Law & Media Program Hosts Greenhouse, Lewis." *Yale Law Report,* Winter 2009.

Lewis, Michael, and Jeannette M. Haviland-Jones, eds. *Handbook of Emotions.* 2nd ed. New York: Guilford Press, 2000.

Linderman, Frank B. *Plenty-coups: Chief of the Crows.* 2nd ed. Lincoln: University of Nebraska Press, 2002.

Lightly, Todd, and Michael Hawthorne. "Illinois Open Records Law Often a Closed Book." *Chicago Tribune,* March 8, 2009.

Lippmann, Walter. *Liberty and the News.* Princeton, NJ: Princeton University Press, 2008.

——. *The Phantom Public.* New Brunswick, NJ: Transaction Publishers, 1993.

——. *A Preface to Morals.* New York: MacMillan, 1929.

——. *Public Opinion.* New York: Free Press, 1965.

Lodge, David. *Consciousness and the Novel: Connected Essays.* Cambridge, MA: Harvard University Press, 2002.

Loewenstein, George, and Jennifer S. Lerner. "The Role of Affect in Decision Making." In Davidson, Scherer, and Goldsmith, *Handbook of Affective Sciences,* 619–42.

Love, Robert. "The Lee Abrams Experience: How to Hear the Man Who Would Transform Tribune." *Columbia Journalism Review,* September–October 2008. Available at http://www.cjr.org/feature/the_lee_abrams_experience.php?page=1.

Mandler, George. *Mind and Body: Psychology of Emotion and Stress.* New York: W. W. Norton & Co., 1984.

Marcus, George E., W. Russell Neuman, and Michael MacKuen. *Affective Intelligence and Political Judgment.* Chicago: University of Chicago Press, 2000.

Marshall, P. David. *Celebrity and Power: Fame in Contemporary Culture.* Minneapolis: University of Minnesota Press, 1997.

Maule, A. John, and G. Robert J. Hockey. "State, Stress, and Time Pressure." In Svenson and Maule, *Time Pressure and Stress in Human Judgment and Decision Making,* 83–101.

McClure, Samuel M., Matthew M. Botvinick, Nick Yeung, Joshua D. Greene, and Jonathan D. Cohen. "Conflict Monitoring in Cognition-Emotion Competition." In *Handbook of Emotion Regulation,* edited by James J. Gross, 204–26. New York: Guilford Press, 2007.

McLuhan, Marshall. *Understanding Media: The Extensions of Man.* Cambridge, MA: MIT Press, 1994.

McNair, Brian. *News and Journalism in the UK.* 4th ed. London: Routledge, 2003.

Medvec, Victoria Husted, Scott F. Madey, and Thomas Gilovich. "When Less Is More: Counterfactual Thinking and Satisfaction among Olympic Medalists." In Gilovich, Griffin, and Kahneman, *Heuristics and Biases,* 625–35.

Menand, Louis. *The Metaphysical Club: A Story of Ideas in America.* New York: Farrar, Straus and Giroux, 2001.

Merleau-Ponty, Maurice. *Phenomenology of Perception.* Translated by Colin Smith. London: Routledge & Kegan Paul, 1962.

———. *Signs.* Translated by Richard C. McCleary. Evanston, IL: Northwestern University Press, 1964.

———. *The Structure of Behavior.* Translated by Alden L. Fisher. Boston: Beacon Press, 1963.

Miller, Peter. "Swarm Theory: Ants, Bees, and Birds Teach Us How to Cope with a Complex World." *National Geographic,* July 2007.

Milton, John. *Areopagitica.* In *The Complete Poetry and Essential Prose of John Milton,* edited by William Kerrigan, John Rumrich, and Stephen M. Fallon, 927–66. New York: Modern Library, 2007.

Mitchell, W. J. T., ed. *On Narrative.* Chicago: University of Chicago Press, 1981.

Mobbs, Dean, Michael D. Greicius, Eiman Abdel-Azim, Vinod Menon, and Allan L. Reiss. "Humor Modulates the Mesolimbic Reward Centers." *Neuron* 40, no. 5 (December 4, 2003): 1041–48.

Moore, Gordon E. "Cramming More Components onto Integrated Circuits." *Electronics Magazine,* April 19, 1965.

Mullainathan, Sendhil, and Andrei Shleifer. "The Market for News." Social Science Research Network (http://www.ssrn.com), 2004.

Nabokov, Peter. *Two Leggings: The Making of a Crow Warrior.* Lincoln: University of Nebraska Press, 1982.

National Opinion Research Center. "Confidence in Press." General Social Surveys, 1972–2006. Available at http://www.norc.org/GSS+Website/Browse+GSS+Variables/Subject+Index.

Neuman, W. Russell, Marion R. Just, and Ann N. Crigler. *Common Knowledge: News and the Construction of Meaning.* Chicago: University of Chicago Press, 1992.

Newspaper Association of America. "Total Paid Circulation, 1940–2007." Available at http://www.naa.org/TrendsandNumbers/Total-Paid-Circulation.aspx.

Niebuhr, Reinhold. *The Nature and Destiny of Man.* Vol. 1, *Human Nature.* Louisville, KY: Westminster John Knox Press, 1996.

Nisbett, Richard, David H. Krantz, Christopher Jepson, and Ziva Kundra. "The Use of Statistical Heuristics in Everyday Inductive Reasoning." In Gilovich, Griffin, and Kahneman, *Heuristics and Biases,* 510–33.

Nisbett, Richard, and Lee Ross. *Human Inference: Strategies and Shortcomings of Social Judgment.* Englewood Cliffs, NJ: Prentice-Hall, 1980.

Norden, Jeanette. *Understanding the Brain.* 4 DVDs. Chantilly, VA: Teaching Co., 2007.

Nussbaum, Martha C. *Love's Knowledge: Essays on Philosophy and Literature.* Oxford: Oxford University Press, 1990.

———. *Upheavals of Thought: The Intelligence of Emotions*. Cambridge: Cambridge University Press, 2001.

Oatley, Keith. "Creative Expression and Communication of Emotions in the Visual and Narrative Arts." In Davidson, Scherer, and Goldsmith, *Handbook of Affective Sciences*, 481–502.

Öhman, Arne, Anders Flykt, and Daniel Lundqvist. "Unconscious Emotion: Evolutionary Perspectives, Psychophysiological Data, and Neuropsychological Mechanisms." In *Cognitive Neuroscience of Emotion*, edited by Richard D. Lane and Lynn Nadel, 296–327. Oxford: Oxford University Press, 2000.

Öhman, Arne, and Stefan Wiens. "On the Automaticity of Autonomic Reponses in Emotion: An Evolutionary Perspective." In Davidson, Scherer, and Goldsmith, *Handbook of Affective Sciences*, 256–75.

"Paleolithic Pornography." *Economist*, May 14, 2009.

Panksepp, Jaak. *Affective Neuroscience: The Foundations of Human and Animal Emotions*. New York: Oxford University Press, 1998.

———. "Basic Emotions Ramify Widely in the Brain, Yielding Many Concepts That Cannot Be Distinguished Unambiguously . . . Yet." In Ekman and Davidson, *The Nature of Emotion*, 86–88.

———. "Subjectivity May Have Evolved in the Brain as a Simple Value-Coding Process That Promotes the Learning of New Behaviors." In Ekman and Davidson, *The Nature of Emotion*, 313–15.

Pascal, Blaise. *Pascal's Pensées*. New York: E. P. Dutton & Co., 1958.

Patterson, Thomas E. "Doing Well and Doing Good: How Soft News and Critical Journalism Are Shrinking the News Audience and Weakening Democracy—and What News Outlets Can Do about It." Shornestein Center on Press, Politics, and Public Policy, Harvard University, 2000.

Pinker, Steven. *The Blank Slate: The Modern Denial of Human Nature*. New York: Viking, 2002.

———. *How the Mind Works*. New York: W. W. Norton & Co., 1997.

———. *The Language Instinct*. New York: Perennial Classics (HarperCollins), 2000.

Plato. "Phaedo." Translated by Hugh Tredennick. In *The Collected Dialogues*, edited by Edith Hamilton and Huntington Cairns, 40–98. Princeton, NJ: Princeton University Press, 1961.

Polivy, Janet. "On the Induction of Emotion in the Laboratory: Discrete Moods or Multiple Affect States." *Journal of Personality and Social Psychology* 41, no. 4 (1981): 803–17.

Popper, Karl R. *The Open Society and Its Enemies*. Vol. 2, *Hegel and Marx*. Princeton, NJ: Princeton University Press, 1971.

Posner, Richard A. "Bad News." *New York Times Book Review*, July 31, 2005.

Postman, Neil. *Amusing Ourselves to Death: Public Discourse in the Age of Show Business*. New York: Penguin Books, 1986.

Pound, Roscoe. "The Cult of the Irrational." Quoted in Schudson, *Discovering the News,* 126–27.

Prior, Markus. *Post-Broadcast Democracy: How Media Choice Increases Inequality in Political Involvement and Polarizes Elections.* Cambridge: Cambridge University Press, 2007.

Putnam, Robert D. "The Strange Disappearance of Civic America." *American Prospect,* Winter 1996. Available at http://www.prospect.org/cs/articles?articles=the_strange_disappearance_of_civic_america.

Ratey, John J. *A User's Guide to the Brain: Perception, Attention, and the Four Theaters of the Brain.* New York: Vintage Books, 2002.

Richards, Robert J. "The Moral Grammar of Narratives in History of Biology: The Case of Haeckel and Nazi Biology." Available at http://home.uchicago.edu./~rjr6/articles/Moral%20Grammar%20of%20Narratives-illustrated.pdf.

Ricoeur, Paul. *Freedom and Nature: The Voluntary and the Involuntary.* Translated by Erazim V. Kohák. Evanston, IL: Northwestern University Press, 1966.

———. *The Rule of Metaphor.* Translated by Robert Czerny with Kathleen McLaughlin and John Costello, SJ. Toronto: University of Toronto Press, 1977.

———. *Time and Narrative.* Vol. 1. Translated by Kathleen McLaughlin and David Pellauer. Chicago: University of Chicago Press, 1984.

———. *Time and Narrative.* Vol. 3. Translated by Kathleen Blamey and David Pellauer. Chicago: University of Chicago Press, 1988.

Root, Waverly. *The Paris Edition: The Autobiography of Waverley Root, 1927–1934.* San Francisco: North Point Press, 1987.

Rozin, Paul. "Introduction: Evolutionary and Cultural Perspectives on Affect." In Davidson, Scherer, and Goldsmith, *Handbook of Affective Sciences,* 839–51.

Sacks, Oliver. *Musicophilia: Tales of Music and the Brain.* New York: Alfred A. Knopf, 2007.

Salopek, Paul. "Hints of Lives Are All That Remain." *Chicago Tribune,* December 4, 2001.

Sapolsky, Robert. *Biology and Human Behavior: The Neurological Origins of Individuality.* 2nd ed. 4 DVDs. Chantilly, VA: Teaching Co., 2005.

Saul, Stephanie. "In Vitro Clinics Face Questions on Risks over Multiple Births." *New York Times,* February 12, 2009.

Schafer, Roy. "Narration in the Psychoanalytic Dialogue." In Mitchell, *On Narrative,* 25–49.

Scherer, Klaus R. "Emotion Serves to Decouple Stimulus and Response." In Ekman and Davidson, *The Nature of Emotion,* 127–30.

Scholes, Robert. "Afterthoughts on Narrative: Language, Narrative, and Anti-Narrative." In Mitchell, *On Narrative,* 200–208.

Schudson, Michael. *Discovering the News: A Social History of American Newspapers.* New York: Basic Books, 1978.

———. *The Sociology of News.* New York: W. W. Norton & Co., 2003.

——. *Why Democracies Need an Unlovable Press.* Cambridge: Polity Press, 2008.

Schwarz, Norbert. "Feelings as Information: Moods Influence Judgments and Processing Strategies." In Gilovich, Griffin, and Kahneman, *Heuristics and Biases,* 534–47.

Scott, D. Travers. "Pundits in Muckrakers' Clothing: Political Blogs and the 2004 U.S. Presidential Election." In Tremayne, *Blogging, Citizenship, and the Future of Media,* 39–57.

Shafer, Jack. "The Lies of Ryszard Kapuściński: Or, If You Prefer, the 'Magic Realism' of the Now Departed Master." *Slate,* January 25, 2007. Available at http://www.slate .com/id/2158315.

Shapiro, Stephanie. "The Return of the Sob Sisters." *American Journalism Review,* June/July 2006.

Shister, Neil. "A Matter of Degree: The Role of Journalists as Activists in Journalism Business and Policy." A Report of the Aspen Institute Forum on Diversity and the Media. Washington, DC: Aspen Institute, 2004.

Shriver, Jube, Jr. "By the Numbers." *American Journalism Review,* June/July 2006.

Shubin, Neil. *Your Inner Fish: A Journey into the 3.5-Billion-Year History of the Human Body.* New York: Pantheon Books, 2008.

Shweder, Richard A. "'You're Not Sick, You're Just in Love': Emotion as an Interpretive System." In Ekman and Davidson, *The Nature of Emotion,* 32–44.

Silverman, David. "Sniper Ends Girl's Dream to Flee Cabrini." *Chicago Tribune,* July 25, 1992.

Smith, Kyle N., Jeff T. Larsen, Tanya L. Chartrand, John T. Cacioppo, Heather A. Katafiasz, and Kathleen E. Moran. "Being Bad Isn't Always Good: Affective Context Moderates the Attention Bias toward Negative Information." *Journal of Personality and Social Psychology* 90, no. 2 (2006): 210–20.

Solomon, Robert C., ed. *Thinking about Feeling: Contemporary Philosophers on Emotions.* Oxford: Oxford University Press, 2004.

Steel, Ronald. *Walter Lippmann and the American Century.* Boston: Atlantic Monthly Press, 1980.

Stemmler, Gerhard. "Methodological Considerations in the Psychophysiological Study of Emotion." In Davidson, Scherer, and Goldsmith, *Handbook of Affective Sciences,* 225–55.

Stephens, Mitchell. "We're All Postmodern Now." *Columbia Journalism Review,* July/August 2005. Available at http://www.journalism.nyu.edu/faculty/files/stephens-postmodern.pdf.

Stone, Linda. Quoted in "A Survey of New Media." *Economist,* April 22, 2006.

Stross, Randall. *Planet Google: One Company's Audacious Plan to Organize Everything We Know.* New York: Free Press, 2008.

Sundar, S. Shyam, Heidi Hatfield Edwards, Yifeng Hu, and Carmen Stavrositu. "Blogging for Better Health: Putting the 'Public' Back in Public Health." In Tremayne, *Blogging, Citizenship, and the Future of Media,* 83–102.

Sunstein, Cass. *Infotopia: How Many Minds Produce Knowledge.* Oxford: Oxford University Press, 2006.

———. *Laws of Fear: Beyond the Precautionary Principle.* Cambridge: Cambridge University Press, 2005.

———. *Republic.com 2.0.* Princeton, NJ: Princeton University Press, 2007.

Svenson, Ola, and A. John Maule, eds. *Time Pressure and Stress in Human Judgment and Decision Making.* New York: Plenum Press, 1993.

Taber, Katherine H., Maurice Redden, and Robin A. Hurley. "Functional Anatomy of Humor: Positive Affect and Mental Illness." *Journal of Neuropsychiatry & Clinical Neurosciences* 19 (November 2007): 358–62.

Tooby, John, and Leda Cosmides. "The Past Explains the Present: Emotional Adaptations and the Structure of Ancestral Environments." *Ethology and Sociobiology* 11 (1990): 375–424.

Tremayne, Mark, ed. *Blogging, Citizenship, and the Future of Media.* New York: Routledge, 2007.

Trow, George W. S. *My Pilgrim's Progress: Media Studies, 1950–1998.* New York: Pantheon Books, 1999.

———. *Within the Context of No Context.* New York: Atlantic Monthly Press, 1981.

Trudeau, Gary. *Doonesbury. Chicago Tribune,* December 25, 2005, comics section.

Turkle, Sherry. *Life on the Screen: Identity in the Age of the Internet.* New York: Simon & Schuster, 1995.

Turner, Fred. *From Counterculture to Cyberculture: Stewart Brand, the Whole Earth Network, and the Rise of Digital Utopianism.* Chicago: University of Chicago Press, 2006.

Tversky, Amos, and Daniel Kahneman. "Extensional versus Intuitive Reasoning: The Conjunction Fallacy in Probability Judgment." In Gilovich, Griffin, and Kahneman, *Heuristics and Biases,* 19–48.

von Uexküll, Jacob. Quoted in Merleau-Ponty, *The Structure of Behavior,* 159.

Wakeman, Frederic. *The Hucksters.* New York: Rinehart & Co., 1946.

Wales, Henry. "Lindbergh Lands in Paris." *Chicago Tribune,* May 22, 1927.

"The Watchmen." Broadcast on National Public Radio. *This American Life,* June 5, 2009. Available at http://www.thisamericanlife.org/radio_Archive.aspx.

Weldon, Michele. *Everyman News: The Changing American Front Page.* Columbia: University of Missouri Press, 2008.

Westen, Drew. *The Political Brain: The Role of Emotion in Deciding the Fate of the Nation.* New York: Public Affairs, 2007.

White, Hayden. "The Value of Narrativity in the Representation of Reality." In Mitchell, *On Narrative,* 1–23.

White, Ryen W., and Eric Horvitz. "Cyberchondria: Studies of Escalation of Medical Concerns in Web Search." Available at http://research.microsoft.com/apps/pubs/default.aspx?id=76529.

Wiebe, Robert H. *The Search for Order, 1877–1920*. New York: Hill and Wang, 1967.

———. *The Segmented Society: An Introduction to the Meaning of America*. London: Oxford University Press, 1975.

———. *Self-Rule: A Cultural History of American Democracy*. Chicago: University of Chicago Press, 1995.

Williams, Joseph M. *Style: Lessons in Clarity and Grace*. 9th ed. New York: Pearson Longman, 2007.

Wilson, Edward O. *Consilience: The Unity of Knowledge*. New York: Alfred A. Knopf, 1998.

———. *On Human Nature*. Cambridge, MA: Harvard University Press, 1978,

Wilson, Gahan. Cartoon in *New Yorker*, February 25, 2005, 47.

Wimmer, Heinz, and Josef Perner. "Beliefs about Beliefs: Representation and Constraining Function of Wrong Beliefs in Young Children's Understanding of Deception." *Cognition* 13 (1983): 103–28.

Wolfe, Tom. "Digibabble, Fairy Dust, and the Human Anthill." *Forbes ASAP*, October 4, 1999.

Wood, Gordon S. *The Creation of the American Republic, 1776–1787*. New York: W. W. Norton & Co., 1972.

Woodward, Bob, and Scott Armstrong. *The Brethren: Inside the Supreme Court*. New York: Simon & Schuster, 1979.

Zak, Paul. J., Robert Kurzban, and William T. Matzner. "Oxytocin Is Associated with Human Trustworthiness." *Hormones and Behavior* 48 (2005): 522–57. Available at http://www.sciencedirect.com.